THE TRUTHS
WE HOLD

ALSO BY KAMALA D. HARRIS

*Smart on Crime: A Career Prosecutor's
Plan to Make Us Safer* (2009)

THE TRUTHS
WE HOLD

An American Journey

KAMALA HARRIS

PENGUIN PRESS

New York

2019

PENGUIN PRESS
An imprint of Penguin Random House LLC
penguinrandomhouse.com

Second insert, page 2, top and bottom, and page 3, bottom: Justin Sullivan via Getty Images;
page 3, top: Bethany Mollenkof/Los Angeles Times via Getty Images; page 10, top: Aaron P.
Bernstein/Getty Images; page 13, bottom: Alex Wong/Getty Images; page 16,
bottom: Zoe Ghertner. All other images courtesy of the author.

ISBN 9780525560715 (hardcover)
ISBN 9780525560722 (ebook)

Printed in the United States of America
1   3   5   7   9   10   8   6   4   2

DESIGNED BY MEIGHAN CAVANAUGH

*Penguin is committed to publishing works of quality and integrity.
In that spirit, we are proud to offer this book to our readers; however,
the story, the experiences, and the words are the author's alone.*

To my darling husband:
Thank you for always being patient, loving,
supportive, and calm. And most of all,
for your sense of "the funny."

CONTENTS

PREFACE

Most mornings, my husband, Doug, wakes up before me and reads the news in bed. If I hear him making noises—a sigh, a groan, a gasp—I know what kind of day it's going to be.

November 8, 2016, had started well—the last day of my campaign for the U.S. Senate. I spent the day meeting as many more voters as I could, and of course cast a vote myself at a neighborhood school up the street from our house. We were feeling pretty good. We had rented a huge place for my Election Night party, with a balloon drop waiting to go. But first I was going out for dinner with family and close friends—a tradition dating back to my first campaign. People had flown in from all across the country, even overseas, to be with us—my aunts and cousins, my in-laws, my sister's in-laws, and more, all gathered for what we hoped would be a very special night.

I was staring out the car window, reflecting on how far we'd come, when I heard one of Doug's signature groans.

"You gotta look at this," he said, handing me his phone. Early results for the presidential election were coming in. Something was happening—something bad. By the time we arrived at the restaurant, the gap between the two candidates had shrunk considerably, and I was inwardly groaning as well. *The New York Times'* probability meter was suggesting it was going to be a long, dark night.

We settled in for a meal in a small room off the main restaurant. Emotions and adrenaline were running high, but not for the reasons we had anticipated. On the one hand, while polls hadn't yet closed in California, we were optimistic that I was going to win. Yet even as we prepared for that hard-earned celebration, all eyes were on our screens as state after state came back with numbers that told a troubling story.

At a certain point, my nine-year-old godson, Alexander, came up to me with big tears welling in his eyes. I assumed one of the other kids in our group had been teasing him about something.

"Come here, little man. What's wrong?"

Alexander looked up and locked eyes with mine. His voice was trembling. "Auntie Kamala, that man can't win. He's not going to win, is he?" Alexander's worry broke my heart. I didn't want anyone making a child feel that way. Eight years earlier, many of us had cried tears of joy when Barack Obama was elected president. And now, to see Alexander's fear . . .

His father, Reggie, and I took him outside to try to console him.

"Alexander, you know how sometimes superheroes are facing a big challenge because a villain is coming for them? What do they do when that happens?"

"They fight back," he whimpered.

"That's right. And they fight back with emotion, because all the best superheroes have big emotions just like you. But they always fight back, right? So that's what we're going to do."

Shortly after, the Associated Press called my race. We were still at the restaurant.

"I can't thank you all enough for being with me every step of the way all the time, all the time," I told my incredibly loving and supportive family and friends. "It means so much to me." I was overwhelmed with gratitude, both for the people in that room and the people I had lost along the way, especially my mother. I tried to savor the moment, and I did, if briefly. But, like everyone else, I soon turned my eyes back to the television.

After dinner, we headed to our Election Night venue, where more than a thousand people had gathered for the party. I was no longer a candidate for office. I was a U.S. senator-elect—the first black woman from my state, and the second in the nation's history, to earn that job. I had been elected to represent more than thirty-nine million people—roughly one out of every eight Americans from all backgrounds and walks of life. It was—and is—a humbling and extraordinary honor.

My team clapped and cheered as I joined them in the greenroom behind the stage. It all still felt more than a little surreal. None of us had fully processed what was happening. They formed a circle around me as I thanked them for everything they'd done. We were a family, too, and we had been through an incredible journey together. Some of the folks in the room had been with me since my first campaign for district attorney. But now, almost two years after the start of our campaign, we had a new mountain to take.

I had written a speech based on the assumption that Hillary Clinton would become our first woman president. As I went onstage to greet my supporters, I left that draft behind. I looked out at the room. It was packed with people, from the floor to the balcony. Many were in a state of shock as they watched the national returns.

I told the crowd we had a task in front of us. I said the stakes were high. We had to be committed to bringing our country together, to doing what was required to protect our fundamental values and ideals. I thought of Alexander and all the children when I posed a question:

"Do we retreat or do we fight? I say we fight. And I intend to fight!"

I went home that night with my extended family, many of whom were staying with us. We all went into our respective rooms, changed into sweats, and then joined one another in the living room. Some of us were sitting on couches. Others on the floor. We all planted ourselves in front of the television.

No one really knew what to say or do. Each of us was trying to cope in our own way. I sat down on the couch with Doug and ate an entire family-size bag of classic Doritos. Didn't share a single chip.

But I did know this: one campaign was over, but another was about to begin. A campaign that called on us all to enlist. This time, a battle for the soul of our nation.

In the years since, we've seen an administration align itself with white supremacists at home and cozy up to dictators abroad; rip babies from their mothers' arms in grotesque violation of their human rights; give corporations and the wealthy huge tax cuts while ignoring the middle class; derail our fight against climate change; sabotage health care and imperil a woman's right to control her own body; all while lashing out at seemingly everything and everyone, including the very idea of a free and independent press.

We are better than this. Americans know we're better than this. But we're going to have to prove it. We're going to have to fight for it.

On July 4, 1992, one of my heroes and inspirations, Thurgood Marshall, gave a speech that deeply resonates today. "We cannot play ostrich," he said. "Democracy just cannot flourish amid fear. Liberty cannot bloom amid hate. Justice cannot take root amid rage. America must get to work. . . . We must dissent from the indifference. We must dissent from the apathy. We must dissent from the fear, the hatred, and the mistrust."

This book grows out of that call to action, and out of my belief that our fight must begin and end with speaking truth.

I believe there is no more important and consequential antidote for these times than a reciprocal relationship of trust. You give and you receive trust. And one of the most important ingredients in a relationship of trust is that we speak truth. It matters what we say. What we mean. The value we place on our words—and what they are worth to others.

We cannot solve our most intractable problems unless we are honest about what they are, unless we are willing to have difficult conversations and accept what facts make plain.

We need to speak truth: that racism, sexism, homophobia, transphobia, and anti-Semitism are real in this country, and we need to confront those forces. We need to speak truth: that, with the exception of Native Americans, we all descend from people who weren't born on our shores—whether our ancestors came to America willingly, with hopes of a prosperous future, or forcibly, on a slave ship, or desperately, to escape a harrowing past.

We cannot build an economy that gives dignity and decency to American workers unless we first speak truth; that we are asking people to do more with less money and to live longer with less security. Wages haven't risen in forty years, even as the costs of health care, tuition, and housing have soared. The middle class is living paycheck to paycheck.

We must speak truth about our mass incarceration crisis—that we put more people in prison than any country on earth, for no good reason. We must speak truth about police brutality, about racial bias, about the killing of unarmed black men. We must speak truth about pharmaceutical companies that pushed addictive opioids on unsuspecting communities, and payday lenders and for-profit colleges that have leeched on to vulnerable Americans and overloaded them with debt. We must speak truth about greedy, predatory corporations that have turned deregulation, financial speculation, and climate denialism into creed. And I intend to do just that.

This book is not meant to be a policy platform, much less a fifty-point plan. Instead, it is a collection of ideas and viewpoints and stories, from my life and from the lives of the many people I've met along the way.

Just two more things to mention before we get started:

First, my name is pronounced "comma-la," like the punctuation mark. It means "lotus flower," which is a symbol of significance in Indian culture. A lotus grows underwater, its flower rising above the surface while its roots are planted firmly in the river bottom.

And second, I want you to know how personal this is for me. This is the story of my family. It is the story of my childhood. It is the story of the life I have built since then. You'll meet my family and my friends, my colleagues and my team. I hope you will cherish them as I do and, through my telling, see that nothing I have ever accomplished could have been done on my own.

—*Kamala, 2018*

One

FOR THE PEOPLE

I still remember the first time I walked into the Alameda County Superior Courthouse, in Oakland, California, as an employee. It was 1988, during the last summer of law school, and I, along with nine others, had been offered a summer internship in the district attorney's office. I had a sense that I wanted to be a prosecutor, that I wanted to be on the front lines of criminal justice reform, that I wanted to protect the vulnerable. But having never seen the job up close, I hadn't made up my mind.

The sun shone brightly on the courthouse. The building stood apart on Lake Merritt, taller and more regal than other buildings nearby. From certain angles, it looked like an architectural marvel from a foreign capital, with its granite base and concrete tower rising to meet a golden rooftop. Though from other angles, it bore an uncanny resemblance to an art deco wedding cake.

The Alameda County District Attorney's Office is itself something of a legend. Earl Warren led the office before becoming attorney general of California and later one of the most influential chief justices of the United States Supreme Court. He was on my mind that morning as I walked past the stunning mosaics in the lobby that depict the early history of California. Warren's words—proclaiming segregation "inherently unequal"—had taken a long fifteen years to make it to Berkeley, California. I was grateful they had come in time for me; my elementary school class was only the second class in my city to be desegregated through busing.

I was the first to arrive at the orientation session. Within a few minutes, the rest of my fellow clerks showed up. There was only one woman among them, Amy Resner. As soon as the session was over, I went up to her and asked her for her phone number. In that male-dominated environment, it was refreshing to have at least one female colleague. She remains one of my closest friends today, and I'm godmother to her children.

As summer interns, we understandably had very little power or influence. Our job was primarily to learn and observe, while assisting where we could. It was a chance to get a taste of how the criminal justice system worked from the inside, what it looked like when justice was served—and when it wasn't. We were placed with attorneys who were trying all kinds of cases, from DUIs to homicides, and had the chance to be in the room—and part of the process—of putting together a case.

I'll never forget the time my supervisor was working on a case involving a drug bust. The police had arrested a number of individuals in the raid, including an innocent bystander: a woman who had been at the wrong place at the wrong time and had been swept up in the dragnet. I hadn't seen her. I didn't know who she was or what she looked like. I didn't have any connection to her, except for the report I was reviewing. But there was something about her that caught my attention.

It was late on a Friday afternoon, and most people had gone home for the weekend. In all likelihood, a judge wouldn't see her until Monday. That meant she'd have to spend the weekend in jail.

Does she work weekends? Is she going to have to explain to her employer where she was? Is she going to get fired?

Even more important, I knew she had young children at home. *Do they know she's in jail? They must think she did something wrong. Who's taking care of them right now? Is there even someone who can? Child Protective Services might get called. My God, she could lose her kids.*

Everything was on the line for this woman: her family, her livelihood, her standing in her community, her dignity, her liberty. And yet she'd done nothing wrong.

I rushed to the clerk of the court and asked to have the case called that very day. I begged. I pleaded. If the judge could just return to the bench for five minutes, we could get her released. All I could think about was her family and her frightened children. Finally, as the minutes in the day wound down, the judge returned. I watched and listened as he reviewed her case, waiting for him to give the order. Then, with the pound of a gavel, just like that, she was free. She'd get to go home to her children in time for dinner. I never did get the chance to meet her, but I'll never forget her.

It was a defining moment in my life. It was the crystallization of how, even on the margins of the criminal justice system, the stakes were extraordinarily high and intensely human. It was a realization that, even with the limited authority of an intern, people who cared could do justice. It was revelatory, a moment that proved how much it mattered to have compassionate people working as prosecutors. Years before I would be elected to run a major prosecutor's office, this was one of the victories that mattered the most. I knew she was going home.

And I knew the kind of work I wanted to do, and who I wanted to serve.

The courthouse wasn't far from where I grew up. I was born in Oakland, California, in 1964 and spent the formative years of my childhood living on the boundary between Oakland and Berkeley.

My father, Donald Harris, was born in Jamaica in 1938. He was a brilliant student who immigrated to the United States after being admitted to the University of California at Berkeley. He went there to study economics and would go on to teach economics at Stanford, where he remains a professor emeritus.

My mother's life began thousands of miles to the east, in southern India. Shyamala Gopalan was the oldest of four children—three girls and a boy. Like my father, she was a gifted student, and when she showed a passion for science, her parents encouraged and supported her.

She graduated from the University of Delhi at nineteen. And she didn't stop there. She applied to a graduate program at Berkeley, a university she'd never seen, in a country she'd never visited. It's hard for me to imagine how difficult it must have been for her parents to let her go. Commercial jet travel was only just starting to spread globally. It wouldn't be a simple matter to stay in touch. Yet, when my mother asked permission to move to California, my grandparents didn't stand in the way. She was a teenager when she left home for

Berkeley in 1958 to pursue a doctorate in nutrition and endocrinology, on her way to becoming a breast cancer researcher.

My mother was expected to return to India after she completed her degree. Her parents had an arranged marriage. It was assumed my mother would follow a similar path. But fate had other plans. She and my father met and fell in love at Berkeley while participating in the civil rights movement. Her marriage—and her decision to stay in the United States—were the ultimate acts of self-determination and love.

My parents had two daughters together. My mother received her PhD at age twenty-five, the same year I was born. My beloved sister, Maya, came two years later. Family lore has it that, in both pregnancies, my mother kept working right up to the moment of delivery— one time, her water broke while she was at the lab, and the other while she was making apple strudel. (In both cases, knowing my mom, she would have insisted on finishing up before she went to the hospital.)

Those early days were happy and carefree. I loved the outdoors, and I remember that when I was a little girl, my father wanted me to run free. He would turn to my mother and say, "Just let her run, Shyamala." And then he'd turn to me and say, "Run, Kamala. As fast as you can. Run!" I would take off, the wind in my face, with the feeling that I could do anything. (It's no wonder I also have many memories of my mother putting Band-Aids on my scraped knees.)

Music filled our home. My mother loved to sing along to gospel— from Aretha Franklin's early work to the Edwin Hawkins Singers. She had won an award in India for her singing, and I loved hearing that voice. My father cared about music just as much as my mother. He had an extensive jazz collection, so many albums that they filled all the shelving against one of the walls. Every night, I would fall asleep to the sounds of Thelonious Monk, John Coltrane, or Miles Davis.

But the harmony between my parents didn't last. In time, things got harder. They stopped being kind to each other. I knew they loved each other very much, but it seemed they'd become like oil and water. By the time I was five years old, the bond between them had given way under the weight of incompatibility. They separated shortly after my dad took a job at the University of Wisconsin, and divorced a few years later. They didn't fight about money. The only thing they fought about was who got the books.

I've often thought that had they been a little older, more emotionally mature, maybe the marriage could have survived. But they were so young. My father was my mother's first boyfriend.

It was hard on both of them. I think, for my mother, the divorce represented a kind of failure she had never considered. Her marriage was as much an act of rebellion as an act of love. Explaining it to her parents had been hard enough. Explaining the divorce, I imagine, was even harder. I doubt they ever said to her, "I told you so," but I think those words echoed in her mind regardless.

Maya was still a toddler at the time of their separation, a little too young to understand what was going on, to feel the hardness of it all. I have often felt a pang of guilt because of something Maya never got to experience: I knew our parents when they were happy together. Maya never really did.

My father remained a part of our lives. We would see him on weekends and spend summers with him in Palo Alto. But it was really my mother who took charge of our upbringing. She was the one most responsible for shaping us into the women we would become.

And she was extraordinary. My mother was barely five foot one, but I felt like she was six foot two. She was smart and tough and fierce and protective. She was generous, loyal, and funny. She had only two goals in life: to raise her two daughters and to end breast cancer. She pushed us hard and with high expectations as she nurtured us. And all the while, she made Maya and me feel special, like we could do anything we wanted to if we put in the work.

My mother had been raised in a household where political activism and civic leadership came naturally. Her mother, my grandmother, Rajam Gopalan, had never attended high school, but she was a skilled community organizer. She would take in women who were being abused by their husbands, and then she'd call the husbands and tell them they'd better shape up or she would take care of them. She used to gather village women together, educating them about contraception. My grandfather P. V. Gopalan had been part of the movement to win India's independence. Eventually, as a senior diplomat in the Indian government, he and my grandmother had spent time living in Zambia after it gained independence, helping to settle refugees. He used to joke that my grandmother's activism would get him in trouble one day. But he knew that was never going to stop her. From them, my mother learned that it was service to others that gave life purpose and meaning. And from my mother, Maya and I learned the same.

My mother inherited my grandmother's strength and courage. People who knew them knew not to mess with either. And from both of my grandparents, my mother developed a keen political consciousness. She was conscious of history, conscious of struggle, conscious of inequities. She was born with a sense of justice imprinted on her soul.

My parents often brought me in a stroller with them to civil rights marches. I have young memories of a sea of legs moving about, of the energy and shouts and chants. Social justice was a central part of family discussions. My mother would laugh telling a story she loved about the time when I was fussing as a toddler. "What do you want?" she asked, trying to soothe me. "Fweedom!" I yelled back.

My mother surrounded herself with close friends who were really more like sisters. My godmother, a fellow Berkeley student whom I knew as "Aunt Mary," was one of them. They met through the civil rights movement that was taking shape in the early 1960s and was being debated and defended from the streets of Oakland to the soap-boxes in Berkeley's Sproul Plaza. As black students spoke out against injustice, a group of passionate, keenly intelligent, politically engaged young men and women found one another—my mother and Aunt Mary among them.

They went to peaceful protests where they were attacked by police with hoses. They marched against the Vietnam War and for civil rights and voting rights. They went together to see Martin Luther King Jr. speak at Berkeley, and my mother had a chance to meet him. She told me that at one anti-war protest, the marchers were confronted by the Hell's Angels. She told me that at another, she and her friends were forced to run for safety, with me in a stroller, after violence broke out against the protesters.

But my parents and their friends were more than just protesters. They were big thinkers, pushing big ideas, organizing their community. Aunt Mary, her brother (my "Uncle Freddy"), my mother and father, and about a dozen other students organized a study group to read the black writers that the university was ignoring. They met on Sundays at Aunt Mary and Uncle Freddy's Harmon Street home, where they devoured Ralph Ellison, discussed Carter G. Woodson, debated W. E. B. Du Bois. They talked about apartheid, about African decolonization, about liberation movements in the developing world, and about the history of racism in America. But it wasn't just talking. There was an urgency to their fight. They received prominent guests, too, including civil rights and intellectual leaders from LeRoi Jones to Fannie Lou Hamer.

After Berkeley, Aunt Mary took a job teaching at San Francisco State University, where she continued to celebrate and elevate the black experience. SFSU had a student-run Experimental College, and in 1966, another of my mother's dear friends, whom I knew as Uncle Aubrey, taught the college's first-ever class in black studies. The campus was a proving ground for redefining the meaning and substance of higher education.

These were my mother's people. In a country where she had no family, they were her family—and she was theirs. From almost the moment she arrived from India, she chose and was welcomed to and enveloped in the black community. It was the foundation of her new American life.

Along with Aunt Mary, Aunt Lenore was my mother's closest confidante. I also cherish the memory of one of my mother's mentors, Howard, a brilliant endocrinologist who had taken her under his wing. When I was a girl, he gave me a pearl necklace that he'd brought back from a trip to Japan. (Pearls have been one of my favorite forms of jewelry ever since!)

I was also very close to my mother's brother, Balu, and her two sisters, Sarala and Chinni (whom I called Chitti, which means "younger mother"). They lived many thousands of miles away, and we rarely saw one another. Still, through many long-distance calls, our periodic trips to India, and letters and cards written back and forth, our sense of family—of closeness and comfort and trust—was able to penetrate the distance. It's how I first really learned that you can have very close relationships with people, even if it's not on a daily basis. We were always there for one another, regardless of what form that would take.

My mother, grandparents, aunts, and uncle instilled us with pride in our South Asian roots. Our classical Indian names harked back to our heritage, and we were raised with a strong awareness of and appreciation for Indian culture. All of my mother's words of affection or frustration came out in her mother tongue—which seems fitting to me, since the purity of those emotions is what I associate with my mother most of all.

My mother understood very well that she was raising two black daughters. She knew that her adopted homeland would see Maya and me as black girls, and she was determined to make sure we would grow into confident, proud black women.

About a year after my parents separated, we moved into the top floor of a duplex on Bancroft Way, in a part of Berkeley known as the flatlands. It was a close-knit neighborhood of working families who were focused on doing a good job, paying the bills, and being there for one another. It was a community that was invested in its children, a place where people believed in the most basic tenet of the American Dream: that if you work hard and do right by the world, your kids will be better off than you were. We weren't rich in financial terms, but the values we internalized provided a different kind of wealth.

My mom would get Maya and me ready every morning before heading to work at her research lab. Usually she'd mix up a cup of Carnation Instant Breakfast. We could choose chocolate, strawberry, or vanilla. On special occasions, we got Pop-Tarts. From her perspective, breakfast was not the time to fuss around.

She would kiss me goodbye and I would walk to the corner and get on the bus to Thousand Oaks Elementary School. I only learned later that we were part of a national experiment in desegregation, with working-class black children from the flatlands being bused in one direction and wealthier white children from the Berkeley hills bused in the other. At the time, all I knew was that the big yellow bus was the way I got to school.

Looking at the photo of my first-grade class reminds me of how wonderful it was to grow up in such a diverse environment. Because the students came from all over the area, we were a varied bunch; some grew up in public housing and others were the children of professors. I remember celebrating varied cultural holidays at school and learning to count to ten in several languages. I remember parents, including my mom, volunteering in the classroom to lead science and art projects with the kids. Mrs. Frances Wilson, my first-grade teacher, was deeply committed to her students. In fact, when I graduated from the University of California Hastings College of the Law, there was Mrs. Wilson sitting in the audience, cheering me on.

When Maya and I finished school, our mother would often still be at work, so we would head two houses down to the Sheltons', whom my mother knew through Uncle Aubrey, and with whom we shared a long-standing relationship of love, care, and connection.

Regina Shelton, originally from Louisiana, was Aubrey's aunt; she and her husband, Arthur, an Arkansas transplant, owned and ran a nursery school—first located in the basement of their own home, and later underneath our apartment. The Sheltons were devoted to getting the children in our neighborhood off to the best possible start in life. Their day care center was small but welcoming, with posters of leaders such as Frederick Douglass, Sojourner Truth, and Harriet Tubman on the wall. The first George Washington Maya and I learned about when we were young was George Washington Carver. We still laugh about the first time Maya heard a classroom teacher talk about President George Washington and she thought to herself proudly, "I know him! He's the one who worked with peanuts!"

The Sheltons also ran an after-school program in their home, and that's where Maya and I would spend our afternoons. We simply called it going to "the house." There were always children running around at the house; lots of laughter and joyful play. Maya and I grew incredibly close to Mrs. Shelton's daughter and foster children; we'd pretend that we were all going to marry the Jackson Five—Maya with Michael and me with Tito. (Love you, Tito!)

Mrs. Shelton would quickly become a second mother to Maya and me. Elegant and warm in equal measure, she brought traditional southern style to her grace and hospitality—not to mention to her pound cake and flaky biscuits, which I adored. She was also deeply thoughtful in both senses of the term—exceptionally smart and uncommonly generous.

I'll never forget the time I made lemon bars to share. I had spent one afternoon making a lemon bar recipe that I'd found in one of my mother's cookbooks. They had turned out beautifully, and I was excited to show them off. I put them on a plate, covered them with Saran wrap, and walked over to Mrs. Shelton's house, where she was sitting at the kitchen table, sipping tea and laughing with her sister, Aunt Bea, and my mother. I proudly showed off my creation to them, and Mrs. Shelton took a big bite. It turned out I had used salt instead of sugar, but, not having tasted them myself, I didn't know.

"Mmmm, honey," Mrs. Shelton responded in her graceful southern accent, her lips slightly puckered from the taste. "That's delicious . . . maybe a little too much salt . . . but really delicious." I didn't walk away thinking I was a failure. I walked away thinking I had done a great job, and just made one small mistake. It was little moments like those that helped me build a natural sense of confidence. I believed I was capable of anything.

Mrs. Shelton taught me so much. She was always reaching out to mothers who needed counseling or support or even just a hug, because that's what you do. She took in more foster children than I can remember and adopted a girl named Sandy who would become my best friend. She always saw the potential in people. I loved that about her, too. She invested in neighborhood kids who had fallen through the cracks, and she did it with the expectation that these struggling boys and girls could be great. And yet she never talked about it or dwelled on it. To her, these deeds were not extraordinary; they were simply an extension of her values.

When I would come home from the Sheltons', I'd usually find my mother reading or working on her notes or preparing to make us dinner. Breakfast aside, she loved to cook, and I loved to sit with her in the kitchen and watch and smell and eat. She had a giant Chinese-style cleaver that she chopped with, and a cupboard full of spices. I loved that okra could be soul food or Indian food, depending on what spices you chose; she would add dried shrimp and sausage to make it like gumbo, or fry it up with turmeric and mustard seeds.

My mother cooked like a scientist. She was always experimenting—an oyster beef stir-fry one night, potato latkes on another. Even my lunch became a lab for her creations: On the bus, my friends, with their bologna sandwiches and PB&Js, would ask excitedly, "Kamala, what you got?" I'd open the brown paper bag, which my mother always decorated with a smiley face or a doodle: "Cream cheese and olives on dark rye!" I'll admit, not every experiment was successful—at least not for my grade school palate. But no matter what, it was different, and that made it special, just like my mother.

While she cooked, she would often put Aretha Franklin on the record player and I would dance and sing in the living room as though it were my stage. We listened to her version of "To Be Young, Gifted and Black" all the time, an anthem of black pride first performed by Nina Simone.

Most of our conversations took place in the kitchen. Cooking and eating were among the things our family most often did together. When Maya and I were kids, our mother sometimes used to serve us what she called "smorgasbord." She'd use a cookie cutter to make shapes in pieces of bread, then lay them out on a tray with mustard, mayonnaise, pickles, and fancy toothpicks. In between the bread slices, we'd put whatever was left in the refrigerator from the previous nights of cooking. It took me years to clue in to the fact that "smorgasbord" was really just "leftovers." My mother had a way of making even the ordinary seem exciting.

There was a lot of laughter, too. My mother was very fond of a puppet show called "Punch and Judy," where Judy would chase Punch around with a rolling pin. She would laugh so hard when she pretended to chase us around the kitchen with hers.

But it wasn't all laughs, of course. Saturday was "chores day," and each of us had our assignments. And my mother could be tough. She had little patience for self-indulgence. My sister and I rarely earned praise for behavior or achievements that were expected. "Why would

I applaud you for something you were supposed to do?" she would admonish if I tried to fish for compliments. And if I came home to report the latest drama in search of a sympathetic ear, my mother would have none of it. Her first reaction would be "Well, what did you do?" In retrospect, I see that she was trying to teach me that I had power and agency. Fair enough, but it still drove me crazy.

But that toughness was always accompanied by unwavering love and loyalty and support. If Maya or I was having a bad day, or if the weather had been gray and depressing for too long, she would throw what she liked to call an "unbirthday party," with unbirthday cake and unbirthday presents. Other times, she'd make some of our favorite things—chocolate chip pancakes or her "Special K" cereal cookies ("K" for Kamala). And often, she would get out the sewing machine and make clothes for us or for our Barbies. She even let Maya and me pick out the color of the family car, a Dodge Dart that she drove everywhere. We chose yellow—our favorite color at the time—and if she regretted having empowered us with the decision, she never let on. (On the plus side, it was always easy to find our car in a parking lot.)

Three times a week, I would go up the street to Mrs. Jones's house. She was a classically trained pianist, but there weren't many options in the field for a black woman, so she became a piano teacher. And she was strict and serious. Every time I looked over at the clock to see how much time was left in the lesson, she would rap my knuckles with a ruler. Other nights, I would go over to Aunt Mary's house, and Uncle Sherman and I would play chess. He was a great player, and he loved to talk to me about the bigger implications of the game: the idea of being strategic, of having a plan, of thinking things through multiple steps ahead, of predicting your opponent's actions and adjusting yours to outmaneuver them. Every once in a while, he would let me win.

On Sundays, our mother would send us off to the 23rd Avenue Church of God, piled with the other kids in the back of Mrs. Shelton's station wagon. My earliest memories of the teachings of the Bible were of a loving God, a God who asked us to "speak up for those who cannot speak for themselves" and to "defend the rights of the poor and needy." This is where I learned that "faith" is a verb; I believe we must live our faith and show faith in action.

Maya and I sang in the children's choir, where my favorite hymn was "Fill My Cup, Lord." I remember one Mother's Day, we recited an ode to moms. Each of us posed as one of the letters in the word "mother." I was cast as the letter T, and I stood there proudly, arms stretched out to both sides. "T is for the time she cares for me and loves me in every way."

My favorite night of the week was Thursday. On Thursdays, you could always find us in an unassuming beige building at the corner of what was then Grove Street and Derby. Once a mortuary, the building I knew was bursting with life, home to a pioneering black cultural center: Rainbow Sign.

Rainbow Sign was a performance space, cinema, art gallery, dance studio, and more. It had a restaurant with a big kitchen, and somebody was always cooking up something delicious—smothered chicken, meatballs in gravy, candied yams, corn bread, peach cobbler. By day, you could take classes in dance and foreign languages, or workshops in theater and art. At night, there were screenings, lectures, and performances from some of the most prominent black thinkers and leaders of the day—musicians, painters, poets, writers, filmmakers, scholars, dancers, and politicians—men and women at the vanguard of American culture and critical thought.

Rainbow Sign was the brainchild of visionary concert promoter Mary Ann Pollar, who started the center with ten other black women in September 1971. Its name was inspired by a verse from the black spiritual "Mary Don't You Weep"; the lyric "God gave Noah the rainbow sign; no more water, the fire next time . . ." was printed on the membership brochure. James Baldwin, of course, had memorably used this same verse for his book *The Fire Next Time*. Baldwin was a close friend of Pollar's and a regular guest at the club.

My mother, Maya, and I went to Rainbow Sign often. Everyone in the neighborhood knew us as "Shyamala and the girls." We were a unit. A team. And when we'd show up, we were always greeted with big smiles and warm hugs. Rainbow Sign had a communal orientation and an inclusive vibe. It was a place designed to spread knowledge, awareness, and power. Its informal motto was "For the love of people." Families with children were especially welcome at Rainbow Sign—an approach that reflected both the values and the vision of the women at its helm.

Pollar once told a journalist, "Hidden under everything we do, the best entertainment we put on, there is always a message: Look about you. Think about this." The center hosted a program specifically for kids through high school age, which included not only arts education but also a parallel version of the adult programming, in which young people could meet and interact directly with the center's guest speakers and performers.

The Bay Area was home to so many extraordinary black leaders and was bursting with black pride in some places. People had migrated there from all over the country. This meant that kids like me who spent time at Rainbow Sign were exposed to dozens of extra-ordinary men and women who showed us what we could become. In 1971, Congresswoman Shirley Chisholm paid a visit while she was exploring a run for president. Talk about strength! "Unbought and Unbossed," just as her campaign slogan promised. Alice Walker, who went on to win the Pulitzer Prize for *The Color Purple,* did a reading at Rainbow Sign. So did Maya Angelou, the first black female best-selling author, thanks to her autobiography, *I Know Why the Caged Bird Sings.* Nina Simone performed at Rainbow Sign when I was seven years old. I would later learn that Warren Widener, Berkeley's first black mayor, proclaimed March 31, 1972, Nina Simone Day to commemorate her two-day appearance.

I loved the electric atmosphere at Rainbow Sign—the laughter, the food, the energy. I loved the powerful orations from the stage and the witty, sometimes unruly audience banter. It was where I learned that artistic expression, ambition, and intelligence were cool. It was where I came to understand that there is no better way to feed some-one's brain than by bringing together food, poetry, politics, music, dance, and art.

It was also where I saw the logical extension of my mother's daily lessons, where I could begin to imagine what my future might hold for me. My mother was raising us to believe that "It's too hard!" was never an acceptable excuse; that being a good person meant standing for something larger than yourself; that success is measured in part by what you help others achieve and accomplish. She would tell us, "Fight systems in a way that causes them to be fairer, and don't be limited by what has always been." At Rainbow Sign, I'd see those values in action, those principles personified. It was a citizen's upbringing, the only kind I knew, and one I assumed everyone else was experiencing, too.

I was happy just where I was. But when I was in middle school, we had to leave. My mother was offered a unique opportunity in Montreal, teaching at McGill University and conducting research at the Jewish General Hospital. It was an exciting step in advancing her career.

It was not, however, an exciting opportunity for me. I was twelve years old, and the thought of moving away from sunny California in February, in the middle of the school year, to a French-speaking foreign city covered in twelve feet of snow was distressing, to say the least. My mother tried to make it sound like an adventure, taking us to buy our first down jackets and mittens, as though we were going to be explorers of the great northern winter. But it was hard for me to see it that way. It was made worse when my mother told us that she wanted us to learn the language, so she was enrolling us in a neighborhood school for native French speakers, Notre-Dame-des-Neiges— Our Lady of the Snows.

It was a difficult transition, since the only French I knew was from my ballet classes, where Madame Bovie, my ballet teacher, would shout, *"Demi-plié,* and up!" I used to joke that I felt like a duck, because all day long at our new school I'd be saying, *"Quoi? Quoi? Quoi?"* ("What? What? What?")

I was sure to take my upbringing with me to Montreal. One day, Maya and I held a demonstration in front of our building, protesting the fact that kids weren't allowed to play soccer on the lawn. I'm happy to report that our demands were met.

Eventually I convinced my mother to let me switch to a fine

arts school, where I tried out violin, French horn, and kettle drum alongside my studies in history and math. One year, we performed "Free to Be . . . You and Me" from start to finish.

By the time I got to high school, I had adjusted to our new surroundings. I still missed home, my friends and family, and was always so happy to return during the summer and holidays, when we'd stay with my father or Mrs. Shelton. But I'd gotten used to most of it. What I hadn't gotten used to was the feeling of being homesick for my country. I felt this constant sense of yearning to be back home. There was no question in my mind I'd return home for college.

I invited both of my parents to come to my graduation, even though I knew they wouldn't speak to each other. I still wanted them both to be there for me. I'll never forget sitting in the first couple of rows of the auditorium, looking out at the audience. My mother was nowhere to be found. "Where is she?" I thought. "Is she not here because my father is?" We were about to get started. And then, all of a sudden, the back door of the auditorium opened and my mother— who, most days, wore jeans and tennis shoes to her lab—walked in wearing a very bright red dress and heels. She was never one to let the situation get the better of her.

During high school, I started thinking more concretely about my future—college and beyond. I'd always assumed I would have a career; I'd seen the satisfaction my parents derived from their work. I'd also seen a series of extraordinary women—Aunt Mary, Mrs. Wilson, Mrs. Shelton, and my mother most of all—leading in their respective fields of influence, and the difference they were making in others' lives.

Though the seed was planted very early on, I'm not sure when, exactly, I decided I wanted to be a lawyer. Some of my greatest heroes were lawyers: Thurgood Marshall, Charles Hamilton Houston, Constance Baker Motley—giants of the civil rights movement. I cared a lot about fairness, and I saw the law as a tool that can help make things fair. But I think what most drew me to the profession was the way people around me trusted and relied on lawyers. Uncle Sherman and our close friend Henry were lawyers, and any time someone had a problem, within the family or the neighborhood, the first thing you'd hear was "Call Henry. Call Sherman. They'll know what to do. They'll know how to make sense of this." I wanted to be able to do that. I wanted to be the one people called. I wanted to be the one who could help.

So when it came to college, I wanted to get off on the right foot. And what better place to do that, I thought, than at Thurgood Marshall's alma mater?

I had always heard stories about what a wonderful place Howard University was, especially from Aunt Chris, who had gone there. Howard is an institution with an extraordinary legacy, one that has endured and thrived since its founding, two years after the Civil War. It endured when the doors of higher education were largely closed to black students. It endured when segregation and discrimination were the law of the land. It endured when few recognized the potential and capacity of young black men and women to be leaders. Generations of students had been nurtured and edified at Howard, equipped with the confidence to aim high and the tools to make the climb. I wanted to be one of them—and in the fall of 1982, I moved into Eton Towers, my first college dorm.

I'll always remember walking into Cramton Auditorium for my freshman orientation. The room was packed. I stood in the back, looked around, and thought, "This is heaven!" There were hundreds of people, and everyone looked like me. Some were children of Howard alumni; others were the first in their families to go to college. Some had been in predominantly black schools their whole lives; others had long been one of only a few people of color in their classroom or their neighborhood. Some came from cities, some from rural communities, and some from African countries, the Caribbean, and throughout the African diaspora.

As was the case for most Howard students, my favorite place to hang out was an area we called the Yard, a grass-covered space the size of a city block, right smack in the heart of the campus. On any given day, you could stand in the middle of the Yard and see, on your right, young dancers practicing their steps or musicians playing instruments. Look to your left and there were briefcase-toting students strolling out of the business school, and medical students in their white coats, heading back to the lab. Groups of students might be in a circle of laughter, or locked in deep discussion. A columnist for *The Hilltop*, the school newspaper, with the star of the football team. A gospel choir singer with the president of the math club.

That was the beauty of Howard. Every signal told students that we could be anything—that we were young, gifted, and black, and we shouldn't let anything get in the way of our success. The campus was a place where you didn't have to be confined to the box of another person's choosing. At Howard, you could come as you were and leave as the person you aspired to be. There were no false choices.

We weren't just told we had the capacity to be great; we were challenged to live up to that potential. There was an expectation that we would cultivate and use our talents to take on roles of leadership and have an impact on other people, on our country, and maybe even on the world.

I dove in with gusto. Freshman year, I ran for my first elected office: freshman class representative of the Liberal Arts Student Council. It was my very first campaign. No opponent I've faced since was as tough as Jersey Girl Shelley Young, and that says a lot, coming from a person from Oakland.

I chaired the economics society and competed on the debate team. I pledged a sorority, my beloved Alpha Kappa Alpha, founded by nine women at Howard more than a century ago. On Fridays, my friends and I would dress up in our best clothes and peacock around the Yard. On weekends, we went down to the National Mall to protest apartheid in South Africa.

While at Howard, in addition to being a student, I had many jobs. I interned at the Federal Trade Commission, where I was responsible for "clips," which meant combing all the morning newspapers, cutting out any articles that mentioned the agency, and pasting them onto sheets of paper to copy and distribute to senior staff. I also did research in the National Archives and was a tour guide at the U.S. Bureau of Engraving and Printing. My fellow tour guides and I were all given walkie-talkies and ID numbers; I was "TG-10," a code name that made me feel like a Secret Service agent. Once, I emerged from my shift to find Ruby Dee and Ossie Davis in the main area, waiting for a VIP tour after hours. They projected an aura like the luminaries they were, yet they made a special point of engaging me in conversation and telling me that it made them proud to see me as a young black woman working in public service. I've never forgotten how it made me feel as a young person to have these two icons, both larger than life, take the time to show an interest in me.

In the summer of my sophomore year, I got an internship with Senator Alan Cranston of California. Who could have known that some thirty years later, I would be elected to the same Senate seat? (I still have, framed, the thank-you letter from his office manager, which hangs in my Senate office near where my own interns sit. When I find myself riding the Senate subway with interns, I often tell them, "You're looking at your future!") I loved going to the Capitol Building every day that summer for work. It felt like the epicenter of change—and even as an intern sorting mail, I was thrilled to be a part of it. But I was even more mesmerized by the Supreme Court Building, across the street. I would walk across the street in the hot, humid summer, when you could cut the air with a butter knife, just so I could stand in awe of its magnificence and read the words engraved in marble above its entrance: EQUAL JUSTICE UNDER LAW. I imagined a world where that might be.

After Howard, I returned home to Oakland and enrolled at UC Hastings College of the Law. I was elected president of the Black Law Students Association (BLSA) during my second year in law school. At the time, black students were having a harder time finding employment than white students, and I wanted to change that. As BLSA president, I called the managing partners of all the major law firms and asked them to send representatives to a job fair we were hosting at a hotel.

When I realized that I wanted to work in the district attorney's office—that I had found my calling—I was excited to share the decision with my friends and family. And I wasn't surprised to find them incredulous. I had to defend my choice as one would a thesis.

America has a deep and dark history of people using the power of the prosecutor as an instrument of injustice. I knew this history well—of innocent men framed, of charges brought against people of color without sufficient evidence, of prosecutors hiding information that would exonerate defendants, of the disproportionate application of the law. I grew up with these stories—so I understood my community's wariness. But history told another story, too.

I knew the history of brave prosecutors who went after the Ku Klux Klan in the South. I knew the stories of prosecutors who went after corrupt politicians and corporate polluters. I knew the legacy of Robert Kennedy, who, as U.S. attorney general, sent Department of Justice officials to protect the Freedom Riders in 1961, and sent the U.S. Marshals to protect James Meredith when he enrolled at Ole Miss the next year.

I knew quite well that equal justice was an aspiration. I knew that the force of the law was applied unevenly, sometimes by design. But I also knew that what was wrong with the system didn't need to be an immutable fact. And I wanted to be part of changing that.

One of my mother's favorite sayings was "Don't let anybody tell you who you are. You tell *them* who you are." And so I did. I knew part of making change was what I'd seen all my life, surrounded by adults shouting and marching and demanding justice from the outside. But I also knew there was an important role on the inside, sitting at the table where the decisions were being made. When activists came marching and banging on the doors, I wanted to be on the other side to let them in.

I was going to be a prosecutor in my own image. I was going to do the job through the lens of my own experiences and perspectives, from wisdom gained at my mother's knee, in Rainbow Sign's hall, and on the Howard Yard.

An important part of what that wisdom told me was that when it came to criminal justice, we were being asked to accept false choices. For too long, we'd been told there were only two options: to be either tough on crime or soft on crime—an oversimplification that ignored the realities of public safety. You can want the police to stop crime in your neighborhood and also want them to stop using excessive force. You can want them to hunt down a killer on your streets and also want them to stop using racial profiling. You can believe in the need for consequence and accountability, especially for serious criminals, and also oppose unjust incarceration. I believed it was essential to weave all these varied strands together.

At the end of my summer internship, I was thrilled to accept a position as deputy district attorney. All I had to do was finish my final year of law school and take the bar exam, and then I'd be able to start my career in the courtroom.

I finished law school in the spring of 1989 and took the bar exam in July. In the waning weeks of summer, my future seemed so bright and so clear. The countdown to the life I imagined had begun.

And then, with a jolt, I was stopped in my tracks. In November, the state bar sent letters out to those who had taken the exam, and, to my utter devastation, I had failed. I couldn't get my head around it. It was almost too much to bear. My mother had always told me, "Don't do anything half-assed," and I had always taken that to heart. I was a hard worker. A perfectionist. Someone who didn't take things for granted. But there I was, letter in hand, realizing that in studying for the bar, I had put forward the most half-assed performance of my life.

F ortunately, I still had a job in the district attorney's office. They were going to keep me on, with clerk duties, and give me space to study to retake the exam in February. I was grateful for that, but it was hard to go into the office, feeling inadequate and incompetent. Just about everyone else who had been hired along with me had passed, and they were going to move on with their training without me. I remember walking by someone's office and hearing them say to someone else, "But she's so smart. How could she have not passed?" I felt miserable and embarrassed. I wondered if people thought I was a fraud. But I held my head up and kept going to work every day—and I passed on my second attempt. I was so proud and so honored the day I was sworn in as an officer of the court, and I showed up at the courthouse ready to start the work. But as it turns out, neither law school nor the bar exam really teach you what to do in court, and in those early days, it can feel like you've landed on another planet, where everyone speaks the language but you. As a clerk, you can represent the people in court under supervision. But this was the first time I'd be in trial on my own.

I had prepared, going over the facts of the case a dozen times. I'd practiced the questions I wanted to ask; internalized the precise wording of my legal motions. I'd researched and rehearsed every practice and custom—down to the skirt suit that was de rigueur for female attorneys, back before women were permitted to wear pants in the courtroom. I'd done everything I could. Still, the stakes were so high, it never felt like enough.

I walked into the courtroom, down the gallery aisle, and past the pews to the bar that separates defendants, families, witnesses, and other spectators from officials of the court. Chairs were arrayed in front of the bar for lawyers waiting for their cases to be called, and I took my seat among them. Nerves, excitement, and adrenaline jockeyed for position in my mind. But most of all, I was honored by and conscious of the immense responsibility I held—the duty to protect those who were among the most vulnerable and voiceless members of our society. When my turn came, I rose from my chair at the prosecutor's desk and stepped up to the podium, saying the words every prosecutor speaks:

"Kamala Harris, for the people."

The reason we have public offices of prosecution in America is that, in our country, a crime against any of us is considered a crime against all of us. Almost by definition, our criminal justice system involves matters in which the powerful have harmed the less powerful, and we do not expect the weaker party to secure justice alone; we make it a collective endeavor. That's why prosecutors don't represent the victim; they represent "the people"—society at large.

I kept that principle front and center as I worked with victims, whose dignity and safety were always paramount for me. It takes an enormous amount of courage for someone to share their story and endure cross-examination, knowing their credibility and most personal details may be on the line. But when they take the stand, they are doing so for the benefit of all of us—so that there will be consequences and accountability for those who violate the law.

"For the people" was my compass—and there was nothing I took more seriously than the power I now possessed. As an individual prosecutor, I had the discretion to decide whether to bring charges against someone and, if so, what and how many charges to bring. I could negotiate plea agreements, and provide sentencing and bail recommendations to the court. I was just starting out as a prosecutor, and yet I had the power to deprive a person of their liberty with the swipe of my pen.

When it came time for closing arguments, I approached the jury box. I decided to do it without notes so I wouldn't be looking down at a piece of paper, reading off my best arguments for why they should convict the defendant. I wanted to look the jurors in the eye. I felt that I should know my case well enough that I could close my eyes and see the entire incident in 360 degrees.

As I finished my closing and headed back to the prosecutor's table, I caught a glimpse of the audience. Amy Resner, my friend from the first day of orientation, was sitting there with a big smile on her face, cheering me on. Now we were both on our way.

The daily work was intense. At any given time, an individual prosecutor might be juggling more than one hundred cases. We started with lower-level work: arguing preliminary hearings, doing misdemeanor trials that covered things like DUIs and petty thefts. As the years passed, I got more and more trials under my belt and moved my way up the hierarchy of the office. In time, I would start prosecuting violent felonies, which took the work to a whole new level.

I would pore over police reports and interview witnesses. I would sit with the coroner and go through autopsy photographs, always cognizant that I was looking at somebody's child or parent. When police arrested a suspect, I would go down to the police station and stand on the other side of a two-way mirror and pass notes back and forth with investigators conducting the interview.

Once I started prosecuting felonies, I was assigned to homicide duty. I'd be given a briefcase on a Friday afternoon containing a pager (high-tech for the early nineties), a pen and pad, a copy of the penal code, and a list of critical numbers to call. For the next week, whenever the pager went off, it meant there had been a homicide and I was needed at the scene. Usually, that meant leaping out of bed between midnight and 6 a.m. My role was to make sure evidence was collected in the proper way, with all appropriate constitutional protections intact, so that it would be admissible in court. I often had to explain to victims and their families that there was a difference between what we knew happened and what we could prove happened. There is a giant chasm between arrest and conviction, and if you want to get from one to the other, you need legally obtained evidence.

I was at home in the courtroom. I understood its rhythm. I was comfortable with its idiosyncrasies. Eventually, I moved into a unit that focused on prosecuting sex crimes—putting rapists and child molesters behind bars. It was difficult, distressing, and deeply important work. I met so many girls, and sometimes boys, who had been abused, assaulted, neglected, all too often by people in relationships of trust.

What made these cases especially difficult was what was often needed to get a conviction: having the assault survivor testify. I spent a lot of those days meeting with survivors at Oakland's Highland General Hospital, walking them through what it would mean to take the stand, what that experience would be like. For some survivors, it was simply unimaginable to get on the witness stand and speak publicly about something they didn't even want to speak about privately.

There is so much pain and anguish associated with having experienced sexual violence. Containing that kind of emotional trauma to take the stand requires an extraordinary amount of courage and fortitude, especially when your abuser is also in the courtroom, when that abuser may be a family member or friend, and knowing you will be cross-examined by defense counsel whose job it is to convince the jury that you aren't telling the truth. I never faulted those who couldn't bring themselves to go through with it.

Often, as in the cases of the youngest children, the challenge of getting a conviction came down to the ability to testify, as much as the willingness. Those were the cases that haunted me most. I'll never forget a tiny, quiet six-year-old girl who was being molested by her sixteen-year-old brother. It was my job to sit with that sweet little child and see if I could get her to tell me her story—and whether she would be able to tell it again in front of a jury. I spent a lot of time with her, playing with toys, playing games, trying to build a relationship of trust. But as much as I tried, I knew—I just knew—that there was no way she could articulate to a jury what she had suffered. I remember walking out of the room and into a bathroom, where I broke down and cried. I wasn't going to have enough evidence to charge her brother. Without her testimony, I'd never be able to prove the allegations beyond a reasonable doubt. Despite all that prosecutorial power, I'm not sure I've ever felt quite so powerless.

These were just some of the challenges of defending children from sexual predators. There was also the jury itself, which sometimes seemed more inclined to believe adults than children. This was especially the case when it came to sexually exploited youth. I often think of a case I had involving a fourteen-year-old who had run away from her foster home with a group of young men from her neighborhood.

Instead of being her allies and protectors, they'd taken her to an empty apartment and gang-raped her. I could tell that she had learned at a young age that she couldn't trust adults; she wore an attitude of skepticism and hostility like a suit of armor. I felt for that poor girl, and the horrific childhood that had led her to this moment. But I was also acutely aware of how the jury might perceive her as she entered the courtroom, chewing gum, potentially coming off as almost contemptuous of the process.

I worried: Would they see her as the child she was, as an innocent victim of serial abuse? Or would they simply write her off as someone dressed "inappropriately," who had it coming?

Jurors are human beings, with human responses and reactions. I knew I had to meet them where they were if I was to have any chance of moving them to a more just interpretation of the facts.

I could see they weren't responding to her well. They didn't seem to like her. "The penal code was not created to protect some of us," I reminded the jury. "It is for all of us. This girl is a child. She needs to be protected from predators who are going to pounce. And one of the reasons the defendants picked her as their victim is that they thought you wouldn't care about her enough to believe her." In the end, we got a conviction, but I'm not sure the verdict meant much to the girl. She vanished after the trial. I asked some investigators to help me try to find her, but, though we had gotten a sketchy report that she was being trafficked on the streets of San Francisco, we could never confirm it. I never saw her again.

It was hard not to feel the weight of the systemic problems we were up against. Putting this young girl's abusers in prison meant they wouldn't be able to hurt other children. But what about the one they had already gotten their hands on? How had our system helped her?

A conviction was never going to make her whole, nor was it enough to get her out of the cycle of violence in which she was trapped. That reality, and what to do about it, bounced back and forth in my head—sometimes in the back of my mind, sometimes at the front of my skull. But it would be a few years before I could tackle it head-on.

In 1998, after nine years in the Alameda County District Attorney's office, I was recruited across the bay to the San Francisco District Attorney's Office. I was hired to run the career criminal unit, which focused on violent and serial offenders. I was hesitant to go at first, and not just because I loved working in the Alameda County courthouse. At the time, the San Francisco DA's office had a dubious reputation.

I was concerned by stories of dysfunction in the office. At the same time, it was a promotion: I would be running a unit, overseeing a team of prosecutors. This was a chance to grow. Plus, my friend and mentor Dick Iglehart, who was then the chief assistant district attorney, was actively encouraging me to come. With some trepidation, I accepted the offer—and soon found that my concerns had been warranted.

The office was a mess. Just one computer for every two lawyers, no filing system, and no database to track cases. It was rumored that when attorneys were finished with a case, some would toss the files in the trash. This was the late 1990s, and yet the office still didn't have email.

There was also a huge backlog of cases that were languishing, uninvestigated, unprosecuted. Lawyers were frustrated with the police for not investigating cases. Police were frustrated with the district attorney because his office was failing to get convictions. The decisions being made at the top appeared to be arbitrary and random, and staff morale was close to rock bottom. That toxic environment was made even worse by a series of firings. One Friday, fourteen lawyers came back from lunch to find pink slips on their chairs. It was devastating. People cried and yelled, and soon their fear turned into paranoia. Lawyers were afraid of one another—afraid of backstabbing by colleagues trying to protect their own jobs. Some people started skipping out on the goodbye parties of their fired compatriots, worried that their attendance would mark them as targets for firing, too.

It was incredibly frustrating, and not just in terms of the day-to-day work. I believed the district attorney was undercutting the whole idea of what a progressive prosecutor could be. My vision of a progressive prosecutor was someone who used the power of the office with a sense of fairness, perspective, and experience, someone who was clear about the need to hold serious criminals accountable and who understood that the best way to create safe communities was to prevent crime in the first place. To do those things effectively, you also need to run a professional operation.

After eighteen months, I got a lifeline. The San Francisco city attorney, Louise Renne, called me with a job offer. Louise was the first woman to hold that office. She was a groundbreaker, and she was fearless, taking on entrenched interests ranging from gun manufacturers and tobacco companies to male-only clubs. There was an opening to lead the division in her office that handled child and family services; she wanted to know if I'd be interested. I told her I would take the job but that I didn't just want to be a lawyer dealing with individual cases; I wanted to work on policy that could improve the system as a whole. Too often, young people in foster care migrated to juvenile detention and then into the adult criminal system. I wanted to work on policies that would stem that devastating flow.

Louise was all for it.

I spent two years at the city attorney's office. I started by co-founding a task force to study the issues of sexually exploited youth. We put together a group of experts, survivors, and community members to help guide the work—a series of recommendations we would present to the San Francisco Board of Supervisors.

Norma Hotaling was my partner in that effort. She had firsthand experience with the challenges we were tackling. She had been abused as a girl, and ended up homeless and addicted to heroin. She was arrested for prostitution more than thirty times. But hers was one of the few such stories that have a happy ending. Norma got clean. She went to college. She got a degree in health education. And as soon as she graduated, she put that degree to use, creating a program designed to rescue women from prostitution that is widely replicated today. I couldn't think of a better person to have teamed up with, and I admire her for having the courage to tell her story and put it to use for the benefit of so many others.

One of our priorities was creating a safe place for prostituted youth to get love and support and treatment. I knew from years of experience that the survivors we were trying to help usually had nowhere to go. In most cases, their parents weren't in the picture. Many of them had run away from foster care. People often wondered why it was that exploited kids picked up by the police would go right back to the pimps or older prostitutes who "took care of them." It didn't seem so strange to me—where else were these kids able to turn?

Our task force proposed establishing a safe house for sexually exploited youth—a sanctuary that would offer substance abuse and mental health treatment; the resources needed to get back to school; and a network of support to keep vulnerable young people safe, healthy, and on track. We advocated for funding to create the safe house, as well as to run a public education campaign. We put posters up in public bathrooms and on buses, where at-risk youth would be able to get the information they needed without their pimp hovering over them.

We also believed it was important to disrupt the network of brothels masquerading as massage parlors, where so many people were being sexually exploited, so we asked the board of supervisors to direct law enforcement to investigate them as one of their top priorities.

To our delight, the board of supervisors adopted and funded our recommendations. We were able to rescue scores of runaways within the first couple of years. Law enforcement, meanwhile, shut down nearly three dozen brothels in the city.

The work was meaningful, empowering, and proof that I could do serious policy work without being a legislator. It also boosted my confidence that when I saw problems, I could be the one to help devise the solutions. All those times my mother had pressed me—"Well, what did *you* do?"—suddenly made a lot more sense. I realized I didn't have to wait for someone else to take the lead; I could start making things happen on my own.

I think it was that realization that turned my sights to elected office. Of all the problems I saw in front of me, few were in more urgent need of fixing than the district attorney's office. While we were making important gains at the city attorney's office, the district attorney's office was self-destructing. Talented career prosecutors were seeing their efforts undervalued and feeling stymied in the vital work to which they'd devoted their lives. Meanwhile, violent felons were walking free. I knew this. We all knew this. But suddenly it wasn't just an important problem to be solved. It was an important problem *I* could solve.

I wanted to honor, support, and empower the DA's office as a whole. But in order to run the office, I would have to run *for* office. A political campaign would be a huge undertaking, and one I clearly couldn't embark upon lightly. I turned to my friends, my family, my colleagues, my mentors. We had long, animated debates (another thesis to defend). We weighed the pros and cons, and then we weighed them all again.

People were generally supportive of the idea, but they were worried, too. My would-be opponent and former boss was already a household name. He also had a reputation as a fighter; in fact, his nickname was Kayo (as in K.O.)—a tribute to the many knockouts he scored in his boxing youth. A campaign would be not only bruising but also expensive, and I had no experience as a fund-raiser.

Was this really the time for me to run? I had no way of knowing. But more and more, I was coming to feel that "wait and see" wasn't an option. I thought of James Baldwin, whose words had defined so much of the civil rights struggle. "There is never a time in the future in which we will work out our salvation," he'd written. "The challenge is in the moment; the time is always now."

Two

A VOICE FOR JUSTICE

K amala, let's go. Come on, we're going to be late." My mother was losing patience. "Just a second, Mommy," I called back. (Yes, my mother was and always will be "Mommy" to me.) We were on our way to campaign headquarters, where volunteers were gathering. My mother often took charge of the volunteer operation, and she didn't dillydally. Everyone knew that when Shyamala spoke, you listened.

We drove from my apartment, near Market Street, past the wealth and attractions of San Francisco's downtown to a predominantly black neighborhood in the southeast part of town known as Bayview–Hunters Point. The Bayview had been home to the Hunters Point Naval Shipyard, which helped to build America's fighting fleet in the mid-twentieth century. In the 1940s, the prospect of good jobs and affordable housing around the shipyard lured thousands of black

Americans who were seeking opportunity and relief from the pain and injustice of segregation. These workers bent the steel and welded the plates that helped our nation win the Second World War.

But like too many similar neighborhoods in America, the Bayview had been left behind in the postwar era. When the shipyard closed, nothing came to take its place. Beautiful old houses were boarded up; toxic waste polluted the soil, water, and air; drugs and violence poisoned the streets; and poverty of the worst kind settled in for the long haul. It was a community disproportionately represented in the criminal justice system and also plagued by unsolved crimes. Families in the Bayview, many of which had generational roots in San Francisco, were cut off—literally and figuratively—from the promise of the thriving city they called home. The Bayview was the kind of place that no one in the city ever saw unless they made it their business to go there. You didn't pass it on the freeway. You didn't cross it to get from one part of the city to another. It was, in deeply tragic ways, invisible to the world beyond it. I wanted to be a part of changing that. So I headquartered my campaign at 3rd Avenue and Galvez, right in the heart of the Bayview.

The political consultants thought I was nuts. They said no campaign volunteers would ever come to the Bayview from other parts of the city. But it was places like the Bayview that had inspired me to run in the first place. I wasn't running so I could have a fancy office downtown. I was running for the chance to represent people whose voices weren't being heard, and to bring the promise of public safety to every neighborhood, not just some. Besides, I didn't believe that people wouldn't come to the Bayview. And I was right: They did come. By the dozens.

San Francisco, like our country as a whole, is diverse yet deeply segregated—more mosaic than melting pot. Yet our campaign attracted people representing the full vibrancy of the whole community. Volunteers and supporters poured in from Chinatown, the Castro, Pacific Heights, the Mission District: white, black, Asian, and Latinx; wealthy and working-class; male and female; old and young; gay and straight. A group of teenage graffiti artists decorated the back wall of campaign headquarters, spray-painting JUSTICE in giant letters. HQ buzzed with volunteers, some calling voters, some sitting together around a table stuffing envelopes, others picking up clipboards so they could go door-to-door talking to people in the community about what we were trying to do.

We pulled up to headquarters just in time. I let my mother out.

"You have the ironing board?" she asked.

"Yeah, of course, it's in the back seat."

"Okay. I love you," she said as she shut the car door.

As I drove away, I could hear her call, "Kamala, what about the duct tape?"

I had the duct tape.

I got back on the road and drove toward the nearest supermarket. It was a Saturday morning, the equivalent of rush hour in the grocery aisles. I pulled into the parking lot, snuck my car into one of the few open spots, and grabbed the ironing board, the tape, and a campaign sign that looked slightly worn from being tossed in and out of the car.

If you think running for office sounds glamorous, I wish you could have seen me striding through the parking lot with an ironing board under my arm. I remember the kids who would look curiously at the ironing board and point, and the moms who would hustle them past. I couldn't blame them. I must have looked out of place—if not totally out of my mind.

But an ironing board makes for the perfect standing desk. I set it up in front of the supermarket entrance, just off to the side, near the carts, and taped up a sign that read KAMALA HARRIS, A VOICE FOR JUSTICE. When the campaign was just getting started, my friend Andrea Dew Steele and I had put together my first piece of campaign literature: a basic, one-page, black-and-white bio and summary of my positions. Andrea would later found Emerge America, an organization that recruits and trains Democratic women to run for elected office nationwide. I put several stacks of my flyer on the ironing board and, next to it, a clipboard with a sign-up sheet. Then I got to work.

Shoppers rolled their carts out the automatic doors, squinting at the sunlight, trying to remember where they parked the car. And then, out of left field:

"Hi! I'm Kamala Harris. I'm running for district attorney, and I hope to have your support."

In truth, I would have settled for them just remembering my name. Early on in the campaign, we did a poll to see how many people in the county of San Francisco had heard of me. The answer was a whopping 6 percent. As in six of every one hundred people had heard of me before. I couldn't help but wonder: Was my mother one of the people they'd randomly called?

But I hadn't gotten into this thinking it would be easy. I knew I'd have to work hard to introduce myself and what I stood for to a whole lot of people who had no idea who I was.

For some first-time candidates, interacting with strangers can feel awkward, and understandably so. It isn't easy to initiate a conversation with someone who passes you on the street, or to try to connect with them at the bus stop on their way home after work, or to walk into a merchant's business and try to strike up a conversation with the owner. I got my share of polite—and occasionally not so polite—rebuffs, like a telemarketer calling during dinner. But more often than not, I encountered people who were welcoming, open, and eager to talk about the issues affecting their daily lives and their hopes for their family and their community—whether that meant cracking down on domestic violence or creating better options for at-risk kids. Years later, I still run into people who remember our interactions at those bus stops.

It may sound strange, but the thing it reminded me of most was jury selection. When I worked as a prosecutor, I spent a lot of time in the courtroom, talking to people who'd been called for jury duty from every part of the community. My job was to ask them questions over the course of a few minutes and, based on that, try to figure out their priorities and perspectives. Campaigning was kind of like that, but without opposing counsel trying to cut me off. I loved being able to engage. Sometimes a mom would come out of the grocery store with a toddler in the shopping cart seat, and we'd find ourselves spending a good twenty minutes talking about her life, and her struggles, and her daughter's Halloween costume. Before we parted, I'd look her in the eye and say, "I hope I can have your support." It's amazing how often people would tell me that no one had ever asked them that directly before.

Still, this process didn't come naturally to me. I was always more than happy to talk about the work to be done. But voters wanted to hear about more than just policy. They wanted to know about me personally—who I was, what my life had been like, the experiences that had shaped me. They wanted to understand who I was on a fundamental level. But I'd been raised not to talk about myself. I'd been raised with the belief that there was something narcissistic about doing so. Something vain. And so, even though I understood what was motivating their questions, it took some time before I got used to it.

There were multiple candidates in my first DA's race, and a runoff was inevitable. But our polling (which had markedly improved over time) suggested that if we just made the runoff, we could win five weeks later.

I spent Election Day on the streets shaking hands, from the predawn commute until the polls closed. Chrisette, one of my closest friends, flew in to help with the last-minute campaigning. It felt like the final quarter-mile sprint at the end of a marathon—thrilling in its own way. My family, friends, senior campaign staff members, and I went out to dinner as the results started rolling in. My campaign manager, Jim Stearns, was at the elections office watching the count and calling in the numbers. Over the course of the meal, my dear friend Mark Leno, who was then a member of the California State Assembly, kept track of the counts along with Maya, my campaign consultant Jim Rivaldo, and my friend Matthew Rothschild. With each precinct that reported, and between bites of pasta, they would update the tally on the paper tablecloth.

Modern campaigns rely on big data, analytics, and sophisticated voter turnout models. But in my experience, I've found that a friend, a pen, and a bowl of spaghetti are just as effective.

We were getting ready to leave when Maya grabbed my arm. A new update had come in.

"Oh, my God, you did it!" she exclaimed. "You made the runoff!" I did the math myself to make sure she was right. I remember looking at Maya and Maya looking at me and both of us saying, "Can you believe it—we're really in this!"

The runoff was held five weeks later. It rained that day, and I spent it getting soaked as I shook hands with voters at bus stops. That night, as I'd hoped, we won a decisive victory.

We held a party at campaign headquarters, and I walked out to speak as "We Are the Champions" blasted through the room. Looking out at the crowd—friends, family, mentors, volunteers from the campaign—I saw one community. There were people from the poorest neighborhoods and the richest. Police officers alongside advocates fighting for police reform. Young people cheering with senior citizens. It was a reflection of what I've always believed to be true: when it comes to the things that matter most, we have so much more in common than what separates us.

At the time of this writing, it's been almost fifteen years since my inauguration as district attorney. I have spent almost every day since working, in some way or another, on reforming the criminal justice system. I spent two terms in its pursuit as district attorney and nearly two terms as attorney general, and I introduced criminal justice reform legislation within my first six weeks as a United States senator. Though I understood, fully, that inauguration morning in 2004, how important the issues were to me, I never could have imagined that they would lead me from San Francisco to Sacramento to Washington, DC.

My inauguration ceremony for district attorney took place in the

Herbst Theatre, in the San Francisco War Memorial and Performing Arts Center—the same stage where the United Nations Charter had been signed in 1945. Now we were making a different kind of history, but unity was still the message of the day. My mother stood between me and Ronald George, the Republican chief justice of the California Supreme Court, who I chose to swear me in. My strongest memory is of looking at her and seeing the pure pride on her face.

The room was packed to overflowing, hundreds of people from all corners of the city. Drummers drummed. A youth choir sang. One of my pastors gave a beautiful invocation. Chinese dragon dancers roamed the aisles. The San Francisco Gay Men's Chorus serenaded us all. It was multicultural, multiracial, a little frenzied in all the best and most beautiful ways.

Jerry Brown, then mayor of Oakland, was sitting in the front row; he told me that his father had taken the same oath of office sixty years ago to the day. And with Gavin Newsom's swearing-in as mayor the same day as mine, there was a palpable sense in the city that a new chapter was opening for San Francisco politics—and what might be possible for us all.

I made my way through the crowd, shaking hands and getting hugs and taking in the joy of it all. As the festivities were winding down, a man came up to me with his two young daughters.

"I brought them here today," he said, "so they could see what someone who looked like them could grow up to do."

After the inauguration, I snuck away to see my new office. I wanted to know what it felt like to sit in the chair. My communications director, Debbie Mesloh, and I drove to the Hall of Justice. Standing right next to the freeway, "850" as it was known (for 850

Bryant Street), was a gray, solemn, and imposing building; I used to joke that it was a "horribly wonderful" place to work. In addition to the district attorney's office, the building housed the police department, the criminal courts, the city tow office, the county jail, and the city coroner's office. There was no doubt this was a place where people's lives were changed, sometimes forever.

"Oh, wow." I surveyed my office. Or, more accurately, I looked around the empty room. It had been stripped of almost everything as part of the transition. A metal cabinet sat against one wall with a 1980s Wang computer on top of it. (Mind you, it was 2004.) No wonder the office hadn't gotten email yet. A plastic-lined wastebasket stood in the corner; a few loose wires stuck out of the floor. Out the window of my new office I could see a row of bail bonds businesses—a daily reminder of the ways in which the criminal justice system is more punishing to the poor. There was no desk in the office, just a chair where the desk had been. But that was okay. It was the chair I had come for. I took my seat.

Now it was quiet. And for the first time since the day began, I was alone with my thoughts, taking it all in, contemplating the surreal.

I had run because I knew I could do the job—and I believed I could do it better than it had been done. Still, I knew I represented something much bigger than my own experience. At the time, there weren't many district attorneys who looked like me or had my background. There still aren't. A report in 2015 found that 95 percent of our country's elected prosecutors were white, and 79 percent were white men.

No part of me would more fully inform my perspective than the decade I had spent on the front lines of the criminal justice system as a line prosecutor. I knew it backward and forward. For what it was, for what it wasn't, and for what it could be. The courthouse was supposed to be the epicenter of justice; but it was often a great epicenter of injustice. I knew both to be true.

I had been around the courtroom long enough to see victims of violence show up years later as perpetrators of violence. I worked with children who had grown up in neighborhoods so crime ridden that they had rates of PTSD as high as those growing up in war zones. I had worked with kids in foster care who changed homes six times before turning eighteen. I had seen them run away, from one bad circumstance into another, only to get caught in the gears of the system, with no prospect for breaking free. I had seen children marked for a bleak future solely because of the circumstances of their birth and the zip codes in which they lived. As deputy DA, my job had been to hold violators of the law accountable. But didn't the system owe them and their communities some accountability, too?

What the system doled out instead was an era of mass incarceration that has further devastated already disadvantaged communities. The United States puts more people in prison than any country in the world. All told, we had more than 2.1 million people locked up in state and federal prisons in 2018. To put that in perspective: there are fifteen American states that have smaller populations than that. The war on drugs pulled a lot of people into the system; it turned the criminal justice system into an assembly line. I saw it up close.

Early in my career, I was assigned to a part of the Alameda County DA's office known as the bridge, where lawyers in small offices would handle drug cases by the hundreds. There were bad actors in the piles, to be sure, plenty of dealers selling to kids or forcing kids to sell for them. But too many case files told a different story: a man arrested for simple possession of a few rocks of crack, a woman arrested for being under the influence while sitting on her stoop.

The cases were as easy to prove as they were tragic to charge. In the rush to clean up the streets, we were criminalizing a public health crisis. And without a focus on treatment and prevention, the crack epidemic spread like a deadly virus, burning through city after city until it had stolen a generation of people.

As I sat alone in my new office, I recalled a time, as a young prosecutor, when I overheard some of my colleagues in the hallway.

"Should we add the gang enhancement?" one of them asked.

"Can we show he was in a gang?" the other said.

"Come on, you saw what he was wearing, you saw which corner they picked him up on. Guy's got the tape of that rapper, what's his name?"

I stepped out into the hallway. "Hey, guys, just so you know: I have family that live in that neighborhood. I've got friends who dress in that style. And I've got a tape of that rapper in my car right now."

I reflected on it all—about why I ran for office, whom I had come there to help, and the difference between getting convictions and having conviction. In the end, I knew I was there for the victims. Both the victims of crimes committed and the victims of a broken criminal justice system.

For me, to be a progressive prosecutor is to understand—and act on—this dichotomy. It is to understand that when a person takes another's life, or a child is molested, or a woman raped, the perpetrators deserve severe consequences. That is one imperative of justice. But it is also to understand that fairness is in short supply in a justice system that is supposed to guarantee it. The job of a progressive prosecutor is to look out for the overlooked, to speak up for those whose voices aren't being heard, to see and address the causes of crime, not just their consequences, and to shine a light on the inequality and unfairness that lead to injustice. It is to recognize that not everyone needs punishment, that what many need, quite plainly, is help.

There was a knock at the door. It was Debbie. "You ready?" she asked, smiling.

"I'll be there in a second," I told her. I breathed in the silence for another moment. Then I pulled a pen and a yellow notepad from my briefcase and started to make a list.

I had just sat down at my desk when my administrative assistant came in. "Boss, there's another mom out here."

"Thanks, I'll be right out."

I walked down the hallway to the lobby to greet her. I'd been on the job only a few weeks, but it was not the first time I'd taken this walk. This was not the first time a woman had shown up and said, "I want to speak to Kamala. I will only speak to Kamala." I knew exactly why she was there. She was the mother of a murdered child.

The woman nearly collapsed in my arms. Her devastation was visceral. She was grieving and exhausted. And yet her being there at all was a testament to her strength. She was there for her baby, the baby she'd lost, a young man killed by gunfire in the streets. It had been months since her son's death, and yet the killer still walked free. The case was one of the more than seventy unsolved homicides languishing in the San Francisco Police Department when I took office.

I had known some of these mothers, and others I had met while I was campaigning. They were almost all black or Latina from high-crime neighborhoods, and all of them loved their children deeply. They had come together to form a group, Mothers of Homicide Victims. It was part support group, part advocacy organization. They leaned on one another to work through their grief. And they organized to get justice for their sons.

They weren't sure if I could help them, but they knew that I would at least see them. And I mean literally see them. See their pain, see their anguish, see their souls—which were bleeding. First and foremost, they knew I would see them as loving, grieving mothers.

This is part of the tragedy. When people hear that a mother has lost a child to cancer or a car accident or war, the natural response is collective sympathy and concern. But when a woman loses her son to violence in the streets, the response from the public is often different, almost a collective shrug, as though it's an expected eventuality. Not the horrific tragedy of losing a child, but rather just another statistic. As though the circumstances of her son's death define the value of his life. As though the loss she has suffered is less valid, less painful, less worthy of compassion.

I walked her back to my office so we could have some privacy to talk. She told me her son had been shot and killed, that no one had been arrested, that no one seemed to care. She described the day she had to go to the coroner's office to identify his body—how she couldn't get that image out of her head, of him lifeless in a place so cold. She had left messages for the homicide inspector, she said, suggesting possible leads, but she never heard back. Nothing had happened, nothing seemed to be happening, and she couldn't understand why. She grasped my hand and looked me straight in the eye. "He mattered," she said. "He still matters to me."

"He matters to me, too," I reassured her. His life should have mattered to everyone. I told my team to get the entire squad of homicide inspectors to convene in my conference room as soon as possible. I wanted to know what was going on with all of these cases.

The homicide inspectors showed up not knowing what to expect. At the time I didn't know it was uncommon for the district attorney to summon them for a meeting. One by one, I asked them to tell me the status of the unresolved homicide cases and pressed them for details about what they were going to do to help us get justice for these families. I had very pointed questions, and I pushed the inspectors hard—harder, I later learned, than they were expecting. This ruffled some feathers. But it was the right thing to do, and it needed to be done—regardless of whether it had ever been done before.

They took my call to action seriously. Within a month of the meeting, the police department launched a new campaign to try to encourage witnesses to step forward. And in time, we were able to reduce the backlog of unsolved homicides by 25 percent. Not every case could be solved, but we made sure we worked hard to ensure that every one that could be was.

Some people were surprised I was so relentless. And I know some others questioned how I, as a black woman, could countenance being part of "the machine" putting more young men of color behind bars. There is no doubt that the criminal justice system has deep flaws, that it is broken in fundamental ways. And we need to deal with that. But we cannot overlook or ignore that mother's pain, that child's death, that murderer who still walks the streets. I believe there must be serious consequences for people who commit serious crimes.

I've handled cases for just about every crime imaginable— including a man who had literally scalped his girlfriend during an argument. I've prosecuted sadistic criminals who have committed the most heinous, unspeakable acts against other people. I've been at homicide scenes where people had been killed, and I've won guilty verdicts against those who did the killing. I've faced cold-blooded murderers in the courtroom as a judge laid down a sentence of life in prison. And I haven't shied away from calling for harsher sentences in certain cases. In 2004, for example, I got a bill passed in California to lengthen the sentences for so-called johns who paid to have sex with underage girls. I believed that should be treated as child sexual assault.

But let's be clear: the situation is not the same—nor should it be—when it comes to less serious crimes. I remember the first time I visited the county jail. So many young men, and they were mostly black or brown or poor. Too many were there because of addiction and desperation and poverty. They were fathers who missed their kids. They were young adults, many of whom had been pulled into gangs with no real choice in the matter. The majority weren't there for violent offenses, and yet they had become drops in the sea of those swept up in a wave of mass incarceration. People whose lives had been destroyed, along with their families and their communities. They represented a living monument to lost potential, and I wanted to tear it down.

In 1977, in the heart of the San Francisco neighborhood known as Western Addition, my friend Lateefah Simon was born. She grew up in what was once a middle-class neighborhood as the crack epidemic was starting to take hold. She saw, firsthand, what it was doing to her community—the self-destructive addiction it fueled, the burden it placed on families that were already struggling to get by with little semblance of a safety net, the way it disappeared fathers and corroded even a mother's most deep-seated instinct to care for her child. When Lateefah was a young girl, her desire was to help people, but as she got older, she became one of the many who needed help. She ended up on probation for shoplifting. She dropped out of high school.

But then someone intervened. Lateefah was a teenager, working eight hours a day at Taco Bell, when an outreach worker told her about an opportunity. There was an organization in San Francisco, the Center for Young Women's Development, that provided social services, including job training, to girls and young women who were on the streets or in trouble. The center was recruiting for new staff to work there. Lateefah saw a lifeline and grabbed hold.

She started working for the center when she was a teenager and raising a daughter of her own; soon she was unstoppable. She was everywhere: at local government meetings, calling for changes to help girls who'd been trafficked; on the streets of poor neighborhoods handing out condoms and candy bars, along with information about how to get help; and at the center itself, working with vulnerable girls from her neighborhood. "I saw resilience in these young women," she recalled. "There were people who had absolutely nothing but were somehow able to make it through the day. And the next day. And the next."

The center's board members were so impressed by Lateefah's tenacity, skills, and leadership that they asked her to become executive director when she was just nineteen years old. She said yes—and that was when I came to know her.

At the city attorney's office, I had been working with the same community of women that Lateefah had. I had been holding "know your rights" sessions for vulnerable women all across the city, and I asked Lateefah to join our efforts. I could see that Lateefah was a genius, and it turned out I wasn't the only one who thought so. In 2003, she became the youngest woman to ever win the prestigious MacArthur "Genius" award (with only a GED).

When I became district attorney, I often thought to myself, "What if Lateefah had been picked up for a bag of weed instead of shoplifting? What if she'd been sentenced to prison instead of probation?" I knew what a felony conviction meant. It wasn't just about the time in prison; it was about what happens afterwards. As a country, we specialize in releasing inmates into desperate, hopeless situations. We give them a little bit of money and a bus ticket and we send them on their way with a felony conviction on their record—not the kind of experience most employers are looking for. In so many cases, finding themselves rejected in the hiring process, they have no way of making money. From the moment they leave, they are in danger of returning. They end up in the same neighborhood, with the same people, on the same corner; the only difference is that they've now served time. Prison has its own gravitational pull, often inescapable; of the hundreds of thousands of prisoners we release as a country every year, nearly 70 percent commit a crime within three years. The status quo isn't working.

I brought a small group of trusted advisers together, including my bold and brilliant chief of policy, Tim Silard, and posed a question: What would it take to put together a reentry program that actually worked? Put another way, if the best way of providing public safety is preventing crime in the first place, what can we do to prevent people from reoffending?

What if we could really get them back on track?

That question would become the name of the program Tim and I developed together: Back on Track. At the heart of the program was my belief in the power of redemption. Redemption is an age-old concept rooted in many religions. It is a concept that presupposes that we will all make mistakes, and for some, that mistake will rise to the level of being a crime. Yes, there must be consequences and accountability. But after that debt to society has been paid, is it not the sign of a civil society that we allow people to earn their way back?

There was tremendous pushback at first. At the time, criminal justice policy was still trending toward things like harsher sentences or militarizing the police. The guiding belief among many was that the criminal justice system wasn't punitive enough. More than a decade later, that attitude has, thankfully, evolved, opening up space for a more balanced approach. Reentry programs like Back on Track are now part of the mainstream conversation. But in those days, I faced intensive backlash, including from people I worked with on a regular basis. They saw a prosecutor's job as putting people in prison, not focusing on what happens to them when they get out. That was someone else's problem. I was accused of wasting precious time and resources. People would say to me, "You should be locking them up instead of letting them out."

But we persevered. It was one of the things I valued about running the office. In the end, it was up to me whether we were going to pursue the initiative. I would hear out my critics, but I wouldn't be constrained by them. I wanted to make a difference. I wanted to prove it could be done.

So Tim and I got to work. We wanted to create opportunities by running participants through a rigorous program that I often compared to boot camp. It would include job training, GED courses, community service, parenting and financial literacy classes, as well as drug testing and therapy. The DA's office led the charge, but we recruited a range of critical partners—from Goodwill Industries, which oversaw community service and employment training, to the San Francisco Chamber of Commerce and its member companies, which helped find jobs for program participants, to local trade unions, which provided valuable apprenticeship opportunities.

Though compassionate in its approach, Back on Track was intense by design. This was not a social welfare program; it was a law enforcement program. All of the first participants were nonviolent first-time offenders who had started their journey to the Hall of Justice in the back of a squad car. Participants had to first plead guilty and accept responsibility for the actions that had brought them there. We promised that if participants completed the program successfully, we would have their charges expunged, which gave them even more reason to put in the effort. We hadn't designed a program that was about incremental improvement around the edges. It was about transformation. We knew what these young people were capable of achieving—and we wanted them to see it in themselves. We wanted every participant to reach for the highest bar.

When it came time to identify someone to run the program, one name immediately came to mind. I called Lateefah.

At first, she was reluctant. She had never imagined herself as the kind of person who would work for the DA. "I never wanted to work for the Man," she told me.

"Well, don't worry," I laughed. "You won't be working for the Man. You'll be working for me."

Lateefah worked incredibly hard. And so did the Back on Track students. And on a night I'll never forget, we got to share in the fruits of that effort together.

Tim, Lateefah, and many others from my office joined me after the court had closed for the evening. We headed down the hall toward the jury assembly room. When we entered, the room was filled with people carrying flowers and balloons. The bustling, joyous mood was not typical in a jury room, to say the least. But this was not a typical night. I walked to the front of the room and opened the ceremonies for the first Back on Track graduation ceremony.

Through the main door, a group of eighteen men and women walked down the aisle to take their seats. With few exceptions, this was the first time in their lives they had ever worn graduation robes. Only a handful of them had ever had an occasion to which they could invite their family, an occasion that would make their loved ones cry happy tears. This celebration was hard-won, and they deserved every minute of it.

In the year since they started the program, each of them had, at a minimum, earned a GED and landed a steady job. They had all done community service—more than two hundred hours of it. The fathers among them had paid all of their outstanding child support payments. And they were all drug free. They proved they could do it—and that it could be done.

In exchange for that effort and that success, we were there to keep our promise. In addition to a diploma, the graduates would have their records cleared by a judge who was standing by.

A number of superior court judges volunteered to preside over Back on Track graduations, including my friend John Dearman, a former social worker who became the longest-serving judge in San Francisco's history. Another among them was Judge Thelton Henderson, an icon in the civil rights movement, who in 1963 lent his car to

Martin Luther King Jr. so Dr. King could make his way to Selma after his own car broke down.

Back on Track quickly proved its merit. After two years, only 10 percent of Back on Track graduates had reoffended, as compared with 50 percent for others convicted of similar crimes. It represented smart, effective stewardship of taxpayer dollars, too: Our program cost about $5,000 per participant. For comparison, it costs $10,000 to prosecute a felony case and another $40,000 or more to house someone for a year in the county jail.

Local officials don't have the ability to make national policy. They have no authority beyond their jurisdiction. But when they land on good ideas, even on a small scale, they can create examples that others can replicate. That was a key goal of ours in creating Back on Track. We wanted to show leaders at every level of government in every state in the union that a reentry initiative could work and was worth trying. So we were especially gratified when the Obama Justice Department adopted Back on Track as a model program.

When I later ran for attorney general, I did so, in no small part, to take the program statewide. And that's exactly what we did, working in partnership with the LA County Sheriff's Department to create Back on Track–Los Angeles (BOT-LA), in the largest county jail system in California.

I remember one day, I went out to visit a group of program participants with two of my special assistant attorneys general, Jeff Tsai and Daniel Suvor. When we arrived, we were told that the men had created a musical group and they wanted to perform a song they'd written for me. "That's great! What do they call themselves?" I asked. The answer made me smile: ContraBand. They were a wonderful sight. There was an older man in a yarmulke; a skinny guy doing his best Michael Jackson imitation; a guitarist who was definitely influenced by Santana; and a keyboardist who was channeling the Eagles. It turned out the song was called "Back on Track." The chorus was "I'm back on track and I'm not going back." They were really getting into it, having so much fun, all of them looking so proud.

We all clapped and cheered. I was laughing, but I found myself tearing up, too. I was so touched by their sincerity, which I hoped others could see in them. There was such beauty in the supposed impossibility of it all.

Whenever we held a Back on Track graduation during my time as DA, we'd make sure that current program participants were there to see what their future could hold. And whenever I spoke at those ceremonies, I'd tell the graduates what I knew to be true: that the program depended a lot more on them than on us. This accomplishment was theirs, and I wanted to make sure they knew it. But I wanted them to know that it was also bigger than themselves.

"People are watching you," I'd tell them. "They are watching you. And when they see your success, they'll think, 'Maybe we can duplicate that. Maybe we should try it back home.' You should feel inspired by that, by knowing that your individual success here will someday create an opportunity for someone you've never met before in some other part of the country."

When I first started as DA and I took out that notepad and made a to-do list, there was a lot I wanted to get done, a lot that needed to get done. I wanted to make sure I accounted for all of it. I even included "Paint the walls." I was serious, too. I've always believed there is no problem too small to fix. I know it may sound trivial, but people were working in offices that hadn't been painted in years. Not only was it a metaphor for the atrophy that had spread across the department—it was just plain depressing. The staff was demoralized. They felt undervalued, disempowered, and beaten down. Painting the walls was a tangible way to signal that I noticed—and that things were going to change.

I sent the staff a survey asking what they needed most to make the job better. One of the most common requests was for new photocopiers. It turned out that lawyers were spending hours pleading with an ancient machine and trying in vain to clear troublesome paper jams. So I ordered new copiers right away, and we celebrated more than you might expect when they arrived.

These were simple things. But the larger goal was restoring professionalism as the highest value. I knew that there was a direct link between professionalizing the operation and making sure it delivered justice. People needed to be at the top of their game. I was leading a DA's office with a former culture that pitted people against one another. I wanted to turn that on its head and make sure we worked as a team. Every Monday afternoon, I'd have all the felony trial lawyers come into the library and present their cases and the verdicts from the previous week to a roomful of their colleagues. When it was your turn, you'd stand up and talk about the legal issues of your case, how the defense was presented, how the judge had responded, any issues you'd had with witnesses, and so on. At the end, I always led the applause, no matter the outcome of the case. It wasn't so much about winning or losing. It was about applauding the professionalism of the performance.

Professionalism, as I see it, is in part about what happens inside an office. But it's also about how people carry themselves outside the office. When I trained younger lawyers, I'd say, "Let's be clear. You represent the people. So I expect you to get to know exactly who the people are." I'd tell my team to learn about the communities where they didn't live, to follow neighborhood news, to go to local festivals and community forums. "For the people" means for *them*. All of them.

The San Francisco District Attorney's Office was certainly not the only government agency that was operating poorly. And I certainly wasn't the first person to take over a mismanaged organization and focus on managing it better. But the stakes of repairing the DA's office were greater than making the trains (or, in San Francisco's case, cable cars) run on time; greater than improving morale and efficiency; greater than budgets and backlogs and conviction rates. At stake was justice itself. In a DA's office, dysfunction necessarily leads to injustice. Prosecutors are human beings; when they are not at their best, they do not perform their best—and that could mean people who should go to prison walk free and people who shouldn't go to prison end up behind bars. Such is the individual power of prosecutorial discretion.

I had divided my to-do list into three categories: short-, medium-, and long-term. Short-term meant "a couple of weeks," medium-term meant "a couple of years," and long-term meant "as long as it takes." It was that far side of the ledger where I wrote down the most intractable problems we were facing—the ones you can't expect to solve on your own, over a term, perhaps even over a career. That's where the most important work is. That's where you take the bigger view—not of the political moment but of the historical one. The core problems of the criminal justice system are not new. There are thinkers and activists and leaders who have been fighting to change the system for generations. I got to meet many of them when I was a child. You don't add the intractable problems to the list because they are new, but because they are big, because people have been fighting against them for dozens—maybe even hundreds—of years, and that duty is now yours. What matters is how well you run the portion of the race that is yours.

It was my mother who had instilled that in me. I grew up surrounded by people who were battling for civil rights and equal justice. But I had also seen it in her work. My mother was a breast cancer researcher. Like her colleagues, she dreamed of the day we'd find a cure. But she wasn't fixated on that distant dream; she focused on the work right in front of her. The work that would move us closer, day by day, year by year, until we crossed the finish line. "Focus on what's in front of you and the rest will follow," she would say.

That is the spirit we need to bring to building a more perfect union: recognition that we are part of a longer story, and we are responsible for how our chapter gets written. In the battle to build a smarter, fairer, more effective criminal justice system, there is an enormous amount of work to do. We know what the problems are. So let's roll up our sleeves and start fixing them.

One of the key issues I focused on during my first year in the Senate was the country's bail system—the process by which you can be released from jail while you await trial. It's an issue that has only begun to get the attention it deserves, given the scope and scale of the injustice it exacts on people's lives.

In this country, you are innocent until proven guilty and—unless you are a danger to others or highly likely to flee the jurisdiction—you shouldn't have to sit in jail waiting for your court date. This is the basic premise of due process: you get to hold on to your liberty unless and until a jury convicts you and a judge sentences you. It's why the Bill of Rights explicitly prohibits excessive bail. That's what justice is supposed to look like.

What it should not look like is the system we have in America today. The median bail in the United States is $10,000. But in American households with an income of $45,000, the median savings account balance is $2,530. The disparity is so high that at any given time, roughly nine out of ten people who are detained can't afford to pay to get out.

By its very design, the cash bail system favors the wealthy and penalizes the poor. If you can pay cash up front, you can leave, and when your trial is over, you'll get all of your money back. If you can't afford it, you either languish in jail or have to pay a bail bondsman, which costs a steep fee you will never get back.

When I was district attorney, I knew that every day, families were leaving the Hall of Justice, crossing the street, walking into those bail bonds offices, having done whatever it took to get the cash to pay the bondsmen—pawning their possessions, securing predatory payday loans, asking for help from their friends or at church. I also knew that people with defensible cases were taking guilty pleas just so they could get out of jail and back to their job or home to their kids.

The New York Times Magazine told the story of a struggling single mother who spent two weeks on Rikers Island, arrested and charged with endangering the welfare of a child, because she'd left her baby with a friend at a shelter while she bought diapers at Target. This young woman could not afford her $1,500 bail, and by the time she was released, her child was in foster care. In another case, sixteen-year-old Kalief Browder was arrested in New York on charges that he had stolen a backpack. When his family couldn't scrape together the $3,000 bail, Kalief went to jail while he awaited his trial. He would end up spending the next three years waiting, endlessly waiting, much of it in solitary confinement, not having ever been tried or convicted of anything. It was a tragic story from beginning to end: in 2015, soon after he was finally released from Rikers, Kalief committed suicide.

The criminal justice system punishes people for their poverty. Where is the justice in that? And where is the sense? How does that advance public safety? Between 2000 and 2014, 95 percent of the growth in the jail population came from people awaiting trial. This is a group of largely nonviolent defendants who haven't been proven guilty, and we're spending $38 million a day to imprison them while they await their day in court. Whether or not someone can get bailed out of jail shouldn't be based on how much money he has in the bank. Or the color of his skin: black men pay 35 percent higher bail than white men for the same charge. Latino men pay nearly 20 percent more. This isn't the stuff of coincidences. It is systemic. And we have to change it.

In 2017, I introduced a bill in the Senate to encourage states to replace their bail systems, moving away from arbitrarily assigning cash bail and toward systems where a person's actual risk of danger or flight is evaluated. If someone poses a threat to the public, we should detain them. If someone is likely to flee, we should detain them. But if not, we shouldn't be in the business of charging money in exchange for liberty. My lead co-sponsor in this effort is Rand Paul, a Republican senator from Kentucky with whom I vehemently disagree on most things. But this is one of those issues that he and I agree on— that all of us should agree on. It's an issue that can—and does— transcend politics, and, one way or another, we're going to get it done.

Something else it's past time we get done is dismantling the failed war on drugs—starting with legalizing marijuana. According to the FBI, more people were arrested for marijuana possession than for all violent crimes in 2016. Between 2001 and 2010, more than seven million people were arrested for simple possession of marijuana. They are disproportionately black and brown. One stark example: during the first three months of 2018, 93 percent of the people the NYPD arrested for marijuana possession were people of color. These racial disparities are staggering and unconscionable. We need to legalize marijuana and regulate it. And we need to expunge nonviolent marijuana-related offenses from the records of the millions of people who have been arrested and incarcerated so they can get on with their lives.

But let's do it with eyes wide open, understanding that there is unfinished business when it comes to legalization. There is no widely used equivalent to a breathalyzer that law enforcement officials agree is consistently reliable. We need to invest in a solution. We also need to acknowledge what we don't know about the effects of marijuana. Because marijuana has been deemed a Schedule 1 drug, doctors and scientists have been able to do only limited research on its effects. We need to understand any risks. And that means committing ourselves to doing the research, listening to what the science tells us, and acting on that information in our approach.

We also need to stop treating drug addiction like a public safety crisis instead of what it is: a public health crisis. When people suffering from drug addiction end up involved in the criminal justice system, our ambition has to be to get them help. It's time that we all accept that addiction is a disease, that it wreaks havoc on people's lives in ways they don't want and never intended. It's time we recognize that addiction does not discriminate, and that our laws shouldn't either. When someone is suffering from addiction, their situation is made worse, not better, by involvement in the criminal justice system. What they need is treatment, and we should fight for a system that provides it.

And even when people have committed offenses that require jail time, we should reject the notion that they are irredeemable or that they don't deserve a second chance. We still have mandatory minimums on the books, many of which have a disproportionate impact across racial lines. And we have to unravel the decadeslong effort to make sentencing guidelines excessively harsh to the point of being inhumane.

Thankfully, we have started to see progress: In the decade after we introduced Back on Track, some thirty-three states have adopted new sentencing and corrections policies aimed at promoting alternatives to incarceration and reducing recidivism. And since 2010, twenty-three states have reduced their prison populations. But there is still much more work to do to ensure that punishments are proportionate to the offense.

We also need to address what happens behind the prison gates. Women now represent the fastest-growing segment of our incarcerated population. Most of them are mothers, and the vast majority are survivors of violent trauma that usually goes undiagnosed and untreated. Many are imprisoned in facilities that don't support basic hygiene or reproductive health. As you read this, there are women being shackled while they're pregnant. In some states, they are shackled while giving birth. I have visited women in prison, heard stories of the ways they face the risk of sexual violence when supervised by male guards in the bathroom or shower. In 2017, I was proud to co-sponsor a bill to deal with some of these issues. This is a conversation we rarely have in this country—and we need to.

In the near term, one of the most urgent challenges is the fight against those who are ripping apart the critical progress we've made in recent years. The current administration has reescalated the war on drugs, reemphasized incarceration over rehabilitation, and rolled back investigations into civil rights violations at police departments that began during the Obama administration. They are even trying to tear up agreements made between the Obama Justice Department and certain police departments that are meant to end policies and practices that violate people's constitutional rights. We can't go backward on these issues when we have only begun to scratch the surface of progress. We have to act with fierce urgency. Justice demands it.

One thing we must do is take on, head-on, the racial bias that operates throughout our criminal justice system. And that effort starts with our stating clearly and unequivocally that black lives matter—and speaking truth about what that means. The facts are clear: Nearly four years after Ferguson, Missouri, became the flashpoint for the Black Lives Matter movement, the state attorney general reported that black drivers there are 85 percent more likely to be pulled over than their white neighbors. Across the nation, when a police officer stops a black driver, he is three times more likely to search the car than when the driver is white. Black men use drugs at the same rate as white men, but they are arrested twice as often for it. And then they pay more than a third more than their counterparts, on average, in bail. Black men are six times as likely as white men to be incarcerated. And when they are convicted, black men get sentences nearly 20 percent longer than those given to their white counterparts. Latino men don't fare much better. It is truly appalling.

It's one thing to say that black lives matter. But awareness and solidarity aren't enough. We need to accept hard truths about the systemic racism that has allowed this to happen. And we need to turn that understanding into policies and practices that can actually change it.

When I was attorney general, I brought the senior leadership of our investigative bureau together, led by Larry Wallace, the director of my office's Bureau of Law Enforcement, and told them that I wanted to institute an implicit bias and procedural justice training program for our agents. Implicit bias lives in split seconds. It is the unconscious shorthand that our brains use to help us make a quick judgment about a stranger. Frontline officers, more than most, have to make split-second judgments all the time, where implicit bias can have a deadly outcome.

The presentation of the subject matter made for a difficult conversation—and understandably so. These senior leaders had dedicated their lives and taken an oath to law enforcement. It wasn't easy to have to reckon with the idea that the men and women of their bureau carry bias with them, that it affects the community, and that they need to be trained to deal with it. But it was an honest conversation, and in the end, the leadership not only agreed it was important, but they also agreed to help create, shape, and lead the training while advocating for its necessity up and down the chain.

Larry and my special assistant attorney general, Suzy Loftus, then worked to develop a curriculum that could be adopted by police academics and offered to law enforcement agencies statewide. We partnered with the Oakland and Stockton police departments and the

California Partnership for Safe Communities to create the training program, and brought in Professor Jennifer Eberhardt from Stanford University to evaluate its effectiveness. It became the first statewide implicit bias and procedural justice course offered anywhere in the country.

None of us were naive about what our training course could accomplish. We knew that such an effort, alone, would not rid the system of bias. And we surely knew that explicit bias, not just implicit bias, permeated the system. Racism is real in America, and police departments are not immune. At the same time, we knew that better training would make a real difference, that for most members of law enforcement, a better understanding of their own implicit biases could be revelatory. We knew that the hard conversations involved in the training course were the kind that stayed with a person, the kind of thing they'd take with them to the streets.

We need to speak another truth: police brutality occurs in America and we have to root it out wherever we find it. With the advent of the smartphone, what was well known only to certain communities is now being seen by the world. People can no longer pretend it isn't happening. It cannot be ignored or denied when we see video of Walter Scott, unarmed, shot in the back as he ran from an officer. We cannot ignore the horrified cries of Philando Castile's girlfriend after he was shot seven times by a police officer while reaching for his driver's license—all with her four-year-old daughter in the back seat. "It's okay, Mommy . . . it's okay. I'm right here with you," the little girl said, in a heartbreaking attempt to comfort. We cannot forget Eric Garner's desperate words—"I can't breathe"—as a police officer strangled him to death during an arrest for selling cigarettes.

And we must remember that tragedies like these occur over and over again, most of them unfilmed and unseen. If people fear murder and beatings and harassment from the police who patrol their streets, can we really say that we live in a free society?

And what does it say about our standards of justice when police officers are so rarely held accountable for these incidents? The Minnesota officer who shot Philando Castile was tried for second-degree manslaughter. But he was acquitted. In Ohio, a police officer climbed onto the hood of a car after a car chase and fired forty-nine times at its occupants, Timothy Russell and Malissa Williams, both of whom were unarmed. The officer was charged—and acquitted. In Pennsylvania, a police officer shot an unarmed driver in the back while he lay facedown in the snow. But he, too, was acquitted of murder.

If there aren't serious consequences for police brutality in our justice system, what kind of message does that send to police officers? And what kind of message does it send to the community? Public safety depends on public trust. It depends on people believing they will be treated fairly and transparently. It depends on a justice system that is steeped in the notions of objectivity and impartiality. It depends on the basic decency our Constitution demands.

But when black and brown people are more likely to be stopped, arrested, and convicted than their white counterparts; when police departments are outfitted like military regiments; when egregious use of deadly force is not met with consequence, is it any wonder that the very credibility of these public institutions is on the line?

I say this as someone who has spent most of my career working with law enforcement. I say this as someone who has a great deal of respect for police officers. I know that most police officers deserve to be proud of their public service and commended for the way they do their jobs. I know how difficult and dangerous the job is, day in and day out, and I know how hard it is for the officers' families, who have to wonder if the person they love will be coming home at the end of each shift. I've been to too many funerals of officers killed in the line of duty. But I also know this: it is a false choice to suggest that you must either be for the police or for police accountability. I am for both. Most people I know are for both. Let's speak some truth about that, too.

Make no mistake: we need to take on this and every aspect of our broken criminal justice system. We need to change our laws and our standards. And we need to elect people who will make it their mission to do so.

So let's recruit more progressives into prosecutors' offices, where many of the biggest problems and best solutions start. Prosecutors are among the most powerful actors in our system of justice. They have the power to prioritize what they work on. They can choose to focus their time and attention on anything from corporate and consumer fraudsters to sexual predators. They have the power to put criminals behind bars, but they also have the discretion to dismiss cases where police used excessive force, or conducted a search and seizure without probable cause. We need people who come from all walks of life and different backgrounds and experiences to sit at the table and wield that kind of power.

We also need to keep the pressure on from the outside, where organizations and individuals can create meaningful change. When I was attorney general, I made sure ours was the first state law enforcement agency to require body cameras for its agents. I did it because it was the right thing to do. But I was able to do it because the Black Lives Matter movement had created intense pressure. By forcing these issues onto the national agenda, the movement created an environment on the outside that helped give me the space to get it done on the inside. That's often how change happens. And I credit the movement for those reforms just as much as anyone in my office, including me.

Engaging in the fight for civil rights and social justice is not for the faint of heart. It is as difficult as it is important, and the wins may never taste as sweet as the losses taste sour. But count yourself as part of the lineage of those who refused to relent. And when we're feeling frustrated and discouraged by the obstacles in front of us, let's channel the words of Constance Baker Motley, one of my inspirations as the first black American woman appointed to the federal judiciary. "Lack of encouragement never deterred me," she wrote. "In fact, I think the effect was just the opposite. I was the kind of person who would not be put down."

Three

UNDERWATER

W e were renters for most of my childhood, and my mother took incredible pride in our home. It was always ready for company, with fresh-cut flowers. The walls were decorated with big posters of artwork by LeRoy Clarke and other artists from the Studio Museum in Harlem, where Uncle Freddy worked. There were statues from her travels in India, Africa, and elsewhere. She cared a great deal about making our apartment a home, and it always felt warm and complete. But I knew my mother always wanted something more. She wanted to be a homeowner.

She would be the first to point out the practical considerations— that it was a smart investment. But it was so much more than that. It was about her earning a full slice of the American Dream.

My mother had wanted to buy her first home while Maya and I were still young—a place to grow up with a sense of permanence. But it would take many years before she could save up enough money for a down payment.

I was in high school when it happened. Maya and I had just gotten home from school when she pulled out the pictures to show us—a one-level dark-gray house on a cul-de-sac, with a shingled roof, a beautiful lawn in front, an outdoor space on the side for a barbecue. She was so excited to show us, and we were so excited to see it—not only because it meant we got to move back to Oakland, but because of the intense joy we saw in her face. She had earned it, quite literally. "This is our house!" I would tell my friends, proudly showing off the pictures. It was going to be our piece of the world.

That memory was on my mind when I traveled to Fresno, California, in 2010, in the midst of a devastating foreclosure crisis in which so many people had their own piece of the world destroyed.

Fresno is the largest city in California's San Joaquin Valley, an area that has been described as the "Garden of the Sun." The San Joaquin Valley is one of the world's most abundant agricultural regions, providing a significant share of the fruits and vegetables consumed in the United States. Amid the acres of almond trees and vineyards full of grapes live about four million people, a population roughly the size of Connecticut's.

Many middle-class families saw a life in Fresno as their best shot at the American Dream. It was a place with promise, a place where they could afford a real single-family home on a suburban street, a place that represented America's vitality, mobility, and hope. In the early 2000s, the population of the San Joaquin Valley was young and growing, and nearly 40 percent Latinx. For so many people who moved there, the six-hour round-trip commute to their jobs in San

Francisco or Sacramento was exhausting, but a worthy price to pay for what they got in exchange: the sense of dignity, pride, and security that came with becoming an American homeowner.

New suburban developments seemed to sprout up every month, taking root in the fertile soil as if they were another cash crop. That wasn't far off. Fresno's real estate boom was fueled by broader economic trends, trends that ultimately sparked an economic inferno.

In the wake of 9/11, central banks around the world slashed their interest rates. This capital-rich environment prompted lenders to become increasingly aggressive, luring more and more borrowers with enticing loan offers like "interest only," "zero down," and even "NINJA" (no income, no job, no assets). High-risk subprime mortgages flooded the housing market, with teaser rates seemed too good to be true. Lenders reassured home buyers (and themselves) that homeowners would just refinance their mortgages before their payments spiked. The reward was worth the risk, because, as they saw it, housing prices were only and always destined to go up.

Meanwhile, global investors were on the hunt for greater returns, which led them toward ever riskier opportunities to place their bets. Wall Street financiers were only too happy to meet this voracious demand, creating newfangled securities backed by the same deeply questionable mortgages. Investors who bought those mortgaged-backed securities believed that the banks had done their due diligence, only bundling together home loans that could and would be paid on time. Few realized they were actually purchasing ticking time bombs.

Remarkably, about half of all of these mortgage-backed securities ended up on the balance sheets of big banks after they realized that holding the securities, rather than the mortgages themselves, would help them avoid traditional regulation. The cycle fed on itself, spinning faster and faster, until it spun right off the rails. In 2006, the housing market peaked. A major housing crisis loomed.

Banks and investors tried to dump their bad securities, which only made things worse. Wall Street started to implode. Bear Stearns failed. Lehman Brothers filed for bankruptcy. Credit started drying up. The economy went into freefall. By 2009, homes in the Fresno area had lost more than half their value, the largest decline in the nation. At the same time, people living in Fresno were losing their jobs in droves; by November 2010, the unemployment rate had soared to 17 percent.

Meanwhile, the teaser rates on loans had expired, and borrowers' mortgages were doubling. Scam artists and fraudsters descended like vultures, promising frantic homeowners relief from foreclosure, only to take their money and run.

This happened all over the country. Consider the story of Karina and Juan Santillan, who bought a home twenty miles east of Los Angeles in 1999. Juan had worked for twenty years at an ink-manufacturing plant, while Karina sold insurance. "A few years after they bought their home, the Santillans say, people started knocking on their door selling financial products," *The Atlantic* reported. "It was easy money, the Santillans were told. Borrow against your house, it's sure to gain value." Like millions of Americans, the Santillans were persuaded to take out an adjustable-rate mortgage on their home. At the time, their monthly payment was $1,200. By 2009 it had risen to $3,000—and Karina had lost her job. Suddenly at risk of losing their house, they contacted a company that promised to protect them. After paying $6,800 for services that were supposed to help, they realized they had been scammed. Ten years after purchas-

My parents met at Berkeley during the civil rights movement. They were married soon after.

My mother and her dear friend Auntie Lenore were part of the protests against Birmingham atrocities.

At twenty-five years old, Mommy had a college degree, a PhD, and me.

Proud daddy on his way to a doctorate in economics at Berkeley. (April 1965)

When I was ten months old, I visited Spanish Town, Jamaica. This is me with my mother and my paternal grandfather, Oscar Joseph.

With my great grandmother Iris Finegan in Jamaica.

Visiting my uncle Freddy in Harlem. Harlem was always
a magical place for me. (September 1966)

Couldn't have been more excited
to welcome my baby sister, May.
(March 1967)

Grandpa and me when we visited him and my grandmother in Lusaka, Zambia. He was sent on a diplomatic mission by India to assist the African nation when it gained independence. Grandpa was one of my favorite people in the world and one of the earliest and most lasting influences in my life.

Christmas 1968. Sisters waiting for Santa Claus.

Mommy, Maya, and me outside of our apartment on Milvia Street
after my parents separated. From then on, we were known
as Shyamala and the girls. (January 1970)

Sporting my 'fro. (Summer of 1970)

My class at Thousand Oaks Elementary School was only the second
in Berkeley to be integrated. This is Mrs. Wilson's first grade.
That's me in the middle, in the white sweater.

This is my sixth birthday party. Included in this photo is Stacey Johnson, my best friend in kindergarten and still one of my closest friends today.

Maya and me at Madam Bovie's Ballet Studio. I loved dancing as a child. I still do.

My favorite pleather jacket at age seven. (December 1971)

Hanging out with my family in Jamaica. Maya is off to the right.

My maternal grandparents came to visit in 1972. You can see my mom's yellow Dodge Dart to the left. We lived just up those stairs, above the nursery school.

Long before "take your kid to work day," my mother often
took us to her lab in Berkeley. She had two goals in life:
to raise her two daughters and to end breast cancer.

This is Maya and me in the front
yard of our building. You can see the
Bancroft Nursery sign just behind us.
We lived upstairs.

My mother always said to me, "Kamala,
you may be the first to do many things.
Make sure you're not the last."

In front of Mrs. Shelton's house, holding her granddaughter Saniyyah. The house was always full of children, good cooking, and lots of love. (Summer 1978)

During my freshman year at Howard University, almost every weekend was spent at the Mall protesting apartheid and calling for divestment. Here I am with Gwen Whitfield. (November 1982)

Visiting my paternal grandmother, Beryl, in Jamaica.

Graduating from University of California Hastings College of the
Law in May 1989. My first grade teacher, Mrs. Wilson (left),
came to cheer me on. My mom was pretty proud, too.

Even after I started working in the Alameda County District Attorney's Office, I would return to Mrs. Shelton's kitchen, where I always knew I would receive a warm hug and delicious food.

We held the campaign kickoff for my DA's race at the Women's Building in San Francisco. My mother is addressing the crowd. She could also regularly be found organizing volunteers, licking envelopes, and generally doing anything that was needed. Also pictured: San Francisco Supervisors Sophie Maxwell and Fiona Ma, and State Assembly Member Mark Leno.

I'm blessed with an amazing family. I'll never be able to thank Auntie Chris, Uncle Freddy, and Aunt Mary enough for their constant encouragement and support. They always showed up for me, as they did here at a campaign event for my DA's race that we held at a San Francisco jazz club.

On Election Night in November 2003, we went to dinner as the vote tallies started to come in. My brother-in-law, Tony West, along with my dear friends Matthew Rothschild and Mark Leno, and my campaign consultant Jim Rivaldo, are writing down early returns on the paper tablecloth. We tore off the tally and I still have it framed in my office.

I won the runoff five weeks later, becoming the first female district attorney of San Francisco. Here I am at campaign headquarters, standing before the word "justice," which volunteers had spray painted on the walls. Behind my left shoulder is my mother. Behind her are Chris Cunnie and City Attorney Dennis Herrera. Chris would later become chief of my bureau of investigations.

After my inauguration, I went over to my new office to see what it would be like. It was totally empty except for a chair in the middle. I was happy to take my seat.

I loved having my mother with me at community events.
Here we are at the Chinese New Year parade. (2007)

ing their home, they were forced to tell their four children they were going to have to leave.

This pattern played out with particular force in Fresno and Stockton. Local leaders pleaded with the federal government to declare the region a disaster area and send help. "Disaster area" was an apt description: entire neighborhoods were abandoned, and the area was suffering one of the highest foreclosure rates in the nation. Sometimes families were struggling so hard to pay their mortgages that they would abruptly pick up and leave. I heard stories of pets being abandoned because their owners could no longer afford to keep them—a phenomenon the Humane Society was reporting all across the country, from Little Rock to Cleveland to Albuquerque. When I visited Fresno, I was told that abandoned dogs had been seen roaming in packs. I felt like I was walking through the aftermath of a natural disaster. But this disaster was man-made.

When the crash finally bottomed out, 8.4 million Americans nationwide had lost their jobs. Roughly 5 million homeowners were at least two months behind on their mortgages. And 2.5 million foreclosures had been initiated.

Two and a half million foreclosures initiated. There is something clinical about saying it that way. Something that makes the human tragedy and trauma seem abstract.

Foreclosure is not a statistic.

Foreclosure is a husband suffering in silence, knowing he's in trouble but too ashamed to tell his partner that he has failed. Foreclosure is a mother on the phone with her bank, pleading for more time— just until the school year is over. Foreclosure is the sheriff knocking at your door and ordering you out of your home. It is a grandmother on the sidewalk in tears, watching her life's possessions being removed from her house by strangers and left exposed in the yard. It is learning from a neighbor that your house was just auctioned off on the steps of City Hall. It is the changing of locks, the immolation of dreams. It is a child learning for the first time that parents can be terrified, too.

Homeowners told me countless stories of personal catastrophe. And as the months dragged on, the news media continued to surface strange reports about irregularities in the foreclosure process. We learned about people whose banks couldn't find their mortgage documents. There were stories of people discovering that they actually owed tens of thousands of dollars less than the banks said they did. A man in Florida had his house foreclosed on and put up for sale—even though he'd bought the house with cash and never *had* a mortgage.

Tales emerged of a process that became known as dual tracking. Through a program with the federal government, banks were working with borrowers on one track to modify loan terms, which was supposed to make it easier for people to stay in their homes. But often borrowers were working on a second track, too, foreclosing on homes anyway, even after making such modifications, even after the home-owner had spent several months paying the new reduced amount. The banks left homeowners with no explanation, no point of contact, and no recourse.

Clearly, something had gone awry. But it wasn't until the end of September 2010 that a major part of the scandal would break wide open. That was when we learned that the country's largest banks—including Bank of America, JPMorgan Chase, and Wells Fargo—had been illegally foreclosing on people's homes since 2007, using a practice that became known as "robo-signing."

We learned that to speed up the foreclosure process, financial institutions and their mortgage servicers hired people with no formal financial training—from Walmart floor workers to hair stylists—and placed them in "foreclosure expert" positions with one responsibility: sign off on foreclosures by the thousands.

In depositions, robo-signers acknowledged that they had little or no familiarity with the documents they were paid to approve. The job wasn't to understand and evaluate; it was simply to sign their name, or to forge someone else's. They got paid $10 an hour. And they got bonuses for volume. There was no accountability. No transparency. None of the due diligence required by law. From the banks' point of view, the faster they got bad loans off their balance sheet, the faster their stock price would rebound. And if that meant breaking the law, so be it. They could afford the fine. It was painful to me when I realized that the banks viewed a fine as just the cost of doing business. It became clear to me that they had built it into their bottom line. It was a damning portrait of an aspect of Wall Street culture that persists, the part that seems to care little—if at all—about the collateral damage caused by recklessness and greed.

I had seen it up close in the district attorney's office, where we'd prosecuted mortgage scammers for defrauding the elderly and veterans. In 2009, as DA, I created a mortgage fraud unit to fill in the areas of chronic under-enforcement by the federal government. But as the foreclosure crisis ballooned, I was eager to take on bigger culprits, to go after the bad-acting banks themselves. And it seemed I might have a chance.

On October 13, 2010, the attorneys general of all fifty states agreed to join together in what's known as a multistate investigation.

It was billed as a comprehensive, nationwide law enforcement effort to uncover the banks' actions in the foreclosure crisis.

I was eager to join the fight, but there was just one small problem: I wasn't yet California's attorney general.

I was in the middle of my campaign when the multistate was announced, and there were still three weeks left until Election Day. The polls were predicting a very close race.

On Election Night 2010, I lost the race for attorney general. Three weeks later, I won.

I'd started the evening with what had become a ritual: a friends-and-family dinner. Then we headed to the Election Night party, which we held on the San Francisco waterfront, in the headquarters of my dear friend Mimi Silbert's Delancey Street Foundation—a leading residential self-help and job training organization for addicts, substance abusers, the formerly incarcerated, and others trying to turn their lives around. We arrived as results started to trickle in from precincts around the state. In the main room, supporters were gathered, waiting in anticipation for the results. Behind them stood risers for TV cameras and press pointed at the stage. We went in through the back and into a side room where my staff was gathered. They had arranged four tables into a square, and most of them were sitting there, staring at their laptops, hitting *refresh* on the websites keeping track of the tally. I greeted everyone, my spirits high, and thanked them for all their hard work.

Then Ace Smith, my chief strategist, pulled me aside.

"How's it looking?" I asked.

"It's going to be a very long night," Ace said. My opponent was in the lead.

I'd always known that I could take nothing for granted. Even plenty of fellow Democrats had considered me a long shot, and some hadn't held back in saying so. One longtime political strategist announced to an audience at UC Irvine that there was no way I could win, because I was "a woman running for attorney general, a woman who is a minority, a woman who is a minority who is anti–death penalty, a woman who is a minority who is anti–death penalty who is DA of wacky San Francisco." Old stereotypes die hard. I was convinced that my perspective and experience made me the strongest candidate in the race, but I didn't know if the voters would agree. The past few weeks, I'd done so much knocking on wood that my knuckles were bruised.

By 10 p.m., we were not much closer to knowing the outcome of the race. I was trailing, but we knew that a lot of precincts had yet to report. Ace suggested that I go out and address the crowd. "The cameras aren't going to stay much longer," he said, "so if you have a message for your supporters tonight, I think you should do that now." It sounded like a smart idea to me.

I left the staff room, spent a few quiet minutes thinking about what I would say, then straightened my suit jacket and walked into the main room and onto the stage. I told the audience that it was going to be a long night, but that it was going to be a good night, too. My opponent was losing ground by the minute, I assured them. I reminded them what our campaign was about and what we stood for. "This campaign is so much bigger than me. It is so much bigger than any one person."

At some point during my speech, I noticed a shift in the room.

People seemed to be getting emotional. Back in the staff room, I later learned, two of my best friends, Chrisette and Vanessa, were sitting on the couch, sipping wine, listening to my speech. Chrisette turned to Vanessa:

"I don't think she knows."

"I don't think she knows, either."

"You gonna tell her?"

"Nope. You?"

"Nope."

I was just finishing my remarks when I saw Debbie Mesloh, my longtime communications adviser, approaching. She mouthed to me, "Get off the stage and go to the back room, now." That wasn't reassuring. I finished my remarks and was making my way to Debbie when I was intercepted by a reporter and her cameraman.

"So what do you think happened?" she asked, putting the microphone in my face.

"I think we ran a really great race and it's going to be a long night." I said.

The reporter seemed confused, and so was I. The more questions she asked, the more it was clear we weren't connecting at all. Clearly something had happened, and I was out of the loop. When I finally got back to the staff room, I learned what. While I'd been onstage, talking about what lay ahead, the *San Francisco Chronicle* had called the race for my opponent. No wonder people were crying! I'd been the only one out there who thought we were still in the game.

Realizing that our hometown paper had called the race against us felt like a punch in the gut. The mood was grim as my team and I huddled together in the greenroom. After so many months of working so hard, excitement was giving way to exhaustion. I looked around at the slumping shoulders and sad expressions. I couldn't bear the thought of sending our volunteers home feeling this way.

Ace called me over. "Listen, I'm looking at the numbers, and a lot of our strongest areas haven't come in. They called the race too early. We're still in this."

I knew he couldn't see the future—but Ace wasn't the kind of person who blew smoke. He knew California down to the precinct level, better than perhaps anyone in the state. If he thought we were still in it, I believed him. I told my supporters we weren't giving up.

My opponent had a different view of things. Around 11 p.m., he stood up in front of the cameras and delivered a speech in Los Angeles declaring victory. But we waited. And waited—getting regular updates from the field and trying to keep one another's spirits high.

Around 1 a.m., I leaned over to my childhood friend Derreck, who was like a cousin and who owned a chicken and waffle restaurant in Oakland. "Is your kitchen still open?"

"Don't worry," he promised. "I'll take care of it."

Sure enough, the next thing I knew, Delancey Street was filled with the mouthwatering aroma of fried chicken and corn bread and greens and candied yams. We all gathered around the aluminum pans and ate. About an hour later, with 89 percent of the precincts in, we were tied.

Finally, I turned to Maya. "I'm exhausted. Do you think anybody's going to have a problem if I leave?"

"Everybody will be fine," she assured me. "People are waiting for you to leave so they can, too."

I went home and got maybe an hour or two of sleep, only to be jolted back awake by the sound of news helicopters circling in the sky.

The Giants were celebrating their first World Series win in more than fifty years with a parade down Market Street. Most of the city was dressed in orange and black.

But the Giants' victory wasn't the only good news. More votes had come in, and I was now ahead in the race, albeit only by a few thousand votes. From the lowest of lows, now it felt like our campaign had vaulted to the peak of the mountain—on a day when music was rising from the streets and confetti raining down from the skies.

With two million votes still waiting to be tallied, there was a good chance we weren't going to know the results for weeks. The counties had about a month to finish counting and certify their tallies.

My phone rang. It was John Keker, a storied lawyer in the Bay Area and a dear friend. He told me that he was assembling a team of top lawyers. "Kamala, we're ready to convene to defend you if there's a recount." If there was going to be a recount, it wasn't going to happen any time soon. The earliest that either of us could request one would be November 30.

In the meantime, members of my campaign staff, led by my campaign manager, Brian Brokaw, activated dozens of volunteers, who put off their vacation plans and got back to work. They fanned out across the state, in county after county, to monitor the vote counting in real time and report any irregularities. Days extended into weeks. Thanksgiving was fast approaching. And all the while, there was a roller coaster of results, making the whole thing pretty excruciating. It reminded me of my days trying cases, when a jury would go off to deliberate and there was nothing left to do but wait. We reconciled ourselves to the fact that nothing was likely to happen with the count over Thanksgiving weekend, so we sent everyone home to be with their families.

Early Wednesday morning, I headed for the airport to catch a flight to New York. I was going to spend the holiday with Maya, my brother-in-law, Tony, and my niece, Meena.

As we were pulling off the highway, I got a text from a district attorney who had supported my opponent. "I look forward to working with you," it read.

I called my campaign team. "What's going on? Have you heard anything?" I asked.

"We're hearing he's going to have a press conference. That's all we know right now." I was just pulling into the airport terminal. "We'll check into it and get back to you." I made it through security and onto the plane without hearing another word. I was in an aisle seat, and fellow passengers, in their Giants caps and jerseys, were walking past me asking, "Kamala, have you won yet? Do you know what's going on?" All I could do was smile and say, "I don't know. I don't know."

I took out my phone and realized that, going through the airport, I'd missed an incoming call. There was a voicemail from my opponent asking me to call him back. I dialed his number as the cabin doors were closing and the flight attendants were directing passengers to put their cell phones away.

"I want you to know I'll be conceding," he said.

"You ran a great race," I said.

"I hope you know how big a job this is going to be," he added.

"Have a nice Thanksgiving with your family," I replied.

And that was it. Of the nearly nine million ballots cast statewide, I had won by the equivalent of three votes per precinct. I was so relieved, so excited, so ready to start. I wanted to call everyone, but the next thing I knew, we were barreling down the runway, and then we were in the air—with no Wi-Fi. My twenty-one-day election night was over, and all I could do was sit there. Alone with my thoughts. For five hours.

Because the count had taken so long, there was only a month to process the victory before my swearing-in. And beyond the election, I was also still processing the grief of my mother's death. She'd passed away the year before, in February 2009, as the long, hard-fought campaign was just getting under way. I will say more about this in a chapter to come, but, needless to say, it was crushing to lose her. I knew what my election would have meant to her. How I wished she could be there to see it.

When January 3, 2011, arrived, I walked down the stairs of the California Museum for Women, History, and the Arts, in Sacramento, to greet the standing-room-only crowd. We had arranged for a wonderful inaugural ceremony, with Bishop T. Larry Kirkland Sr. giving the opening invocation and a gospel singer at the close. Flags were waving, dignitaries were there, observers peered down from the balcony. Maya held Mrs. Shelton's Bible as I took the oath of office. But what I remember most vividly about the day was the worry I felt about saying my mother's name in my address while keeping my composure. I'd practiced over and over again, and choked up every time. But it was important to me that her name be spoken in that room, because none of what I had achieved would have been possible without her.

"Today, with this oath," I told the crowd, "we affirm the principle that every Californian matters."

It was a principle that would be put to the test in the heady weeks that followed. Later that month, 37,000 homeowners lined up in Los Angeles to plead with banks to modify their mortgages so they could stay in their homes. In Florida, there were lines that quite literally stretched for days. "In the 1930s, we had bread lines," said Scott Pelley on *60 Minutes,* during a segment on the foreclosure crisis. "Venture out before dawn in America today and you'll find mortgage lines."

On my first day in office, I gathered my senior team and told them that we needed to get involved right away in the multistate investigation into the banks. I had appointed Michael Troncoso, a longtime member of my team, as chief counsel in the attorney general's office, and Brian Nelson as special assistant attorney general. I asked them to dig in and get us up to speed.

Inside the office we were preparing for battle. Outside the office, we were constantly reminded of who we were fighting for. At every event we held, there was always a group of people—sometimes five or ten or twenty—who had come in the hope of seeing me and asking for my help, face-to-face. Most brought their paperwork with them— accordion folders and manila envelopes overflowing with mortgage documents and foreclosure notices and handwritten notes. Some had driven hundreds of miles to find me.

I'll never forget the woman who interrupted a small health care event I was doing at Stanford. She stood up in the audience, tears streaming down her face, desperation in her voice. "I need help. You need to help me. I need you to help call the bank and tell them to let me stay in my home. Please, I'm begging you." It was heartbreaking.

I also knew there were tens of thousands of people just like her, fighting for their lives, who didn't have the ability to track down the attorney general in person. So we went directly to them, holding roundtable meetings in community centers across the state. I wanted them to see us. I also wanted my team to see them, so that when we were sitting across from the bank executives in a conference room, we'd remember who we were representing. At one of these convenings, I was speaking to a man about the problems he was having with the banks. His young son was playing quietly nearby. And then the little boy came over and looked up at his father.

"Daddy, what does 'underwater' mean?"

I could see the awful fear in his eyes. He thought his father was literally drowning.

It was a terrible thing to contemplate. But the metaphor was apt: a lot of people had gone under. Still more were clinging by their fingernails to the edge. And every day that went by, more and more of those desperate people were losing their grip.

Over the course of our battle with the banks, we'd heard so many stories that underscored that these issues weren't intellectual or academic; they were about people's lives. At one homeowners' roundtable, a woman described with pride the home she had saved up to buy in 1997—the first home she'd ever purchased as an adult. After falling one month behind on a loan payment in early 2009, she'd called her lender asking for advice. Representatives for the lender said they could help, but after months of their insisting she produce and fax them endless paperwork, of sending her documents without explanation and demanding that she sign, of keeping her in the dark as she sought answers to her questions, her home was foreclosed upon from under her feet.

Fighting back tears as she shared her story with me, she said, "I'm sorry. I know it's just a house . . ." But she knew, as we all do, that it's never "just a house."

My first opportunity to get personally involved in the multistate talks arrived in early March. The National Association of Attorneys General—whose acronym, NAAG, is appropriate—was holding its annual multiday meeting at the Fairmont hotel, in Washington, DC. I flew in with my team. All fifty attorneys general were there, seated in alphabetical order by state. I took my spot between Arkansas and Colorado.

As the conversation turned from general business to the multistate investigation, it suddenly became clear to me that the investigation wasn't complete; there were still many unanswered questions. Yet they were talking settlement. They had a number on the table, and I got the impression that it was basically a done deal. All that seemed left to do was divide the money among the states—and that was exactly what was happening.

I was dumbfounded. What was the number based on? How did they come up with it? How could we negotiate a settlement when we hadn't completed an investigation?

But what shocked me most wasn't the choosing of an arbitrary dollar figure. It was that in exchange for settling, the banks were going to be given a wholesale release against any potential future claims—a blank check of immunity for whatever crimes they might have committed. That meant that by settling with them on the issue of robo-signing, we could be prohibited from bringing a future case against them that related to the mortgage-backed securities that had caused the crash.

During a break in the session, I gathered my team. The settlement was going to be on the agenda again in the afternoon.

"I'm not going to that meeting," I told them. "This thing is baked." I knew that if I joined the meeting, the conversation would just pick up where it had left off. They weren't going to turn back just because a new AG expressed concerns. But if they knew I would pull out of the negotiations if I had to, that might move some minds. California had more foreclosures than any other state, making it the biggest exposure of liability for the banks. If the banks couldn't get a settlement with me, they weren't going to settle with anyone. It was one thing to know I had this leverage; it was another to convince the others I was willing to use it. If I skipped the afternoon session, my empty chair would express that message better than I ever could.

My staff and I left the Fairmont and took a cab to the Justice Department. We called Tom Perrelli on the way, to let him know we were coming. Perrelli was the U.S. associate attorney general. It was his job, among other things, to oversee the multistate investigation on behalf of the federal government. I told him that of the ten cities hit hardest by the foreclosure crisis at the time, seven were in California; that it was my job to get to the bottom of it; and that I couldn't sign on to anything that was going to preclude me from doing my own investigation.

Perrelli made the case that my investigation wouldn't yield what I hoped it would, that going after the big banks was not something any one state could do, even the biggest in the nation. And, he added, that kind of litigation was going to take many years. By the time I got what California deserved, the people who needed help would have already lost their homes. This was the reason there hadn't been a thorough investigation; there simply wasn't time.

Later that afternoon, I met with Elizabeth Warren, who at that time was working at the Treasury Department, building what would become the Consumer Financial Protection Bureau. I raised the same concerns with her, and she was sympathetic and supportive. As an administration official, she couldn't outright tell us to go our own way, but I got the strong sense that she would understand if I persisted.

We flew home that night and got right to work. I had been told that, as things stood, California was going to get somewhere between $2 billion and $4 billion in the settlement. Some of the lawyers in the office thought it was a big number, big enough to take. My point to them was: Compared with what? If the banks' illegal scheme had caused a lot more than $2 billion to $4 billion in damage, then those really big numbers would start to look really small.

The immediate challenge was that our office wasn't equipped to answer that riddle. It was a problem that required economists and data scientists, not lawyers. Recognizing the hole in our game, I decided to hire some experts and put them to work crunching the numbers. I wanted to know how many underwater homeowners there were county by county so that we could target relief to the highest pain points. I also wanted to understand what we were dealing with in very human terms: How many people was the money going to help? How many would be left to fend for themselves? How many children were affected by the foreclosure crisis?

The results were as unacceptable as I had feared. Compared with the devastation, the banks were offering crumbs on the table, nowhere near enough to compensate for the damage they had caused.

"We need to be prepared to walk away from the settlement," I told my team. "There's no way I'm taking this offer." I told them that it was time to open up our own independent investigation. "Look, we're a guest at someone else's party and we don't have our own car," I said. "We need our own ride so that when we're ready to leave, we can leave."

Even before taking office, I'd planned with my team to launch a statewide effort to investigate the fraud. Now was the time. That May, we announced the California Attorney General's Mortgage Fraud Strike Force, a unit of the best and brightest lawyers from our consumer fraud, corporate fraud, and criminal divisions, as well as sworn investigators.

The robo-signing settlement was a critical part of the investigation, but our scope was even wider. I wanted to go after Fannie Mae and Freddie Mac, which owned 62 percent of new mortgages nationwide. I wanted to investigate the mortgage-backed securities that JPMorgan Chase had sold to the California public employee pension fund. And I wanted to go after the predators who had exploited these vulnerable communities, promising to save homeowners from foreclosure for a price—only to steal what little they had left.

The fact that we were doing our own investigation aggravated the multistate negotiators. The banks were furious that I was causing trouble. The settlement was now in doubt. But this had been my goal. Now, instead of merely noting my concerns, the state attorneys general and the banks would have to answer them, too.

Over the course of the summer, we focused on two tracks: the investigation on one, the settlement talks on the other. For my team, that meant working all hours of the day and night—traveling up and down the state and back and forth to Washington. Still, the negotiations were getting nowhere. The banks balked at our demands. At the same time, the rate of foreclosures picked up significantly in California.

In August, the New York attorney general pulled out of the multistate negotiations. In the aftermath, it seemed that everyone's eyes had turned to me. Would I leave the negotiations, too?

I wasn't yet ready to do that. I wanted to exhaust every reasonable possibility that the banks would meet our demands. There were important reforms that were part of the negotiation, and I wanted to see them implemented. We were being presented with a false choice: the reforms or the money. I wanted both.

And I knew that time was of the essence. In a homicide case, the body is cold; you're talking about punishment and restitution after the fact. In this situation, the harm was still unfolding. While negotiations went on, hundreds of thousands of more homeowners had gotten foreclosure notices. It was happening every day and in real time. There were huge areas, entire zip codes, where people were hundreds of thousands of dollars underwater. My team and I pored over the numbers weekly—a dashboard of despair, describing how many people were thirty, sixty, ninety days from losing their homes.

Before I walked away from the table, I wanted to take one last shot at getting a fair deal and some real relief for my state.

To that point, the day-to-day negotiations had been led by Michael and a team of veterans of the California Department of Justice. The next meeting was being held in September, and the general counsels of the major banks had asked me to attend. I was sure they wanted me there so they could size me up from across the table—this new attorney general from out of nowhere. Good. I wanted to size them up, too.

We arrived at the offices of Debevoise & Plimpton, the Washington law firm that was hosting the meeting. We were led into a large conference room where more than a dozen people were gathered.

After a few polite hellos, we took our seats around a long, imposing conference table. I sat at one head of the table. The chief counsels of the big banks were there, along with a team of Wall Street's best lawyers, including a man known as the "trauma surgeon of Wall Street."

The meeting was tense from the moment it began. Bank of America's counsel opened by turning to my negotiating team and complaining about the terrible pain we were putting the banks through. I'm not kidding. She said that the process was frustrating, that the bank had been through enormous trauma, that employees there were working to respond to all the investigations and regulatory changes since the crash. Everyone was exhausted, she told us. And she wanted answers from California. What was the holdup?

I ripped right in. "You want to talk about pain? Do you have any understanding of the pain that you've caused?" I felt it viscerally. It made me so angry to see homeowners' suffering downplayed or dismissed. "There are a million children in California who aren't going to be able to go to their school anymore because their parents lost their home. If you want to talk about pain, I'll tell you about some pain."

The bank representatives were calm but defensive. They essentially said the homeowners were to blame for getting into mortgages they couldn't afford. I wasn't having any of that. I kept thinking about what the home-buying process looks like in real life.

For the vast majority of families, buying a home is the biggest financial transaction they will ever be involved in. It's one of the most affirming moments in a person's adult life, a testament to all your hard work. You trust the people involved in the process. When the banker tells you that you qualify for a loan, you trust that she's reviewed the numbers and won't let you take on more than you can handle. When the offer is accepted, the broker is so happy for you, you'd think he's going to move into the house with you. And when it comes time to finish the paperwork, it's basically a signing ceremony. You might as well be popping champagne. Your broker is there, your banker is there, and you believe they have your best interests at heart. When they put a stack of paper in front of you, you trust them, and you sign. And sign. And sign. And sign.

I surveyed the roomful of lawyers, and I was certain that not one of them had read every word of their own mortgage documents before buying their first house. When I bought my apartment, I didn't.

The bankers spoke about mortgages seemingly without any sense of what they represented to the people involved, or who those people were. To me, it sounded as though they had made terrible assumptions about the character and values of struggling homeowners. I'd met many of those people. And for them, buying a home was not just about an investment. It was about attainment, self-fulfillment. I thought about Mr. Shelton, who was always in the front yard, pruning his roses in the morning, always mowing or watering or fertilizing. At one point, I asked one of the lawyers, "Haven't you ever known somebody who was proud of their lawn?"

The back and forth continued. They seemed to be under the misimpression that I could be bullied into submission. I wasn't budging. Toward the end of the meeting, the general counsel of JPMorgan chimed in with what he apparently thought was a smart tactic. He told me that his parents were from California and that they had voted for me and liked me. And he knew there were a lot of voters back home who would be really happy with me if I just settled. It was great politics—he was sure of it.

I looked him straight in the eye: "Do I need to remind you this is a law enforcement action?" The room went quiet. After forty-five minutes, the conversation had gone on long enough.

"Look, your offer doesn't come near acknowledging the damage you have caused," I told them. "And you should know that I mean what I say. I'm going to investigate everything. Everything."

The general counsel of Wells Fargo turned to me.

"Well, if you're going to keep investigating, why should we settle with you?"

"You have to make that decision for yourself," I told him.

As I left the meeting, I made the decision to pull out of the negotiations altogether.

I wrote a letter announcing my decision—but I waited to release it until Friday evening, after the markets had closed. I knew that my words could move markets, and that wasn't my intention. This wasn't about grandstanding or making a scene or tanking share prices. This was about trying to get justice for millions of people who needed and deserved help.

"Last week, I went to Washington, DC, in hopes of moving our discussions forward," I wrote. "But it became clear to me that California was being asked for a broader release of claims than we can accept and to excuse conduct that has not been adequately investigated. After much consideration, I have concluded that this is not the deal California homeowners have been waiting for."

I started getting phone calls. From friends who were afraid that I had made too powerful an enemy. From political consultants who warned me to brace myself because the banks were going to spend tens of millions of dollars to throw me out of office. From the governor of California: "I hope you know what you're doing." From White House officials and cabinet secretaries, trying to bring me back to the talks. The pressure was intense—and constant—and it was coming from all sides: from longtime allies and longtime adversaries and everyone in between.

But there was another kind of pressure, too. Millions of homeowners had raised their voices, along with activists and advocacy organizations that were mobilizing based on our strategy. We knew we weren't alone.

Still, this period was hard. Before bed, I would say a small prayer: "God, please help me do the right thing." I'd pray that I was choosing the right path, and for the courage to stay the course. Most of all, I'd pray that the families counting on me remained safe and secure. I knew how much was at stake.

I often found myself thinking about my mother and what she would have done. I know she would have told me to hold fast to conviction; to listen to my gut. Tough decisions are tough precisely because the outcome isn't clear. But your gut will tell you if you're on the right track. And you'll know what decision to make.

During those days, Beau Biden, Delaware's attorney general, became an incredible friend and colleague. The banks were in Beau's backyard, and the foreclosure crisis hadn't hit Delaware as hard as it had other states. By some measures, he had every reason to keep his head down and toe the line. But that wasn't who Beau was. Beau was a man of principle and courage.

From the very beginning, he had consistently objected to the deal. He hammered on the points that I was making, too: not enough money; no investigation into the scope of the fraud. Like me, he wanted testimony and documents. He wanted proof that the banks even owned the mortgages they were foreclosing on. And he never budged from that position. He had also opened up his own investigation, and we were actively sharing the information we uncovered. There were periods, when I was taking heat, when Beau and I talked every day, sometimes multiple times a day. We had each other's backs.

I had other great allies in the fight, too. Martha Coakley, then the attorney general of Massachusetts, was tough and smart and meticulous in her work. My now–Senate colleague Catherine Cortez-Masto was Nevada's attorney general at the time, and she became a formidable ally as well. Nevada, like California, had been pummeled by the crisis, and Catherine, who'd been in office since 2007, had formed her own Mortgage Fraud Strike Force in 2008. She, like me, was determined to fight the banks, and in December 2011 she and I joined forces to probe foreclosure fraud and misconduct. I could not have asked for better or more resolute teammates.

At the height of this period, I was constantly traveling the country with my team. I'll never forget the time we flew out to Washington, DC, dressed for the winter, only to find out that we would need to go to Florida the following day. Brian and I ended up racing into a clothing store in Georgetown to find more weather-appropriate attire. It was an awkward moment of levity as we critiqued each other's choices off the rack.

By January, the banks were exasperated. Michael came into my office.

"I just got off the phone with the general counsel of JPMorgan," he said. "I told him what the deal was—that we weren't budging off our position."

"What did he say?" I asked.

"He wouldn't stop screaming at me. He says it's over. That we pushed too far. It was really intense. And then he hung up."

I pulled my team into my office and we tried to figure out a next step—if there was one to be taken. Had we killed the possibility of any deal? Was there still a chance? I needed to be sure. We sat in silence for a while, thinking it through, until an idea popped into my head. I shouted for my assistant next door (which was the same intercom system we had used growing up). "Get me Jamie Dimon on the phone." Dimon was and—as of this writing—remains the chairman and CEO of JPMorgan Chase.

My team freaked out. "You can't call him. He's represented by an attorney!"

"I don't care. Get him on the phone."

I was tired of feeling caged, of talking through lawyers and other intermediaries in endless obfuscation. I wanted to go right to the source, and I believed the situation demanded it.

About ten seconds later, my assistant popped her head into my office. "Mr. Dimon is on the line." I took off my earrings (the Oakland in me) and picked up the receiver.

"You're trying to steal from my shareholders!" he yelled, almost as soon as he heard my voice. I gave it right back. "*Your* shareholders? *Your* shareholders? *My* shareholders are the homeowners of California! You come and see them. Talk to them about who got robbed." It stayed at that level for a while. We were like dogs in a fight. A member of my senior team later recalled thinking, "This was either a really good or a colossally bad idea."

I shared with Dimon the way his lawyers were presenting his position, and why it was unacceptable to me. As temperatures cooled, I got into the details of my demands so that he would understand exactly what I needed—not through the filter of his general counsel, but directly from me. At the end of the conversation, he said he would talk to his board and see what they could do.

I'll never know what happened on Dimon's side. But I do know that two weeks later, the banks gave in. When all was said and done, instead of the $2 billion to $4 billion that was originally on the table, we secured an $18 billion deal, which ultimately grew to $20 billion in relief to homeowners. It was a tremendous victory for the people of California.

As part of the settlement, the federal government was going to assign a monitor to make sure the banks complied. But given how much exposure California had, that didn't satisfy me. I was going to hire our own monitor and authorize her to oversee the agreement's implementation in our state.

I had been asked to fly to Washington to be part of the larger announcement, a major press conference and celebration that would take place at the Department of Justice and the White House. But I wanted to be at home with my team. It was our victory to share together. And we needed to gear up for the next battle ahead.

The settlement was just the beginning. In addition to money, the agreement required banks to provide homeowners with a number of reforms to make the process of fighting a foreclosure easier. But the settlement required those measures to be in place for only three years. If we wanted to protect homeowners in California from abuses in the future, we were going to need legislation to make the terms of the settlement permanent. I wanted the banks to be permanently prohibited from engaging in their notoriously predatory practices. And I wanted individual homeowners to have the right to sue when banks broke the rules. In coordination with our allies in the legislature, we put these ideas together into what we named the California Homeowner Bill of Rights.

But getting a new law that related to the banks passed through the legislature was going to be a problem. The banks had enormous influence in Sacramento. California legislators had tried to pass similar legislation on at least two prior occasions, only to be defeated by bank resistance. This was going to have to be a full-court press.

The reception to the bill was cold at first. People told me it was dead on arrival. They said the banking lobby was too strong to overcome. The rightness of the legislation seemed to have little to do with the calculation.

I met with John Pérez, who was speaker of the state assembly at the time, to come up with a strategy to turn the bill into law. John is an exceptional man, savvy in both policy and politics. He and I were in complete agreement about the importance of a Homeowner Bill of Rights, and he was ready to work to leverage his power to take on the banks.

I remember at one point during this effort, Speaker Pérez invited me to the Democratic policy retreat of the state assembly at the Leland Stanford Mansion, in Sacramento. Pérez, who had made sure to be in charge of seating assignments, strategically placed me at a table with a couple of strong allies, as well as a few legislators who needed some persuading. We spent much of the dinner talking about the bill. By that point, I knew more than I ever imagined I would about how the banks had acted, all the ways in which they had victimized homeowners. Being able to talk through those experiences with the group seemed to help. When the dinner was over, I had the sense that I had changed one or two of their minds.

None of the legislators ever explicitly said they were siding with the banks. But in conversation after conversation, they would try to find any technical excuse they could for why they couldn't support the bill. *If only you'd done this. If only you'd done that. If only that semicolon wasn't there.*

I'll never forget one Democratic legislator saying to me, "Well, Kamala, I don't know what's so bad about these foreclosures. They're good for our local economy. Because when a house is foreclosed upon and abandoned, that means they have to hire painters and gardeners to clean it up." Really? Really? Did this guy also support arson because it keeps fire extinguisher companies in business? It was stunning to me how people would justify being in the pocket of the banks.

While Speaker Pérez spent time focusing on the inside game, I went on the road, using the bully pulpit to evangelize for a fairer, more just system for homeowners. I was joined in the effort by a number of groups that had been championing homeowner rights and were mounting a pressure campaign to get the bill passed. Organized labor was critically important to this effort. Their ability to mobilize supporters was stunning. So many people called their legislators that they crashed the phone lines.

But it wasn't just labor's organizing efforts that mattered. It was their very presence. There was a cynical way of thinking in Sacramento: When a home is foreclosed on, the family living there is likely to move out of your district. They will no longer be your constituents. So their anger is only a temporary problem for you. The banks, on the other hand, are a permanent presence in the state capital, and their anger could result in retribution. What organized labor made clear was that there was also a permanent presence in the capital that was going to fight intensely for workers, not just so they could have better wages, but so they could be treated with dignity in every aspect of their lives, including buying a home. It sent a powerful message: Side with the banks, answer to labor.

As the vote drew near, I started walking the halls of the capitol building, knocking unannounced on legislators' doors. A lot of people refused to see me. I dispatched key members of my team as well. Brian Nelson, my special assistant attorney general, recalls that I would sometimes call him at his desk, and if he answered, he was in trouble. "Why are you sitting at your desk?" I'd ask. "Why aren't you walking the halls of the capitol? I know you have important work, but nothing is more important than this. You gotta be walking the halls! No one should be able to avoid having a face-to-face conversation with one of us."

When the bill came to the floor for a vote, we still didn't have a majority. Many legislators were planning not to vote so they wouldn't have to take a position one way or the other. But we needed forty-one people to vote yes. Abstentions were tantamount to voting no.

Speaker Pérez had a plan. He was going to hold the vote open while we continued to pressure people to come to our side. If they didn't want to vote, he implied, the vote was just going to stay open forever. At the beginning of the proceeding, he had an ally make a point of parliamentary inquiry.

"What's the longest the roll has ever been open?" the legislator asked.

"To my understanding," Pérez said, "the longest the roll has ever been open was an hour and forty-five minutes, and you know how competitive I am. I'm willing to go a lot longer than that!" At that point, everyone understood he was serious, and green lights started flashing as votes were cast.

I was in the office of Darrell Steinberg, the senate president pro tem, who had also played an instrumental role, watching the floor action on a closed-circuit television. I watched for legislators who weren't yet on the floor or who were milling around in the back. "I saw you didn't vote," I would text. "Go vote. It's time." We moved person to person, one by one, as John repeated the same phrase over and over again. "Have all members voted who decided to vote? Have all members voted who decided to vote?" He sounded like an auctioneer.

It felt like it lasted forever. But in reality it took only about five minutes of this before we got our forty-first vote cast. John closed the vote, and we declared victory. The bill passed the state senate as well and was signed into law by the governor. We had done what we had been told was impossible. It was as gratifying a moment as I can remember, and a reminder that even in the sausage making of politics, inspiring things can happen and good work can be done.

Meanwhile, the Mortgage Fraud Strike Force was pushing hard. The unit would go on to investigate and prosecute a number of major mortgage scams. The head of one of the larger scams was sentenced to twenty-four years in state prison. Because of the efforts of a truly extraordinary team, we were able to secure—on top of the $18 billion—$300 million from JPMorgan to reimburse the state pension system for losses on investments in mortgage-backed securities. We also secured $550 million from SunTrust Mortgage, $200 million from Citigroup, and another $500 million from Bank of America— all in connection with the mortgage crisis.

These were important wins, to be sure. But they weren't the kinds of victories we wanted to celebrate, because, for all the people these actions helped, millions of Americans across the country were still hurting. And despite the billions we recovered, a lot of people still lost their homes. The structural damage to the economy was so profound that, even with some relief, many people couldn't pay their mortgages and still make ends meet. The jobs weren't there. And neither were the wages.

Countless Americans saw their credit destroyed. Parents' dreams of financing their children's education evaporated like mist. Families faced multiple stresses simultaneously—from joblessness to homelessness to abruptly having to switch school districts. One analysis published in *The Lancet* suggested that "the rise in US unemployment during the recession [was] associated with a 3.8% increase in the suicide rate, corresponding to about 1330 suicides."

In many ways, the impact of the crash is still with us in 2018. In Fresno, the overwhelming majority of homes are still valued below their prerecession levels. Nationally, middle-class wealth was nearly wiped out and much of it hasn't returned.

Studies suggest that the burden hit black families disproportionately. An independent report of the Social Science Research Council, commissioned by the American Civil Liberties Union, found that, whereas white and black families alike were hit hard by the 2007–2009 crisis, by 2011 "the typical white family's losses slowed to zero, while the typical black family lost an additional 13 percent of its wealth." The consequence: "For a typical Black family, median wealth in 2031 will be almost $98,000 lower than it would have been without the Great Recession."

In other words, tomorrow's generations will suffer as a result of yesterday's folly and greed. We cannot change what has already happened. But we can make sure it never happens again.

The culture on Wall Street hasn't changed. Only some of the rules have. And the banks are waging a full-scale battle to repeal the Obama-era Wall Street reforms that have helped hold them in check. Where they have failed to repeal them, they have done everything they can to get around them. According to an analysis from *The Wall Street Journal*, between 2010 and 2017, major banks invested $345 billion in subprime loans—funneling the money to nonbank financial institutions, or so-called shadow banks.

"Banks say their new approach of lending to nonbank lenders is safer than dealing directly with consumers with bad credit and companies with shaky balance sheets," noted the *Journal*. "Yet these relationships mean that banks are still deeply intertwined with the riskier loans they say they swore off after the financial crisis."

Meanwhile, in 2017, the president appointed a man to run the Consumer Financial Protection Bureau who has referred to that very bureau as "a joke," and who set about actively dismantling it from the inside. In 2018, instead of tightening the rules on Wall Street, Congress rolled back essential protections, releasing midsize banks from the regulations meant to keep them in check. This is more than unacceptable. It's outrageous.

There is still much to be done. If we agree that we are tired of banks getting away with such reckless behavior, if we agree that we can't let the banks drag us into another recession, if we agree that homeowners deserve to be treated with dignity and respect, not as lines on a balance sheet to be packaged and sold, then there's only one way to achieve the change we seek: with our voices and our votes.

Four

WEDDING BELLS

Whenever I travel to a country for the first time, I try to visit the highest court in the land. They are monuments of a certain kind, built not just to house a courtroom but to convey a message. In New Delhi, for example, the Supreme Court of India is designed to symbolize the balancing scales of justice. In Jerusalem, Israel's iconic Supreme Court building combines straight lines—which represent the immutable nature of the law—with curved walls and glass that represent the fluid nature of justice. These are buildings that speak.

The same can be said of the United States Supreme Court Building, which, to my mind, is the most beautiful of them all. Its architecture harks back to the earliest days of democracy, as though you are standing in front of a modern-day Parthenon. It is grand and commanding while also dignified and restrained. As you walk up the steps toward an extraordinary portico of Corinthian columns, you can see a nation's founding aspirations in its architecture. It is there that the words EQUAL JUSTICE UNDER LAW are engraved in stone. And it was that promise that brought me to the Supreme Court Building on March 26, 2013.

When I arrived, the building was admittedly not looking its finest. It was encased in scaffolding, part of an overdue repair effort after a large chunk of marble broke off and fell to the ground. To minimize the unsightly view, a life-size, high-resolution photograph of the facade had been printed on a scrim and draped across the entrance. It was about as realistic as one of those oversize beach T-shirts with a bikini body printed on the front. Even so, the majesty of the building was unmistakable.

I was escorted to my seat in the courtroom. Because the Supreme Court justices don't allow photography or video inside, this is a place that most of the country never sees. I certainly hadn't before that day. I gazed around in awe: the stunning pink marble; the vivid red draping and intricate ceiling; the imposing bench with its nine empty chairs. I kept thinking about all the history that had been made inside these walls. But unlike a museum or a place like Gettysburg, where history is preserved for posterity, the Supreme Court is a place where history is active and alive, where it continues to unfold with every decision.

A little after 10 a.m., we rose as the nine justices entered the courtroom and took their seats.

"We'll hear argument this morning in Case 12-144, *Hollingsworth v. Perry*," said Chief Justice John Roberts.

This was the case against Proposition 8, a California ballot initiative that passed in 2008, prohibiting marriages for same-sex couples in the state. It had been a long time coming.

California may have a reputation as a bastion of liberalism, but in the year 2000, California voters approved a ballot initiative—Prop 22 (also known as the Knight Initiative, after its author, state senator William "Pete" Knight)—that required the state to define marriage as a union between people of the opposite sex. For years we fought it—in the streets, at the ballot box, and in the courts. Even my then school-aged niece, Meena, got in on the action; I remember one time going to pick her up at her high school and being told she was in a student meeting. When I got to the classroom, young Meena was in front, rallying her peers: "This isn't a Knight Initiative—it's a nightmare!"

During Valentine's Day week in 2004, then–San Francisco mayor Gavin Newsom decided to allow marriages for same-sex couples to proceed anyway.

I was on my way to the airport to catch a flight to Los Angeles, but I decided to pass by San Francisco City Hall before I left. There were throngs of people lined up around the block, waiting to get in. They were counting down the minutes before a government would finally recognize their right to marry whomever they loved. The joy and anticipation were palpable. Some of them had been waiting decades.

I got out of my car and walked up the steps of City Hall, where I bumped into a city official. "Kamala, come and help us," she said, a glowing smile on her face. "We need more people to perform the marriages." I was delighted to be a part of it.

I was quickly sworn in, along with numerous city officials. We stood together performing marriages in the hallway, crowded into every nook and cranny of City Hall. There was all this wonderful excitement building as we welcomed the throngs of loving couples, one by one, to be married then and there. It was unlike anything I had ever been a part of before. And it was beautiful.

But not long after, the marriages were invalidated. The couples who had been so happy and hopeful received letters telling them that their marriage licenses would not be recognized under the law. It was, for each and every one of them, a devastating setback.

In May 2008, the California Supreme Court came to the rescue. The court held that the same-sex marriage ban was unconstitutional, which paved the way for LGBTQ couples to realize the equal dignity they had always deserved. Ronald George, who had sworn me in as district attorney of San Francisco, wrote the majority opinion. And over the next six months, eighteen thousand same-sex couples exchanged wedding vows in California.

But in November 2008, on the same night that Barack Obama was elected president, the people of California narrowly voted to pass Prop 8, an amendment to the California Constitution that stripped same-sex couples of their right to marry. Because this was a constitutional amendment, it couldn't be overturned by the legislature or the state court system. No new marriages could be performed. Couples who had already been married were placed in a cruel limbo.

There was one clear route left to justice: the federal courts. The American Foundation for Equal Rights, then led by Chad Griffin, decided that the best way to respond was to bring suit against the state of California, arguing that Prop 8 violated the protections granted to every citizen in the Fourteenth Amendment: equal protection and due process under the law. This was a matter of civil rights and civil justice, and Griffin and his team planned to take the case all the way to the Supreme Court. The organization hired the lawyers who had argued against each other in *Bush v. Gore,* then filed a lawsuit on behalf of two same-sex couples—Kris Perry and Sandy Stier; Paul Katami and Jeff Zarrillo—whose job was to represent in court the millions of people just like them, people who simply wanted to be accorded the human dignity of marrying the person they loved.

It would take eight months for the lawsuit to make its way to the first stage of the fight: the U.S. federal district court. Inside that courtroom, a judge would hear from witnesses, review evidence, and, based on the facts before him, decide whether Prop 8 had violated the civil rights of Kris, Sandy, Jeff, and Paul. On August 4, 2010, Chief Judge Vaughn Walker ruled in their favor, concluding that Prop 8 was indeed unconstitutional and affirming the right of same-sex couples to marry. It was fantastic and important news. But, as is common practice, the judge decided he was going to wait to enforce the ruling until it was appealed to a higher court—a legal concept known as a stay.

I was in the middle of my race for attorney general when the ruling came down, and it quickly became a central issue in the campaign. The California attorney general had the right to appeal the decision. Jerry Brown, whom I was running to succeed, had refused to defend the measure in court. I, too, made clear that I had no intention of spending a penny of the attorney general's office's resources defending Prop 8. My opponent took the other view—a sharp distinction between us. I understood that it wasn't just about principle; it was about practical outcomes. If California refused to appeal the ruling, the lower court judge could lift the stay and the state could start issuing marriage licenses again right away. If California did appeal the ruling, on the other hand, it would take years before marriages could begin.

When I won the election, my refusal to appeal the decision should have been the end of it. But proponents of Prop 8 were unwilling to give up the fight. In an unusual move, they joined together to appeal the ruling themselves. In my view, they had no basis for doing so. Your right to free speech doesn't give you the right to intervene in a court proceeding. You don't get to be a party in a lawsuit simply because you have strong feelings about something. In order to bring a case in court, you are required to have standing, which means, among other things, that you have suffered or might suffer an actual injury. (In more colloquial terms, I think of it as my New Jersey–raised husband might explain it: you have to be able to provide a concrete answer to the question "Whatsittoya?")

Kris Perry had standing to sue the state when Prop 8 passed because it injured her; it stripped her of a civil right. We had a law on the books that treated one group of Americans differently from all other Americans, and fundamentally that was unfair. But when Prop 8 was invalidated in federal court, that decision gave protections to one group without taking away anything from anyone. The constitutional principle was clear. Those people who wanted to deny same-sex couples the benefits of equal protection and due process under the U.S. Constitution could not do so simply because they didn't like the notion. They would always have their freedom of expression. But they did not have the power to deny other Americans their fundamental rights.

And yet the appeal proceeded. The ruling stayed on hold. It would take more than a year before the Ninth Circuit Court of Appeals issued its decision. Each day of delay represented justice denied—and much, much more. Each day of delay was a day a devoted couple couldn't consecrate their commitment. Each day of delay was a day a grandmother passed away before the wedding she would have loved to see. Each day of delay was a day a child was left wondering "Why can't my parents get married, too?"

There was much to applaud in the Ninth Circuit's ruling. A three-judge panel affirmed the lower court's decision that Prop 8 had deprived same-sex couples of their civil rights in California. But the court didn't take issue with the Prop 8 proponents' right to appeal. Instead, the court issued a stay in its ruling and allowed them to appeal once again—this time to the Supreme Court.

As I sat listening to the oral arguments, the Supreme Court justices homed in on the issue of standing. Justice Stephen Breyer questioned whether the Prop 8 proponents were "no more than a group of five people who feel really strongly." Justice Sonia Sotomayor wanted to know how the lower court's ruling had caused the proponents an injury "separate from that of every other taxpayer to have laws enforced." But when the arguments were over, there was really no way to tell what the decision would be.

As I left the Supreme Court, there were hundreds of people gathered, waving rainbow flags, holding signs, waiting anxiously for justice. It made me smile. They were why I had become a lawyer in the first place. It was in the courtroom, I believed, that you could translate that passion into action and precedent and law.

I looked out at their faces and imagined all the people who had stood in the same place for similar reasons: black parents with their children, fighting against segregation in schools; young women marching and shouting, holding signs that said KEEP ABORTION LEGAL; civil rights activists demonstrating against poll taxes and literacy tests and laws prohibiting interracial marriage.

In everyday life, they might have seemed like they had nothing in common. But on these steps, they shared something profound: in one form or another, they had faced treatment "directly subversive of the principle of equality," as Chief Justice Earl Warren had once put it.

And in one way or another, they believed the Constitution could set them free. They revered that document, in the words of Franklin Roosevelt, "not because it is old but because it is ever new, not in the worship of its past alone but in the faith of the living who keep it young, now and in the years to come." So they marched. And they fought. And they waited.

I knew that nothing was certain. The Supreme Court had made some terrible decisions in its past. In 1889, it upheld a law—still not overturned—that specifically excluded Chinese people from immigrating to America. In 1896, it held that racial segregation did not violate the Constitution. In 1944, it held that there was nothing unconstitutional about the forced internment of Japanese Americans. In 1986, it held that gay relationships could be criminalized. In 2010, it ushered in an era of dark money in politics with its ruling in *Citizens United*. And on the day before we would hear the ruling in our case, the Court's conservative justices invalidated—and gutted—a critical part of the Voting Rights Act. Nothing was certain.

But on the morning of June 26, 2013, we received wonderful news. The Supreme Court agreed that Prop 8 proponents had no standing to appeal, and dismissed the case in a 5–4 decision. That meant the lower court ruling would stand. And that meant marriage equality was the law again in California—finally.

I was in my Los Angeles office when the word came through. A spontaneous celebration broke out, with whoops and applause ricocheting through the hallways. After so many years of struggle and setback, love had finally conquered all.

I gathered my team to discuss a plan of action. I wanted the marriages to begin right away. But that couldn't happen until the Ninth

Circuit Court of Appeals lifted its stay, and the appellate court said it would take weeks to do so. This was unacceptable to me.

As I headed to a press conference to discuss the victory, my staff cautioned against challenging the court to act. There was decorum around these things, and my publicly weighing in might offend. But this was no time for decorum. Our fellow Americans had been waiting far too long. And so I leaned into the microphone and called on the Ninth Circuit to lift the stay as quickly as possible.

Two days later, I was in my San Francisco office with my team for a Friday afternoon strategy meeting, where we were discussing transnational criminal organizations ranging from drug smugglers to human and weapons traffickers. We were deep in conversation about a recently opened investigation when my assistant Cortney Bright came in and passed me a note. "The Ninth Circuit made a decision." I read the note to the team, and we lost all ability to focus on the work at hand. We needed to know the answer.

A short while later, Cortney was back. The Ninth Circuit had lifted the stay. The state could begin issuing marriage licenses right away. We erupted in cheers.

My phone rang, and it was Chad Griffin. He was with Kris Perry and Sandy Stier.

"Kamala, we're coming to San Francisco. Sandy and Kris are going to be the first marriage, and we want you to perform the ceremony."

"Of course! I would love to!" I told Chad. "Nothing would make me more proud."

Normally, I had to travel by official car, but this time I insisted that we walk. As my team and I made our way to City Hall, I recalled the famous image of Thurgood Marshall striding purposefully with

Autherine Lucy, who had been denied admission to the University of Alabama, one of the first tests of integration. Though we were the only ones in the street this time, it felt like we were leading our part of a parade—one that stretched through generations. We were following in the footsteps of giants, and widening the trail for our time.

When we reached City Hall, we made our way to the clerk's office, where a crowd was already gathering in the hallway. Kris and Sandy arrived soon after, beaming and ready to go.

"Congratulations!" I exclaimed as I hugged them both. They had been through so much, for so long. We were laughing and chatting when a reporter and a cameraman came over to ask me a question. He'd heard there might be an appeal and wanted to know what I thought about it.

I just looked at him and smiled. "Wedding bells are about to ring!"

Meanwhile, news started to spread, and people started coming to City Hall by the hundreds. Some to celebrate. Some to get married. Some just to bear witness. We could hear the Gay Men's Chorus singing, their voices soaring in the rotunda. As we filed into that confined space together, everyone experiencing pure joy, the feeling was magical.

We were preparing for the ceremony when somebody pulled me aside to say that the clerk in Los Angeles was refusing to issue marriage licenses until he heard from the state. He clearly needed direction. It was as simple as passing me the phone.

"This is Kamala Harris," I said. "You must start the marriages immediately."

"All right!" he responded, sounding relieved. "I will take that as our notice and we will issue the licenses now."

I thanked him. "And enjoy it!" I added. "It's going to be fun."

A short time later, I took my spot on the balcony and watched Kris and Sandy, followed by their loved ones and friends, walk up the stairs of City Hall. They made an elegant pair, in matching beige and white. Sandy was holding a bouquet of white roses. Two days earlier, they had become living symbols of justice. Now, as they took their final steps toward me—through the same building in which Harvey Milk had lived and died defending the dignity of all people—I could feel history being made.

"Today we witness not only the joining of Kris and Sandy, but the realization of their dream—marriage. . . . By joining the case against Proposition 8, they represented thousands of couples like themselves in the fight for marriage equality. Through the ups and downs, the struggles and the triumphs, they came out victorious."

Kris and Sandy exchanged their vows, and their son, Elliott, handed over the rings. I had the honor and privilege to say, "By virtue of the power and authority vested in me by the state of California, I now declare you spouses for life."

There were hundreds of weddings that day, all across the state, each one of them an expression of love and justice and hope. San Francisco City Hall was lit in the colors of the rainbow—a beautiful tribute to the beautiful words "I do!"

When I got home that evening, I had a chance to reflect on the day. My thoughts turned to a man I wished could have been there to see it. Jim Rivaldo was a San Francisco political strategist, one of the co-founders of *The National Lampoon,* and a leading member of the gay community who had been a key player in getting Harvey Milk elected to the San Francisco Board of Supervisors in 1977. He was truly brilliant, and when I first ran for district attorney, he was one of my most important advisers. My family and I loved him, especially my mother. In the years after my first election, we would see him often. He spent Thanksgiving with us the year before he died, in 2007. My mother cared for him at his bedside, trying to keep him comfortable in his final days.

I wanted to talk to him. I wanted to share the moment with him. But even in his absence, I knew exactly what he would have said: *We're not done yet.*

It would take another two years before the Supreme Court recognized marriage equality in all fifty states. And today, it is still the case under federal law that an employer can fire an employee if they identify as LGBTQ. It is still the case, in statehouses across the country, that transgender rights are getting trampled. This is still very much an active civil rights battle.

What happened with Prop 8 was an important part of a longer journey, one that began before America was its own nation and one that will continue for decades to come. It is the story of people fighting for their humanity—for the simple idea that we should all be equal and free. It is the story of people fighting for the promise made to all future generations at the signing of the Declaration of Independence: that no government has the right to rob us of our life or our liberty or our humble pursuit of happiness.

In the years to come, what matters most is that we see ourselves in one another's struggles. Whether we are fighting for transgender rights or for an end to racial bias, whether we are fighting against housing discrimination or insidious immigration laws, no matter who we are or how we look or how little it may seem we have in common, the truth is, in the battle for civil rights and economic justice, we are all the same. In the words of the great Bayard Rustin, organizer of the 1963 March on Washington, "We are all one, and if we don't know it, we will learn it the hard way."

A few months after Kris and Sandy got married, I was on my way to an event at a nonprofit organization called the California Endowment, run by my friend Robert K. Ross, a health philanthropist. The endowment is headquartered in a beautiful, modern space, and during my time as attorney general, we often used it to hold big events. On this particular day, the topic for discussion was one few might have expected to be on an attorney general's agenda. I was there to talk about elementary school truancy, and to initiate a discussion about solutions.

When I first started as attorney general, I told my executive team that I wanted to make elementary school truancy a top priority for my office. Those who didn't know me must have thought I was joking. Why would the state's top law enforcement official want to focus on whether seven-year-olds are going to school or not? But those who had been with me for a while knew I wasn't messing around. Indeed, instituting a statewide plan on truancy was part of the reason I'd run for the office in the first place.

When I was district attorney, much of the work I had done in crime prevention focused on interventions later in life. Back on Track, for example, was all about helping young adults avoid prison time and the consequences that flow from a felony conviction. But I was equally concerned about early interventions, about the kinds of steps we could take as a community—and a country—to keep children safe and on track to begin with. I wanted to identify key moments in a child's life when my office could make a difference.

It was during that process that I started connecting a series of research-related dots. The first dot concerned the importance of third-grade reading proficiency. Studies show that the end of third grade is a critical milestone for students. Up until that point, the curriculum focuses on teaching students to learn to read. In fourth grade, there's a shift, and students transition to reading in order to learn. If students can't read, they can't learn, and they fall further behind, month after month and year after year—which forces them onto a nearly inescapable path to poverty. The door of opportunity closes on them when they're barely four feet tall. I believe it is tantamount to a crime when a child goes without an education.

At the same time, I was focused on a rash of homicides in the city and county of San Francisco. It was an issue for leaders across the area, in and out of government, so there was a lot of activity and concern about what we should do to address it. When we studied the data, we learned that more than 80 percent of prisoners were high school dropouts.

I went to see the school district superintendent, a wonderful woman named Arlene Ackerman, to ask her about the high school dropout rate. She told me that a significant percentage of their habitually truant high school students had missed their elementary school classes, too—for weeks, even months at a time. That, to me, was a call to action. The connections were so clear. You could map the path for children who started drifting away from the classroom when they were young. The truant child became the wanderer . . . who became the target for gang recruiters . . . who became the young drug courier . . .

who became the perpetrator—or the victim—of violence. If we didn't see that child in elementary school, where they belonged, chances were we'd see them later in prison, in the hospital, or dead.

Some of my political advisers worried that tackling truancy would not be a popular issue. Even today, others don't appreciate the intention behind my approach; they assume that my motivation was to lock up parents, when of course that was never the goal. Our effort was designed to connect parents to resources that could help them get their kids back into school, where they belonged. We were trying to support parents, not punish them—and in the vast majority of cases, we succeeded.

Still, I was willing to be the bad guy if it meant highlighting an issue that otherwise would have received too little attention. Political capital doesn't gain interest. You have to spend it to make a difference.

My office joined with the city and the school district, and we developed a truancy initiative. I'm proud to say that by 2009, we had reduced truancy among San Francisco's elementary school children by 23 percent.

As we dug into the issue, what we found was quite different from what a number of my colleagues expected. Stereotypes held that a child becomes a chronically truant student because his or her parents don't care about the child's future. But the truth is different. The truth is that the vast majority of parents have a natural desire to parent their children well. They want to be good fathers and mothers. They just may not have the skills or the resources they need.

Imagine a single parent, working two minimum-wage shift jobs, six days a week, and still trapped below the poverty line. She gets paid hourly, with no vacation or sick leave. If her three-year-old daughter runs a fever, she can't bring her to the day care she took a second job to pay for. There's no money for a babysitter, but if she stays home, she's not going to be able to afford diapers for the rest of the month. It's already been hard enough saving money to buy new shoes for her eleven-year-old son, whose feet seem to grow a whole size every few months.

What amounts to a headache for those with means takes the form of desperation for those without. If a parent in that situation asks her son to stay home from school for a day in order to take care of his little sister, we can't accuse her of loving her children any less. This is a matter of circumstance and condition, not of character. She wants to be the best parent she can.

The goal of our truancy prevention initiative was to step in and provide support. We wanted the schools to reach out to parents with information: not only about the links between high truancy, illiteracy, and high crime, but, importantly, about resources they might not have been aware of—support the city and school district offered to make it easier to get their kids to school.

When we were first putting the initiative together, the draft guidance to the school districts told them to notify the parent with whom the child lived in case there was a truancy issue. This was usually the mother.

"Wait a minute," I asked. "What about the father?"

"Well, in a lot of these cases," one of my staffers explained, "the kids don't live with the father and the father isn't paying child support."

"So what?" I replied. "He may not be paying child support. It doesn't mean he doesn't want his child to go to school every day." And sure enough, in one of these cases, a young man found out that his daughter wasn't going to school every day and ended up changing his schedule to take her there each morning. He even started volunteering in her classroom.

When I became attorney general, I wanted to use the power of my office to expose the truancy crisis across the state. I knew the cameras would show up for a lot of what I did, and I wanted to shine a spotlight on this issue and appeal to people's self-interest. Like it or not, most people prioritize their own safety over the education of someone else's child. I wanted to make them see that if we didn't prioritize education now, it would be a public safety matter later.

Our first report, the results of which I was announcing that day at the California Endowment, estimated that we had approximately a million truant elementary school kids across the state. And in too many schools, nearly everyone was truant: one school had a truancy rate higher than 92 percent.

And so as I took the stage, what might have seemed like a tangential topic for the state's attorney general became the heart of impassioned remarks, in which I called on educators and policy makers, inside the room and beyond it, to step up and acknowledge the severity of the crisis.

While I was speaking, I noticed that two of my staffers were whispering to each other while pointing to a man in the audience. I couldn't hear them, but I knew exactly what they were saying: "Who's that guy? Is that him?" And I knew they were saying it because that guy was Doug.

Six months earlier, I hadn't known who that guy Doug was, either. I just knew that my best friend, Chrisette, was blowing up my phone. I was in the middle of a meeting, and my phone wouldn't stop buzzing. I ignored her call the first several times, but then I started to get worried. Her children are my godchildren. Had something happened?

I stepped out and called her.

"What's going on? Is everything okay?"

"Yes, everything is great. You're going on a date," she said.

"I am?"

"You are," she replied with total certainty. "I just met this guy. He's cute and he's the managing partner of his law firm and I think you're going to really like him. He's based in Los Angeles, but you're always here for work anyway."

Chrisette is like a sister to me, and I knew there was no use in arguing with her.

"What's his name?" I asked.

"His name is Doug Emhoff, but promise me you won't Google him. Don't overthink it. Just meet him. I already gave him your number. He's going to reach out."

Part of me groaned, but at the same time, I appreciated Chrisette's take-charge approach. She was one of the only people to whom I could talk candidly about my personal life. As a single, professional woman in my forties, and very much in the public eye, dating wasn't easy. I knew that if I brought a man with me to an event, people would immediately start to speculate about our relationship. I also knew that single women in politics are viewed differently than single men. We don't get the same latitude when it comes to our social lives. I had no interest in inviting that kind of scrutiny unless I was close to sure I'd found "the One"—which meant that for years, I kept my personal life compartmentalized from my career.

A few nights later, I was on my way to an event when I received a text from a number I didn't recognize. Doug was watching a basket-ball game with a friend, and he'd worked up the courage to send me an awkward text. "Hey! It's Doug. Just saying hi! I'm at the Lakers game." I wrote back to say hi, and we made plans to talk the follow-ing day. Then I punctuated it with my own bit of awkwardness—"Go Lakers!"—even though I'm really a Warriors fan.

The next morning, I was leaving the gym before work when I noticed that I had missed a call from Doug. Even though I had sug-gested we connect the following day, I hadn't expected him to reach out that early. But I found it pretty endearing, I'll admit. In fact, while I was writing this chapter, I sat down with Doug and asked him to explain what was going through his head when he made that call. This is what he said:

> I got up early that morning. I had an early meeting. And as I was driving to work, I couldn't get you off my mind. And I kept saying to myself, "It's eight thirty a.m., it's way too early to call her. That would be ridiculous. Don't be that guy. Just don't. Don't call her. Don't do it." And then, "Oh no, I just rang her number," and, "Oh no, it's ringing.

The voicemail, which I still have saved to this day, was long and a little rambling. He sounded like a nice guy, though, and I was in-trigued to learn more. Doug, on the other hand, was pretty sure that he had ruined his chances. The way he tells it, he thought his voice-mail had been disastrous and that he'd likely never hear from me again. He had to restrain himself from calling again and leaving an-other long-winded message trying to explain away the first one.

But fate was smiling on us. As it happens, I own an apartment in San Francisco, and, after saving up for years to redo my kitchen, the work was finally about to start. That day, I was supposed to meet the contractor and his team to show them in and give them keys, but when I got to the apartment, I learned the contractor was running late, and I would have to wait.

In other words, I found myself with a free hour for lunch—something that almost never happened. So I decided I'd give Doug a call. Maybe he was on a lunch break, too.

He answered, and we ended up on the phone for the entire hour. It sounds corny, I know, but the conversation just flowed; and even though I'm sure that both of us were trying extra hard to seem witty and interesting, most of all I remember us cracking each other up, joking and laughing at ourselves and with each other, just the way we do now. By the time the contractor arrived, I was genuinely excited to meet this Doug guy in person. We made dinner plans for Saturday night in Los Angeles. I could hardly wait to fly down.

Doug suggested that we meet first at his place. I suggested that he pick me up instead. "Okay, but I just need you to know I'm not a really good driver," he said. "Thanks for letting me know," I replied with a chuckle. There was no pretense or posing with Doug, no arrogance or boasting. He seemed so genuinely comfortable with himself. It's part of why I liked him immediately.

The morning after our first date, Doug emailed me with all of his available dates for the next couple of months. "I'm too old to play games or hide the ball," the email read. "I really like you, and I want to see if we can make this work." In fact, he was eager to see me that Saturday, but I had a long-scheduled girls' weekend on the calendar.

"That's no problem," he said. "I could come up and you and I could just sneak off on the margins." I appreciated his enthusiasm, but I had to explain to him that, no, that's not how a girls' weekend works. We planned a second date for later that week instead.

For our third date, Doug decided that a grand gesture was in order. He flew to Sacramento to meet me for dinner. After that, we knew we had something special. We agreed to commit to each other for six months, and to reevaluate our relationship at the end of it. Attending a speech about the ills of truancy isn't exactly what most people think of as a romantic date, but the event was Doug's coming out—the first time I'd invited him to join me at a professional gathering. Hence the whispering and pointing among my team, who had heard rumors of his existence but hadn't seen him with their own eyes. They would later refer to that era as A.D.—"After Doug." They loved how much he made me laugh. I did, too.

Doug had been married once before, and he had two kids, Cole and Ella—named after John Coltrane and Ella Fitzgerald. When Doug and I first started dating, Ella was in middle school and Cole was in high school; Doug shared custody with his first wife, Kerstin. I had—and have—tremendous admiration and respect for Kerstin. I could tell from the way Doug talked about his kids that she was a terrific mother—and in later months, as Kerstin and I got to know each other, we really hit it off ourselves and became friends. (We sometimes joke that our modern family is almost a little too functional.)

After our second date, Doug was ready to introduce me to Cole and Ella, and I was eager to meet them, too. But as a child of divorce, I knew how hard it can be when your parents start to date other people. So I slowed things down. Other than occasionally talking to the kids when Doug had me on speakerphone in the car, I wanted to make sure that Doug and I had something real and lasting before I waded into Cole's and Ella's lives.

Doug and I put a lot of thought into when and how that first meeting should transpire. We waited until about two months after we'd met, although in my memory it feels like we'd been together for a long time—maybe because the buildup was so great, or because, by the time the big day finally arrived, I felt like I'd loved Doug for years.

I woke up that morning feeling incredibly excited, but also with some butterflies in my stomach. Until that moment, I'd known Cole and Ella as gorgeous faces in Doug's photographs, charming characters in his stories, the central figures in his heart. Now I was finally going to meet these two amazing young people. It was a momentous occasion.

On my way home from my LA office, I picked up a tin of cookies and tied a festive ribbon in a bow around it. I got rid of my suit, changed into jeans and my Chuck Taylors, took a few deep breaths, and got a ride to Doug's house. On the way over, I tried to imagine how the first few minutes would go. I ran scenarios in my head and tried to land on the perfect things to say. The tin of cookies was sitting beside me on the seat, a silent witness to my rehearsing. Would the kids think the cookies were really nice or really weird? Maybe the ribbon was too much.

The ribbon was probably too much. But Cole and Ella could not have been more welcoming. They'd been wanting to meet me, too. We talked for a few minutes, then piled into Doug's car for dinner together. Doug and I had decided the kids should choose where we ate, to make everything as comfortable as possible. They'd picked a place that had been a favorite since they were younger—a seafood hut off the Pacific Coast Highway called the Reel Inn. It was about an hour away in traffic, which gave us some quality car time to get to know one another. Cole, it turned out, was a music aficionado, and he was excited to share some of his latest discoveries with me.

"I just started listening to Roy Ayers," he said. "Do you know him?"

I sang back: "Everybody loves the sunshine, sunshine, folks get down in the sunshine . . ."

"You know it!"

"Of course I know it!"

We put on the song, and then another and another. The four of us sang together with the windows rolled down as we drove up the coast to dinner.

The Reel Inn was casual and unpretentious. It was hard not to feel at ease. We waited in line with trays at a counter, the menu of fresh fish written on a blackboard on the wall. The cashier gave us numbers, much like at a deli, and when our order was called, we took our trays to some picnic tables with a view of the ocean, just as the sun was beginning to set. When we were done eating, Cole and Ella told us that they were going to head over to Cole's school to see an art show where some of their friends' work would be displayed. They wanted to know if we wanted to join them.

"Of course!" I said, as if this was a totally normal thing. It sounded great to me. Then Doug whispered to me, "They must like you. They never invite me to anything." We went to the school together, and Ella—a gifted artist—expertly guided us through the exhibit. Lots of their friends were there, too, and we had fun mingling and making conversation with the students and their parents. Doug later joked that I got completely inundated with their lives that night, but I think it's more accurate to say that I was hooked, and Cole and Ella reeled me in.

At the end of March 2014, I had two trips planned. One was to Mexico, where I was coordinating with senior officials in the fight against transnational criminal organizations and human traffickers. The other was to Italy, where Doug and I were looking forward to a romantic getaway. The respective itineraries were, in a word, different. At home, Doug and I stayed up late looking at pictures and guidebooks and planning our itinerary for Florence. At the office, I was working to put together and lead a bipartisan delegation of state attorneys general to join me in Mexico City.

Mexico-based transnational crime was—and is—a major threat, and California was a primary target. That March, my office had released a report that found, for example, that 70 percent of the U.S. supply of methamphetamine was coming through the San Diego port of entry on California's southern border. The report also drew attention to ways in which Mexican-based drug trafficking was being amplified in the United States as cartels formed alliances with gangs on California streets and in California prisons.

The challenges posed to California law enforcement—and thereby the rest of the country—were significant, and I wanted to meet with Mexican officials to work through a joint plan to take on the cartels.

We spent three days in Mexico—four other state attorneys general and I—and were able to come away with a plan for concrete action. We signed a letter of intent with the National Banking and Securities Commission of Mexico to establish an anti-money-laundering enforcement effort. Money laundering fuels transnational criminal organizations, and by creating a communication and cooperation agreement with

Mexico, we hoped to improve our ability to investigate and disrupt this financing.

On March 26, 2014, I arrived back at my apartment in San Francisco, feeling like the trip had been a real success. But it was late in the evening when I got home, and now I had a small problem: my trip with Doug was starting early the next morning, and I'd had no time to pack.

Shortly after I arrived at my apartment, Doug texted to say he was on his way from the airport. When he got to the apartment, I was in the middle of a frantic search. I couldn't find my black pants, and I was intensely frustrated about it.

It was ridiculous, of course, but it was one of those moments when the balancing act caught up with me—a balancing act that many working women, and some men, know all too well. Just like my mother, I've internalized the idea that everything I do deserves 100 percent, but sometimes it feels like the numbers won't work. There just isn't enough of me to go around. This was one of those times. I had a hundred things racing through my mind in the aftermath of the Mexico trip, and a hundred more as I contemplated the work I'd missed while I was away. Meanwhile, I was trying to shift mental gears for a getaway with my sweetheart—but my packing list and my to-do list were competing hard for real estate in my brain. I was beating myself up for trying to do too much, even as I worried that I wasn't doing quite enough, and all of this stress coalesced in the form of a search for my black pants.

Which I couldn't find. My closet was a mess.

As a result, I was frazzled, and when Doug arrived he seemed out of sorts as well. He was acting strange—a little stiff, a little quiet.

"Do you mind if we get takeout instead of going out to eat?" I asked him. "I didn't plan for this very well and I need time to pack."

"Of course," he said. "How about the Thai place we like?"

"Sounds great," I replied. I rifled through a kitchen drawer and produced a tattered paper menu. "How about pad thai?"

Doug turned to me. "I want to spend my life with you."

That was sweet, but he was always sweet like that. Truth be told, I didn't register the significance of what he'd said at all. I didn't even look up. My mind was still on the black pants.

"That's nice, honey," I said, rubbing his arm as I looked over the menu. "Should we have chicken or shrimp on the pad thai?"

"No, I want to spend my life with you," he said again. When I looked up, he was getting down on one knee. He'd concocted an elaborate plan to propose to me in front of the Ponte Vecchio, in Florence. But once he had the ring, it was burning a hole in his pocket. He couldn't keep it secret.

I looked at him there, on one knee, and burst into tears. Mind you, these were not graceful Hollywood tears streaming down a glistening cheek. No, I'm talking about snorting and grunting, with mascara smudging my face. Doug reached for my hand and I held my breath and smiled back. Then he asked me to marry him, and I bellowed a tear-soaked "Yes!"

Doug and I were married on Friday, August 22, 2014, in an intimate ceremony with the people we loved. Maya officiated; Meena read from Maya Angelou. In keeping with our respective Indian and Jewish heritage, I put a flower garland around Doug's neck, and he stomped on a glass. And then it was done.

Cole, Ella, and I agreed that we didn't like the term "stepmom." Instead they call me their "Momala."

One of my favorite routines is Sunday family dinner. This is a routine I instituted once Doug and I got engaged. When he and I first started dating, he was a single dad sharing custody with Kerstin. Family dinner had been Chinese takeout and plastic forks, which the kids spirited off to their bedrooms. I changed that. Now everyone knows that Sunday family dinner is nonnegotiable, that we come together, all of us around the table, relatives and friends always welcome, and I cook a meal for us to share. It's really important to me.

Everyone quickly got into the routine and found their role to play. Cole sets the table, picks the music, and pitches in as sous chef in the kitchen. Ella makes restaurant-quality guacamole and exquisite desserts, including a gorgeous fresh fruit tart, where she folds the dough in magnificent ways, topped off with homemade whipped cream. Doug bought himself a pair of onion goggles, which he dons with great fanfare when it's time to chop—and let me tell you, there is nothing more attractive than a man in onion goggles.

I make the main dish—maybe a rich pork stew or spaghetti Bolognese or an Indian biryani or chicken with feta cheese, lemon rind, and fresh oregano from the garden. Usually I'll start cooking on Saturday, and sometimes even Friday, though if I've been on the road I'll pull it all together quickly—something simpler, like fish tacos. It doesn't always go as planned: sometimes the pizza dough doesn't rise or the sauce won't thicken or we're missing a key ingredient and I have to improvise. That's all okay. Sunday family dinner is about something more than the meal.

When dinner is finished, the kids do the dishes. I once told them the story of Uncle Freddy. Because he lived in a small basement apartment in Harlem with a tiny kitchen, Uncle Freddy would clean every single dish or utensil he used as soon as he was done using it.

And in time, the kids turned "Uncle Freddy" into a verb. When it's time to clean, they promise to "Uncle Freddy" the place. And they do a pretty good job!

I know that not everyone likes to cook, but it's centering for me. And as long as I'm making Sunday family dinner, I know I'm in control of my life—doing something that matters for the people I love, so we can share that quality time together.

E arly one morning in that busy summer of 2014, my phone rang at the side of my bed. I picked it up to find Eric Holder, then the U.S. attorney general, on the other end of the line. He told me he had a question.

"I'm going to be stepping down soon. Are you interested?"

It was, needless to say, a lot to take in. Did I want to be United States attorney general? Did I want to hold the office that Bobby Kennedy once held? Of course I did. This was the kind of job I used to daydream about during lectures in law school. And this wasn't just any moment or any president. This was Barack Obama, my friend and my president, whose leadership I so admired and whom I had been so proud to support. To join his cabinet would have been the honor of my life.

And yet I wasn't sure if I truly wanted the job. By the time Holder stepped down, there would be fewer than two years left in the administration. What kind of opportunity would I have to create a real agenda?

The next time Holder and I spoke, I brought up Back on Track. I said that if there was a budget at the Department of Justice to fund and create incentives for local reentry initiatives, then I would be interested in the job. I wanted to be able to create real reform at a national level, with an approach that prioritized prevention. Alas, as Holder explained, there wasn't any existing budget for such an effort, and any new funding would have to be approved by Congress— which we both knew was not going to happen.

That was disheartening. But I still knew the job wasn't something to be turned down lightly. Like every lawyer I know, I listed the pros and cons on a yellow pad. I batted the options back and forth with Doug and other members of the family. I did my best to argue both sides.

One day, one of my best friends suggested we take a hike in the Windy Hill Open Space Preserve, near Palo Alto. She thought the outdoor air and beautiful rolling hilltops might refresh my state of mind—and she was right. Away from the office, the contours of my choice came into sharper relief. With every step, I saw more clearly what I wanted to do, and why.

Inevitably, there would be limitations that came with the job. I took that as a given. But as I talked with my friend, and she raised all the right questions, I realized the real reason behind my resistance to the offer: I already had a job I loved, and work I still wanted to do.

I thought about my first days as California attorney general, when I'd learned that we had a big backlog of rape kits. I thought about all the work we were putting in to reduce the backlog, about the innovations we deployed to triple the number of cases that could be handled. Earlier in 2014, my Rapid DNA Service team received an award from the Department of Justice for our achievements. I thought about our work on human trafficking, too, which had been an unseen problem for so long, and our efforts to combat the brutal criminal organizations and street gangs that traded in human lives.

I thought about the fight I'd been able to lead, first as district attorney and then as attorney general, to stop defendants in hate crimes from using what's known as the "gay and trans panic defense." In 2002, a seventeen-year-old woman, Gwen Araujo, had been brutally beaten and murdered in Newark, California. Her killers, two of whom had been involved with her sexually, had tried to justify their actions in court by claiming that they had panicked upon learning that Araujo was transgender, to the point of temporary insanity. It was ludicrous. As district attorney, I had organized a conference of prosecutors and law enforcement officials from across the country to push back against the idea that criminal conduct could be mitigated by prejudice. And as attorney general, in that summer of 2014, I was working with the governor and state legislature on what would be a successful effort to ban such a defense statewide. I thought about how much that meant to me.

I thought about the Bureau of Children's Justice, a new initiative I was still developing with one of my special assistant attorneys general, Jill Habig, which would be entirely devoted to making sure the rights of all of California's children were protected. There was a lot on that agenda, and I was eager to see it all through.

I thought about the work we were doing to prepare to open up state crime data to the public, a first-of-its-kind transparency initiative led by special assistant attorneys general Daniel Suvor and Justin Erlich, which we would call OpenJustice.

Likewise, we were taking Back on Track and my truancy initiative statewide.

And then there were the corporate predators who took advantage of students and veterans and homeowners and the poor. I loved being the voice and advocate for the people they mistreated. The lawyers on my team knew how serious I was about holding corporate predators accountable. They would joke that "Kamala" meant "Get more commas in that settlement price."

And of course, the banks. The fight with them was still ongoing. We were still bringing lawsuits, and I had no plans of backing down.

By the time our hike was over, my friend and I both knew I'd made my decision. It wouldn't be about the title or the perception of prestige. What mattered to me was the work. And when it came to the work that mattered most, I wasn't finished yet.

Later that evening, I called Holder to let him know. Then Doug and I curled up on the couch with the kids and a big bowl of popcorn and, for the second time, watched *Iron Man 2*.

Five

I SAY WE FIGHT

I 'll always remember how I felt in November 1992, as a twenty-eight-year-old prosecutor, driving across the bridge from my home in Oakland into San Francisco to celebrate the victory of newly elected U.S. senators Barbara Boxer and Dianne Feinstein. They were the first female senators from California, and the first two women to represent any state at the same time. Their election was a highlight of the so-called Year of the Woman, and an inspiration to girls and women everywhere, including me.

I recalled that celebration twenty-two years later when, in early January 2015, Senator Boxer posted a video of herself in conversation with her oldest grandchild, Zach. She talked about the issues she cared about, the issues for which she'd fought over three decades in Congress—a strong middle class, a woman's right to choose, the environment, civil rights, human rights—and underscored that she wasn't going to give them up. But, as she told Zach, she wanted to come home to California. And so she wouldn't be running for re-election.

November 2016 was almost two years away, but I had a decision to make. Should I run to replace Senator Boxer? It would be an opportunity to take the issues we were driving forward in the California attorney general's office and bring them to the national stage. Becoming a U.S. senator would be a natural extension of the work I was already doing—fighting for families feeling the burden of stagnant wages, soaring housing costs, and diminishing opportunity; for people imprisoned in a broken criminal justice system; for students exploited by predatory lenders and burdened by skyrocketing tuition; for victims of fraud and white-collar crime; for immigrant communities, for women, for older people. I knew it mattered whose voice was represented at the table where national priorities and policies are set.

I announced my candidacy on January 13, 2015. Eventually, so did thirty-three others. Doug, for whom it was his first major campaign, had to get used to a new kind of scrutiny. We still laugh about the time a reporter asked me who would play me in a movie about my life. I deflected—said I didn't know. Doug was not as prudent. He answered the question and the resulting article said he was "delighted" at the prospect of being played by Bradley Cooper.

I tackled the race as I had every other, meeting as many people as I could, listening carefully to their concerns, mapping a plan of action to address them. As the campaign rolled on, my team and I crisscrossed the state in what we called the Kamoji bus, because of the giant emoji caricature of me painted on the back door.

Because of California's unique "jungle primary," I ultimately found myself in a runoff against fellow Democrat Loretta Sanchez, a long-time member of Congress. She was a tough, determined opponent who kept fighting until the end. I was fortunate enough to have on my team some of the best people in the business—my brilliant campaign manager, Juan Rodriguez, and my longtime strategic advisers Sean Clegg and Ace Smith, along with Ellie Caple, and an extraordinarily dedicated group of staff and volunteers. My goddaughter, Helena, was among them. She started a newsletter, interviewing the staff and chronicling our efforts. Our team was in it together every step of the way, and I couldn't have done it without them.

The two-year campaign passed both fast and slow. But even as I focused on my state, my campaign, and the work before me, something ugly and alarming was infecting the presidential election. The Republican primary was turning into a race to the bottom—a race to anger, a race to blame, a race to fan the flames of xenophobic nativism. And the man who prevailed crossed every boundary of decency and integrity—bragging about sexually assaulting women; mocking people with disabilities; race baiting; demonizing immigrants; attacking war heroes and Gold Star families; and fomenting hostility, even hatred, toward the press.

As a result, Election Night 2016 was not a night for cheering. It was no longer about the race that had just ended. It was about the fight that was clearly now beginning. Drawing on the words of Coretta Scott King, I reminded the audience that freedom must be fought for and won by every generation.

"It is the very nature of this fight for civil rights and justice and equality that whatever gains we make, they will not be permanent. So we must be vigilant," I said. "Understanding that, do not despair. Do not be overwhelmed. Do not throw up our hands when it is time to roll up our sleeves and fight for who we are."

I didn't know, when I spoke to my supporters that night, exactly what was to come. But I did know this: we would need to stand strong and stand together.

On Thursday, November 10, less than forty-eight hours after my election, I visited the headquarters of the Coalition for Humane Immigrant Rights of Los Angeles (CHIRLA).

CHIRLA is one of Los Angeles's oldest immigrant rights advocacy organizations. It was founded in 1986, after President Reagan, a former California governor, signed the Immigration Reform and Control Act, which, among other things, gave legal status to undocumented immigrants who had entered the United States before 1982. CHIRLA's original mission was to inform immigrants about the process by which they could apply for legal status and about their rights to work. It trained community organizers, challenged anti-immigrant laws like California's Proposition 187, which prohibited undocumented immigrants from getting nonemergency public services, and it eventually took on a national portfolio by building coalitions all across the country. It was the first place I wanted to speak officially as senator-elect.

Angelica Salas, CHIRLA's indefatigable executive director, was there to greet me when I arrived. The room was full. It was full of strong, brave women—young women to mothers to grandmothers to great-grandmothers—working women who did everything from domestic work to home health care work, some of whom spoke fluent English and some of whom spoke only Spanish, all of them ready to fight.

In their courage, their dignity, and their determination, they reminded me of my mother. Standing among them, I thought about the duality of the immigrant experience in America.

On the one hand, it is an experience characterized by an extraor-

dinary sense of hopefulness and purpose, a deep belief in the power
of the American Dream—an experience of possibility. At the same
time, it is an experience too often scarred by stereotyping and scape-
goating, in which discrimination, both explicit and implicit, is part of
everyday life.

My mother was the strongest person I have ever known, but I always felt protective of her, too. In part, I suppose, that instinct to
protect comes from being the older child. But I also knew my mother
was a target. I saw it, and it made me mad. I have too many memories
of my brilliant mother being treated as though she were dumb because of her accent. Memories of her being followed around a department store with suspicion, because surely a brown-skinned woman
like her couldn't afford the dress or blouse that she had chosen.

I also remember how seriously she took any encounter with government officials. Whenever we would come back from traveling
abroad, my mother made sure Maya and I were on our best behavior
as we went through customs. "Stand up straight. Don't laugh. Don't
fidget. Have all your stuff. Be prepared." She knew that every word
she spoke would be judged, and she wanted us to be ready. The first
time Doug and I went through customs together, my muscle memory
kicked in. I was preparing myself in the usual way, making sure we
had everything just right and in order. Meanwhile, Doug was as re-
laxed as ever. It frustrated me that he was so casual. He was genuinely
perplexed, innocently wondering, "What's the problem?" We had
been raised in different realities. It was eye-opening for us both.

For as long as ours has been a nation of immigrants, we have been
a nation that fears immigrants. Fear of the other is woven into the fab-
ric of our American culture, and unscrupulous people in power have

exploited that fear in pursuit of political advantage. In the mid-1850s, the first significant third-party movement in the United States, the so-called Know-Nothing Party, rose to popularity on an anti-immigrant platform. In 1882, an act of Congress banned Chinese immigrants to the country. In 1917, Congress overrode President Woodrow Wilson's veto in order to establish a host of new restrictions on immigrants, including a literacy requirement. Concerns about growing numbers of newcomers from Southern and Eastern Europe resulted in the imposition of immigration quotas in 1924. In 1939, nearly 1,000 German Jews fleeing the Nazis in a ship called the *St. Louis* were turned away from the United States. A plan to allow 20,000 Jewish children into the country was outright rejected. And shortly after, the U.S. government interned some 117,000 people of Japanese ancestry.

More recently, as globalization has robbed the country of millions of jobs and displaced huge swaths of the middle class, immigrants have become convenient targets for blame. When the Great Recession ravaged rural America, a number of Republican politicians pointed to immigration as the problem, even as they filibustered a bill that would have created new jobs. Despite the profound role they have played in building and shaping America, immigrants who come here to seek a better life have always made for an easy scapegoat.

Our country was built by many hands, by people from every part of the world. And over the centuries, immigrants have helped to lift and fuel the economy—providing labor to industrialize it and brainpower to create society-altering innovations. Immigrants and their children were the creative minds behind many of our best-known brands—from Levi Strauss to Estée Lauder. Sergey Brin, the co-founder of Google, was a Russian immigrant. Jerry Yang, co-founder of Yahoo!, came here from Taiwan. Mike Krieger, the co-founder of

Instagram, is an immigrant from Brazil. Arianna Huffington, co-founder of *The Huffington Post,* was born in Greece. In fact, in 2016, researchers at the National Foundation for American Policy found that more than half of Silicon Valley's billion-dollar startups were founded by one or more immigrants.

I stood by the podium at CHIRLA, with an American flag and stars-and-stripes balloons in the backdrop, as a mother—a house cleaner from the San Fernando Valley—spoke in Spanish about her fears of deportation. I could barely translate her words, but I understood their meaning and I could feel her anguish. It was visible in her eyes, in her posture. She wanted to be able to tell her children that everything would be okay, but she knew she couldn't.

I thought of the nearly six million American children who live in a home with at least one undocumented family member and the trauma and stress that the election had wrought. I had heard many stories of safety plans that were being put in place—mothers telling their children, "If Mommy doesn't come home right after work, call your aunt or uncle to come and get you." It reminded me of the safety plans I'd seen when I was working with victims of domestic abuse. In both cases, there needed to be a contingency plan to mitigate against an impending harm.

Advocates working with families told us how children were afraid to go to school, not knowing if their parents would still be there when they got home. Parents canceled their children's pediatrician appointments out of fear that ICE would be waiting for them. Likewise, I knew that parents, at that moment, were facing harrowing decisions about what to do with their American children if they were deported. Should the children stay with a relative in the United States? Should they go with their parents to a country that they had never known?

Either option was heartbreaking to imagine. And I knew it wasn't just undocumented people who were terrified. According to research published in *American Behavioral Scientist,* all Latinx immigrants—whether citizens, legal residents, or undocumented—experience the fear of deportation at the same rates. I wanted them to know I had their back.

"This is a time in our country for coalition building," I said, reminded of the work I had seen and done through the years. "We are going to fight for the ideals of this country," I told them, "and we are not going to let up until we have won."

I left CHIRLA two days after the election feeling both encouraged and worried. I knew we were preparing for battle together. But I knew, too, that we were underdogs in the fight. We were going to have to steel ourselves for all that was to come.

T hings moved very quickly. The following week, Doug and I flew across the country to Washington for new senators' orientation. A bipartisan group of senators and their spouses hosted us for three jam-packed days of sessions, during which we were informed about Senate rules and procedures, ethics, and how to set up a Senate office. Doug studied the spouses' binder like a Talmudic scholar.

Nathan Barankin, my number two in the California Department of Justice, agreed to move his family to Washington, and he began the intensive process of selecting and vetting my new team as my chief of staff. We had only the period between Election Day and New Year's to build the office virtually from scratch—poring over some five thousand résumés to fill a host of positions from policy and constituent relations to communications, correspondence, and more. Hiring a diverse staff was important to me—veterans, women, people of color. I wanted my staff in Washington and our state offices to reflect the people we represent.

Ella was now in her senior year of high school, which meant that Doug would be spending at least every other week in Los Angeles. This was the hardest part of it all, being away from Ella. Before becoming a senator, I had gone to every one of her swim meets, every one of her basketball games. Kerstin and I usually embarrassed Ella as we sat together and loudly cheered her name. I hated that I would have to miss some of those games now. And I hated that we would have so much less quality time in person, especially because she was about to go off to college, as Cole had done several years earlier. I was committed to flying home as many weekends as I could, which was important to me for so many reasons—to see my constituents, feel the pulse on the ground, and, crucially, cook Sunday family dinner.

The worst was several months later when I realized I wasn't going to be able to go to Ella's graduation. Fired FBI director James Comey had been invited to testify before the Senate Intelligence Committee that same day about the Russia investigation and his firing, and, given the significance to our national security, there was no way I could miss it. When I called to tell her, she was so understanding, but I felt awful about it. I had conversations with some of my female colleagues afterwards. Maggie Hassan bucked me up. "Our kids love us for who we are and the sacrifices we make," she said. "They get it." In the case of Ella and Cole, I'm so lucky to know that's true. When the hearing was over, I dashed to the airport and flew back to California. I missed the graduation ceremony but made it home in time for family dinner that night.

Doug and I rented a temporary apartment not far from the Capitol, along with minimal furniture—a pair of stools, a bed, a foldout couch for when the kids came to visit, and, for Doug, a big-screen TV. With things happening so quickly, there wasn't much time on the margins for grocery shopping or cooking, though I did make turkey chili one night and froze enough to last us for weeks.

I was sworn in on January 3, 2017, by Vice President Joe Biden during his final month in office, and moved into a basement office alongside other newly elected senators. While not every Senate committee had available seats, I was appointed to four based on my expertise and background: Intelligence, Homeland Security, Budget, and Environment and Public Works.

One week later, the Homeland Security Committee held a confirmation hearing for General John Kelly, who had been nominated for secretary of Homeland Security. I chose to focus my questions to him on the Deferred Action for Childhood Arrivals program (DACA), which was created in 2012 by the Obama administration to protect eligible undocumented youth from deportation and allow them to obtain work permits.

"Hundreds of thousands of DACA recipients around the country are afraid right now for what this incoming administration might do to them and also what it might do to their unauthorized family members," I said.

I went on to explain that in order to qualify for the program, recipients had submitted extensive paperwork to the federal government, including detailed information about themselves and their loved ones. Each person's case was reviewed and vetted according to specific criteria. The young person must not have been convicted of a felony, a significant misdemeanor, or three or more misdemeanors.

They must not have been deemed a threat to public safety or national security. They had to be in school or have already earned a high school diploma or certificate, or been honorably discharged from the armed forces. They had to provide proof of identity, proof of time and admission in the United States, proof of school completion or military status, and biometric information. Only if they cleared this extensive vetting would they get DACA status.

In addition, when they applied, the Department of Homeland Security (DHS) assured them it would follow its long-standing practice not to use their information for law enforcement purposes except in very limited circumstances. "These young people," I said to General Kelly, "are now worried that the information they provided in good faith to our government may now be used to track them down and lead to their removal." Hundreds of thousands of them have relied on our representations.

"Do you agree that we would not use this information against them?" I asked. Kelly wouldn't directly answer the question. I next read to him from a government document—frequently asked questions about the DACA program. There was a question that asked "If my case is referred to ICE [U.S. Immigration and Customs Enforcement] for immigration enforcement purposes or if I receive an NTA [Notice to Appear], will information related to my family members and guardians also be referred to ICE for immigration enforcement purposes?" The answer to the question on the government document was no.

"Are you willing to maintain that policy?" I asked. Again, Kelly deflected. I pressed harder. "Do you intend to use the limited law enforcement resources of DHS to remove [DACA recipients] from the country?" Once again, he refused to answer the question directly.

"Would you agree that state and local law enforcement agencies are uniquely situated to protect the public safety of their own communities?"

"I would agree," he said.

"Are you aware that state and local law enforcement leaders across the country have publicly stated that they depend on the cooperation of immigrant communities" to prosecute criminal activity and come forward as witnesses to crime?

"I've read that."

"And are you aware that when the government has applied indiscriminate immigration sweeps, many local law enforcement agencies have been concerned and have complained that there has been a decrease in immigrants reporting crimes against themselves and others?"

"I was not aware of that."

"Will you make it your priority to become aware of the impact on immigrant communities, in terms of their reluctance to report crimes against themselves, their family members, or others, when they are concerned that DHS may direct sweeps against entire immigrant communities?"

"You have my commitment. I'll get briefed on this. Again I fall back on, really—the law will guide me, if confirmed, in everything that I do."

That wasn't enough.

As a former district attorney and attorney general, I had a lot of experience with this issue. I knew that victims of crime—be it rape, be it child sexual assault, be it fraud—simply will not come forward if they believe they are the ones who will be treated as criminals. I also knew that predators use this knowledge to their advantage, exploiting the vulnerability of certain groups who they know will keep quiet. I don't ever want a victim of a crime to be afraid to wave down a passing patrol car to get help. Such a system serves the predators, not the public. It renders all of us less safe. As attorney general, I had crafted legislation to help ensure that undocumented immigrants who stepped forward to testify about crimes, or to report them, were shielded from deportation for doing so. I knew this would help prosecutors obtain convictions while strengthening the relationship of trust between law enforcement and immigrant communities.

In the end, I voted against John Kelly's confirmation and pressed my colleagues to do the same. He wasn't prepared to keep the nation's promises, and I wasn't prepared to put him in charge of them.

Whether he ever got briefed on the consequences of indiscriminate immigration enforcement, I will never know. What I do know is that in the first hundred days of the administration, immigration arrests increased by more than 37 percent. The administration chose to make all unauthorized immigrants a priority for deportation, regardless of whether they were otherwise law-abiding members of the community. Arrests of undocumented immigrants with no criminal record nearly doubled.

The policies have had far-reaching consequences for children. As the Center for American Progress documented, ICE officials raided a meatpacking plant in Tennessee where they arrested ninety-seven workers. It was one of the largest workplace raids in ten years. All told, 160 children had a parent arrested in the raid. The next day, 20 percent of the Latinx students in a nearby county were absent from school as parents feared that they—or their children—would be arrested as well. In 2016, a quarter of all kids in the United States under the age of five lived in immigrant families. These children have had to live in the grip of the fear that, at any moment, their parents could be abruptly taken away from them.

Children of immigrants also faced a new kind of torment. Teachers around the country have reported spikes in bullying that echoes the administration's rhetoric. Kids are being taunted by other kids, told they will be deported, told their parents will be deported, told they should go back where they came from. The words of one prominent, powerful bully have been mimicked and adopted as the rallying cry of bullies everywhere.

Of course, it's not just the children of immigrants who are affected. According to the Migration Policy Institute, for example, at least 20 percent of early childhood educators are immigrants. Immigrants also represent a large percentage of people working in the early child care industry—and those numbers have tripled over the past two decades. These caregivers—primarily women—nurture millions of children each and every day. The risks to their safety and security in this country due to overbroad immigration enforcement are a risk to us all. This cannot be overlooked.

On January 20, 2017, I attended the presidential inauguration, along with fellow members of the United States Congress. My Senate colleagues and I gathered in the Senate chamber and walked, two by two, through the Capitol Building, exiting the West Front onto the inaugural platform, where risers and chairs were arrayed for the ceremony. As we walked to our seats, we were handed plastic ponchos in case of rain. Doug was sitting with his new pals in the spouses' section, closer to the stage than I was. He turned around and gave me a wave.

By some twist of fate, the skies opened up just as the transition of power was complete. Some supporters of the president took the rain as a sign of blessing, but for me and so many others, dark clouds were settling in.

Renewal, it turned out, decided to reveal itself the next day. In the runup to Inauguration Day, activists had planned a Women's March in cities all across the country. But given the organic, decentralized way the march had come together—sparked by a Facebook post from a grandmother in Hawaii the day after the election and organized in a matter of weeks by a diverse group of activists, many of whom had never met before—no one knew exactly how it would unfold.

Reality exceeded all expectations: more than four million people showed up in the streets nationwide, with sister marches in countries around the world.

In Washington, the crowd was so massive that it packed the entire route, end to end—a vibrant sea of pink-hatted people of all ages, races, genders, and orientations. Marchers carried handmade signs that expressed the full range of emotions we all felt, from disbelief to determination, horror, purpose, and hope: IT'S 2017. WTF? . . . STILL I RISE . . . GIRLS JUST WANT TO HAVE FUNDAMENTAL RIGHTS . . . MEN OF QUALITY DON'T FEAR EQUALITY . . . WE THE PEOPLE.

I saw white-haired grandmothers and blue-haired college students; flannel-clad hipsters and down-jacketed soccer moms; toddlers in strollers and teenagers in the trees; men and women in solidarity, side by side. Amazingly, amid the throng, I ran into Aunt Lenore, who engulfed me in a giant bear hug. She told me that her daughter Lilah, who was at the time a leader in the Service Employees International Union (SEIU), was in the crowd as well. They had come out to march together, carrying forward the banner of social justice that Lenore and my mother had held high as students at Berkeley half a century before.

I had been asked to speak, and as I climbed up to the stage, I was overwhelmed by the size and spirit of the crowd stretching out before me as far as I could see. There were so many people that cellular networks had gone down, yet the energy was electric. No one could move, but everyone seemed to understand that the march was a glimpse of a new kind of coalition whose true strength had yet to be tested. "Even if you're not sitting in the White House, even if you are not a member of the United States Congress, even if you don't run a big corporate super PAC, you have the power. And we the people have the power!" I told the marchers. "And there is nothing more powerful than a group of determined sistahs, marching alongside with their partners and their determined sons and brothers and fathers, standing up for what we know is right!"

I talked about women's issues, at least what I see as women's issues: the economy, national security, health care, education, criminal justice reform, climate change. I said that if you are a woman who is an immigrant and you don't want your family torn apart, you know that immigration reform is a women's issue. I said that if you are a woman who is working off student loans, you know that the crushing burden of student debt is a women's issue. I said that if you are a black mother trying to raise a son, you know that Black Lives Matter is a women's issue. "And if you are a woman, period, you know we deserve a country with equal pay and access to health care, including a safe and legal abortion, protected as a fundamental and constitutional right." I affirmed that together we are powerful, and cannot be written off.

A few days later, Doug and I were in our new apartment in DC, eating dinner on stools at our kitchen counter, when breaking news cut across the television. The president had signed an executive order banning travel to the United States from seven Muslim-majority countries—Iraq, Iran, Libya, Somalia, Sudan, Syria, and Yemen—for a period of 90 days. He barred refugees from coming to the United States for 120 days and barred refugees from Syria indefinitely.

Travelers started getting detained at airports, unable to speak with lawyers. Families were panicking as their loved ones failed to emerge from airport security. I received calls from activists and lawyers, including Meena, who had rushed to airports to try to help people who were being detained. There was chaos.

So I called John Kelly. By then he had been confirmed as secretary of homeland security, and I needed to find out what was going on and to make sure that anyone being detained would get access to a lawyer. There were a lot of ways Secretary Kelly could have shown his responsiveness, a lot of information he could have provided. Indeed, the American people had a right to this information, and, given my oversight role on the Senate Homeland Security Committee, I intended to get it. Instead, he said gruffly, "Why are you calling me at home with this?" That was his chief concern.

By the time we got off the phone, it was clear that he didn't understand the depth of what was going on. He said he'd get back to me, but he never did. And by the next day, the nation had erupted in spontaneous protest, knowing full well that the travel ban was really a Muslim ban, and that there were few things more antithetical to our founding ideals. Enshrined in the First Amendment is the notion that not only would America establish no official religion of its own, but the government has no authority to prohibit anyone's activities based on their religion.

I was new to Washington and still learning how things worked. This episode taught me that calling this secretary of homeland security was a wasted effort. We needed a law. The first bill I introduced in the Senate was the Access to Counsel Act, which prohibits federal officials from denying access to a lawyer for anyone detained trying to reach the United States. But we were in an uphill fight, made harder by the political circumstances of the moment.

Four days after the travel ban was executed, Neil Gorsuch was nominated to the Supreme Court to fill a seat that had been open since Antonin Scalia's death almost a year earlier. President Obama had nominated a highly respected United States circuit judge, Merrick Garland, to serve. But in an unprecedented show of partisan obstruction, Republicans refused to hold even one hearing on Garland's nomination. They were rewarded for their recalcitrance. Gorsuch was confirmed by the Senate in April 2017, shifting the balance of power on the Court back toward the conservative justices. Fifteen months later, Justice Gorsuch cast the deciding vote in one of the most shameful decision's in the Court's recent history: the decision to uphold the president's travel ban.

Six

WE ARE BETTER
THAN THIS

On February 16, 2017, I gave my maiden speech on the floor of the United States Senate. It was a humbling experience. In recent years, the Senate has been known largely as a body of gridlock and partisanship. Once revered as the country's most deliberative body, it has often proved to be anything but. And yet as I stood there, it was the giants of the Senate who came to mind, and the extraordinary work that had been done on that very floor. It was here that the New Deal came to life and the economy was saved. It was here that Social Security earned passage and, later, Medicaid and Medicare. The Civil Rights Act, the Voting Rights Act, the War on Poverty—all fought for and won right here in this body. At my Senate desk once sat Eugene McCarthy, who sponsored the Immigration and Nationality Act of 1965, which ended quotas and established rules aimed at reunifying immigrant families.

I opened my speech exactly as those who know me would have expected. "Above all, I rise today with a sense of gratitude for all those upon whose shoulders we stand. For me, it starts with my mother, Shyamala Harris."

I told her immigration story, the story of her self-determination, the story that made Maya and me, and made us Americans. "And I know she's looking down on us today. And, knowing my mother, she's probably saying, 'Kamala, what on earth is going on down there? We have got to stand up for our values!'"

I didn't mince words. I talked about the unprecedented series of executive actions taken in the early weeks of the administration, actions that hit our immigrant and religious communities like a cold front, "striking a chilling fear in the hearts of millions of good, hard-working people."

I talked about the outsize impact on the state of California, because I believe California is a microcosm of who we are as Americans. I explained that we have farmers and environmentalists, welders and technologists, Republicans, Democrats, Independents, and more veterans, and more immigrants—documented and undocumented—than any state in the nation. When it came to DACA, I reiterated what I had said in Kelly's confirmation hearing: that we had promised recipients that we would not use their personal information against them, and that we could not go back on our promise to these kids and their families.

I spoke as a lifelong prosecutor and former attorney general of the largest state in this country when I said that the administration's Muslim ban and immigration actions presented a real and present threat to our public safety. Instead of making us more safe, the increased raids and executive orders instill fear. "For this reason," I said, "studies have shown Latinos are more than 40 percent less likely to call 911 when they have been a victim of a crime. This climate of fear drives people underground and into the shadows, making them less likely to report crimes against themselves or others. Fewer victims reporting crime and fewer witnesses coming forward."

I also talked about the economic consequences, noting that immigrants make up 10 percent of California's workforce and contribute $130 billion to our state's gross domestic product. "Immigrants own small businesses, they till the land, they care for children and the elderly, they work in our labs, attend our universities, and serve in our military. So these actions are not only cruel. They cause ripple effects that harm our public safety and our economy."

I closed my remarks with a call to action: that we have a responsibility to draw a line and say no—that as a coequal branch of government, it is our duty to uphold the ideals of this country.

The next month, I invited a young woman from Fresno who is a University of California at Merced alumna, a biomedical researcher, and a DACA recipient to be my guest at a joint session of Congress. Yuriana Aguilar's parents moved their family from Mexico to Fresno when Yuriana was just five years old. None of them had papers. Her parents were agricultural workers who supported the family by selling vegetables. Still, as Yuriana recalls, "somehow they knew in order to succeed, you have to have an education." Yuriana took her parents' message to heart—literally. Today she works at Rush Medical College, in Chicago, studying how the heart's electrical system functions. DACA made it possible for her to pursue her education and earn a PhD.

Yuriana has described how, when she first heard about the creation of DACA, she cried with relief. Then she went back to her research, doing her part to help others live healthier lives. As she says, "Science

doesn't have borders—there are no limitations on its advancement."
My mother would have loved her.

When we talk about DACA recipients, Yuriana's commitment to
giving back to our country is the rule, not the exception. The vast
majority of DACA recipients are employed—more than 75 percent of
them. They wear our nation's uniform, they study at our colleges and
universities, and they work in U.S. companies large and small. In fact,
if DACA recipients were deported, it is estimated that the U.S. economy as a whole could lose as much as $460 billion over a decade. These
young people are contributing to our country in meaningful ways.

I kept Yuriana top of mind over the course of the drama that
would unfold through the year. She was the first person I thought of
when, on September 5, 2017, Attorney General Jeff Sessions cruelly
and arbitrarily announced that the administration was ending the
DACA program, throwing the fates of hundreds of thousands of people into limbo.

Without DACA, eligible young people who had been brought to
the United States as children are faced with a terrible choice: they can
live here without papers and in fear of deportation or leave the only
country they've ever known. They have no path to citizenship. They
can't leave the country and get in line to immigrate here. There is no
line. And for this administration, that's the point.

Congress can fix this. There is bipartisan legislation in the House
and the Senate that I've co-sponsored—the DREAM Act—which
gives these young people a permanent path to citizenship. Every day
that the DREAM Act goes unpassed is another day they have to live
in fear—despite having done everything we asked them to.

I've met many Dreamers over the years, and on a nearly daily basis
throughout my first year in the U.S. Senate. They bravely came to

Washington to meet with members of Congress and tell their stories. There was one day when I was supposed to meet with five Dreamers from California who were in town as part of a group from all over the country. The others wanted to join, too, so I invited them into my conference room. It was packed, standing room only, with people lined up against the walls.

I was struck by one of the California kids, Sergio, who was a student at the University of California at Irvine. He talked about his mother working in Mexico, unable to make ends meet, and the decision she had made to come to the United States to give him a chance at a better life. He talked about how hard he had worked through school and how he had focused a lot of his energy on doing outreach to help people get health care. Like so many Dreamers, he was taking on a life of service. That's the thing about the Dreamers: they really do believe in the promise of this country. It is their country, too.

There was so much passion in Sergio's eyes. But I knew he was also frightened. The administration's decision to end DACA had been so dispiriting and demoralizing, so counter to the better history of our country, so counter to the promise of opportunity on which he had relied. And as he and most of them searched my eyes, looking for confidence that they would be okay, I fought the pain of knowing how wrong and unfair the situation was, and that I could not, on my own, control the outcome. It pains me still today.

Three days after Sessions announced his actions, the University of California filed suit against the administration "for wrongly and unconstitutionally violating the rights of the University and its students" by rescinding the DACA program on "nothing more than unreasoned executive whim." The president of the University of California system, Janet Napolitano, had served as President Obama's homeland security secretary and had been responsible for drafting and overseeing the DACA program as originally conceived. For her, and for all of us, this was personal.

On January 10, 2018, the federal court sided with the university, issuing a temporary nationwide injunction blocking the government's decision. This was a huge relief, as it restarted the DACA program and halted the administration action. But the operative word is "temporary." Congress must still act to provide these young people with permanent protection from deportation, which can come only through legislation. Until then, Dreamers will remain in constant fear that a new court decision could rip them away from their families and the only country they've called home. And with a solid conservative majority on the Supreme Court, there's every reason to believe that such a reversal could be forthcoming.

February 2018 was a pivotal month in the immigration fight. The administration continued its cruel and outrageous conduct, going so far as to remove a reference to the United States as "a nation of immigrants" from the mission statement of the agency responsible for citizenship and immigration services. Meanwhile, the administration and many congressional Republicans effectively held the Dreamers hostage.

As part of the budget bill debates to fund the government, the Senate had agreed to take a vote on the DREAM Act, which would create a path to citizenship for the Dreamers. But there was a catch. In exchange, the legislation included $25 billion in taxpayer money to build a wall on the border with Mexico.

There were a number of reasons why I opposed this. Purely from a dollars-and-cents perspective, it was a total waste of taxpayer money.

I am a strong believer in border security—but experts agree that a wall will not secure our border. Moreover, I worried that those billions of dollars would be used to implement the administration's anti-immigrant agenda—including raids that target California and its residents, and families across the country. For the same price tag, we could do anything from funding a full-scale effort to combat the opioid crisis to expanding rural broadband and upgrading critical infrastructure.

But there was a bigger reason to oppose the border wall. A useless wall on the southern border would be nothing more than a symbol, a monument standing in opposition to not just everything I value, but to the fundamental values upon which this country was built. The Statue of Liberty is the monument that defines to the world who we are. Emma Lazarus's words—"Give me your tired, your poor, your huddled masses yearning to breathe free"—speak to our true character: a generous country that respects and embraces those who have made the difficult journey to our shores, often fleeing harm; that sees our quintessentially optimistic, can-do spirit in those who aspire to make the American Dream their own. How could I vote to build what would be little more than a monument, designed to send the cold, hard message "KEEP OUT"?

The immigration debate is so often defined by false choices. I remember a town hall I held in Sacramento, where a group of the president's supporters showed up. One man said he thought I cared more about undocumented immigrants than I cared about the American people. It was a false choice. I care deeply about them both. Similarly, the budget debate was offering a false choice: fund the government or oppose the wall. I believed we could do both.

In the end, we were presented with two bills. I was proud to support the first, a bipartisan compromise drafted by Senators Chris Coons, a Democrat from Delaware, and the late John McCain, a Republican from Arizona, which included measures to protect Dreamers from deportation and provide them with a path to citizenship, and did not include funding for the wall. The other proposal—which included the DREAM Act in exchange for the wall—was something I simply couldn't get behind, regardless of the pressure. I voted against it. Ultimately, neither of the bills became law.

The fight on behalf of Dreamers continues. And here's what I believe: These young people were brought into our country, in many cases before they could walk or talk, through no choice of their own. This is the only country they've ever known. This is their home, and they're contributing. So I won't let up until they are recognized as the Americans they are.

There's a region in Central America known as the Northern Triangle, which includes three countries: El Salvador, Guatemala, and Honduras. Together these countries have the menacing distinction of being among the most violent in the world. Between 1979 and 1992, El Salvador was undone by civil war that left as many as 75,000 dead. Between 1960 and 1996, Guatemala's civil war resulted in the deaths of 200,000 civilians. Honduras didn't have a civil war of its own, but the violence in neighboring countries bled across its borders and made it, too, one of the world's most dangerous places to live.

Even after the wars ended, the violence didn't. A broken economy with deep poverty and few jobs, awash in weapons and generational destruction, led to the formation of organized criminal organizations that used murder, rape, and other sexual violence to control territory and take over large swaths of the region. In the years since, more people have been killed and kidnapped in the Northern Triangle than in some of the world's most brutal wars. Between 2011 and 2014, nearly fifty thousand people were murdered in the Northern Triangle, and just 5 percent of the deaths resulted in judicial convictions.

For residents of these countries, life is often defined by terror. Gang violence, drug trafficking, and corruption are rampant. The largest and most notorious of these transnational criminal organizations, MS-13 and the Mara 18, are reported to include as many as 85,000 members worldwide. They extort small business owners and residents in poor neighborhoods into paying hundreds of millions of dollars each and every year. Those who don't pay risk death, for them and their families. The gangs recruit young men to join their ranks through threats and intimidation, and they force teenage girls to endure sexual violence as so-called gang girlfriends.

Indeed, for women and girls in these countries, violence is systemic. In July 2014, the UN Special Rapporteur on Violence Against Women reported that violent deaths of women in Honduras had risen by 263.4 percent between 2005 and 2013. There are stories of children being robbed, raped, murdered—including an eleven-year-old girl in Honduras whose killers slashed her throat and stuffed her underwear in it. If there was a ground zero for brutality and bleakness, the Northern Triangle would be it.

The only option is escape. And so hundreds of thousands of people have fled the region into neighboring countries and up through Mexico to the United States. In the past, we have welcomed asylum seekers in accordance with international law, granting them special protected status because of the severity of the hardships they face. Sometimes they come as families. But all too often, the journey is impossible to afford, leaving parents with an excruciating choice: Do they keep their children close but in the midst of mortal peril, or do they send them to the United States, knowing that if they survive the perilous journey they will have a chance to be safe and free?

In the summer of 2014, an unprecedented surge of tens of thousands of children and adolescents fled the violence of the Northern Triangle through human smuggling networks that brought them to the United States.

I was attorney general at the time, sitting at home watching the evening news, when I saw an image that struck a chord. In Murrieta, California—a town roughly halfway between Los Angeles and San Diego—several buses carrying roughly 140 undocumented children and parents were on their way to a processing center. A crowd had gathered, blocking the street, waving flags and signs and yelling, "Nobody wants you!" "You're not welcome!" "Turn around and go back home!" There were children inside the buses, looking out of their windows at faces filled with hate and vitriol. Their only wrong was that they had fled horrific violence.

And it wasn't just the protesters in the streets. At the same time, a big push was coming out of DC to expedite the decision-making process so that they could quickly turn undocumented kids and families back. The aim was to assess and reach asylum decisions in about two weeks. Now, to be clear, the process requires someone to make a decision about whether the asylum seeker was fleeing real harm. That means that children have to share facts and tell their story in a comprehensive way.

I knew, having prosecuted child sexual assault, that in these types of cases, it takes a long time to earn a child's trust, and for a child to be able to tell his or her story in a court of law. What was worse, I learned that these asylum-seeking kids had no right to a lawyer to guide them through the process. And that mattered a great deal. If you don't have a lawyer, there's about a 90 percent chance that you will lose your asylum case. If you have legal advice, there's about a 50 percent chance you will prevail. Given that deportation would take these children back into the heart of danger, whether or not they had a lawyer was a matter of life and death.

I had to do something about this, and I knew there wasn't any time to waste. So I personally got on the phone with managing partners of some of the most prestigious law firms in California, as well as corporate lawyers from big entertainment companies like Walt Disney and Warner Bros. Entertainment, and asked them to come to my office to help me make sure these children, some as young as eight years old, had lawyers, and thus had access to due process. Representatives from dozens of law firms convened in the conference room of my downtown Los Angeles office, and I took on the role of auctioneer.

"Okay, can I get five hundred hours of pro bono from you? How about you? And you? What about your firm? What can you guys do for us?" Soon after, we held a similar meeting in Northern California, where I did the same. We rallied the private lawyers to work through one of the community agencies that was offering legal services to help unaccompanied kids. Then I sponsored legislation to provide $3 million to other nonprofits that were providing these children with legal representation.

This was my first experience with the crisis in the Northern

Triangle and the consequences it had wrought on children and families. But it wouldn't be the last.

In January 2017, one of the new administration's first orders of business was signing an executive order that revoked the temporary protected status of immigrants from the Northern Triangle. As a result, some 350,000 immigrants are in the process of losing their right to live and work in the United States. The administration also ordered a change in the way asylum cases are considered, making it more difficult for immigrants to establish a legal basis for staying in the United States. Between February and June 2017, the number of applicants found to be eligible for asylum dropped by 10 percent.

In March 2017, Secretary Kelly went on CNN, where he was asked about a report that, in order to deter more people from the Northern Triangle from coming to the United States, he was actively considering the possibility of forcibly separating parents from their children at the border. "I would do almost anything to deter the people from Central America from getting on this very, very dangerous network that brings them up through Mexico into the United States," he said, confirming that it was under consideration.

Shortly thereafter, Elaine Duke, the deputy secretary of homeland security, appeared before the Homeland Security Committee. "Do you know when this is supposed to take effect?" I asked her, trying to gauge the likelihood that something so atrocious could be under way.

"It is not a decision," she said. "The Secretary—I talked to him personally about it. He considers it still a possibility. They are looking at a wide range of deterrents, and it was raised as a possible method of deterrence but there is no decision made and there is no implementation plan currently."

It was an unacceptable answer. The next month, when Kelly appeared before the committee, I grilled him on the issue. He was evasive about whether this policy was under consideration, but he refused to rule it out.

"So are you unwilling, sir, to issue a written directive that it is the policy of this department to not separate children from their mothers unless the life of the child is in danger?"

"I don't need to do that."

I continued to press for answers through the end of 2017 and into 2018, but DHS was not forthcoming. Then, on April 6, 2018, Attorney General Sessions announced a zero-tolerance policy at the border, meaning that the administration would refer for criminal prosecution any adult crossing the border illegally, regardless of the reason, and that this could include separating children from their parents. We learned through a *New York Times* report several days later that, despite DHS's insistence that there was no separation policy, seven hundred children had been separated from their parents since the previous October, including one hundred who were under the age of four.

There are few things more cruel, more inhumane, more fundamentally evil than ripping a child from her parent's arms. We should all know this to be true on a gut level. But if we needed more proof, we could look at a statement released by Dr. Colleen Kraft, president of the American Academy of Pediatrics, on behalf of the organization, stating that she was appalled by the new policy. Dr. Kraft wrote about the extraordinary stress and trauma of family separation, which "can cause irreparable harm, disrupting a child's brain architecture and affecting his or her short- and long-term health." These findings are shared by the American Medical Association, which has called for an end to the policy, noting that the children the U.S. government is forcibly separating from their parents may be scarred for life.

The administration claimed that it wouldn't separate families seeking asylum if they arrived at an official port of entry, as opposed to other parts of the border. But that didn't hold true. There were reports of a six-year-old girl from the Democratic Republic of Congo who was taken from her mother when they arrived at the San Diego port of entry seeking asylum, even though the mother was able to establish a credible fear of persecution. This was just one of many documented cases of family separation at ports of entry. A blind six-year-old was taken from her mother. So was an eighteen-month-old. This wasn't just a tragedy; it was a violation of international law. It was a human rights abuse. And the toll it took was not just on the children. After a man from Honduras was separated from his wife, after his three-year-old son was ripped from his arms, after he was placed in an isolation cell, the trauma led him to take his own life.

On May 15, Kirstjen Nielsen, who had been confirmed as homeland security secretary after Kelly was named White House chief of staff, came before our committee. I told her that I was extremely concerned about the administration's repeated attacks on some of the most vulnerable communities, children and pregnant women in particular, as enforced by DHS. I pointed to the DACA program, to the separation of children at the border, and to an agency directive that allows for more detentions of pregnant women. I expressed concern about a new information-sharing system between the Office of Refugee Resettlement and ICE that is likely to have a chilling effect on sponsors who otherwise would be willing to come forward to provide care for unaccompanied minors, because of fear that doing so would lead to their own deportation.

I also noted that the previous week, *The Washington Post* had reported that Nielsen was considering undermining an agreement that ensures standards of care for immigrant children, such as the provision of meals and recreation, and calls for them to be placed in the least restrictive setting possible.

I told her that the administration had routinely provided misleading information to the committee and had even gone so far as to claim that policies many consider to be cruel, such as routinely separating families, are carried out in the best interest of the child.

"So my question to you is, last Thursday, *The New York Times* reported that the president has directed you to separate parents from children when they cross into the United States as a way to deter illegal immigrants, is that correct? Have you been directed to separate parents from children as a method of deterrence of undocumented immigration?"

"I have not been directed to do that for purposes of deterrence, no."

"What purpose have you been given for separating parents from their children?"

"So my decision has been that anyone who breaks the law will be prosecuted. If you're a parent or you're a single person or you happen to have a family, if you cross between the ports of entry we will refer you for prosecution. You have broken U.S. law."

Again I pressed. "So your agency will be separating children from their parents—"

"No, what we'll be doing is prosecuting parents who have broken the law, just as we do every day in the United States of America."

"But if that parent has a four-year-old child, what do you plan on doing with that child?"

"The child, under law, goes to HHS for care and custody."

"They will be separated from their parent. And so my question—"

"Just like we do in the United States every day."

"So they will be separated from their parent, and my question then is when you are separating children from their parents, do you have a protocol in place about how that should be done and are you training the people who will actually remove a child from their parent on how to do that in the least traumatic way? I would hope you do train on how to do that, and so the question is, and the request has been, to give us the information about how you are training and what the protocols are for separating a child from their parent."

"I'm happy to provide you with the training information," she said, though she never did. Once again, Nielsen made the false claim that she had stuck with through the entire process: "Again, we do not have a policy to separate children from their parents," she said. "Our policy is if you break the law, we will prosecute you. You have an option to go to a port of entry and not illegally cross into our country."

Let's call this what it is. The White House and DHS were using children—babies—as pawns in a profoundly misguided and inhumane policy to deter immigration. Attorney General Sessions admitted as much—proudly, it appeared, while quoting scripture to justify the abuse:

"Persons who violate the law of our nation are subject to prosecution. I would cite you to the Apostle Paul and his clear and wise command in Romans 13 to obey the laws of the government because God has ordained them for purpose and order," he said, seemingly forgetting or omitting all of the teachings of Christ in the process.

For an added dose of cruelty, Sessions got rid of the right of women and children to seek asylum because of domestic abuse.

I often describe the balance of our democracy as resting on four legs: three independent, coequal branches of government and a free, independent press. As this horror unfolded, the press worked tirelessly to safeguard our true values. Crews of reporters went down to our southern border, filming, filing, and reporting in real time, showing Americans what was really going on, bringing the crisis into our living rooms. The vivid daily coverage informed and inspired a public outcry that eventually forced the administration to backtrack, at least temporarily.

On June 20, 2018, the president signed an executive order that ended its family separation practice. But that did not put an end to the story. Rather than separating families, the new administration policy was to hold those families indefinitely behind bars. As of this writing, jailing innocent children remains the policy of the United States. Children remain separated from their parents. And in the aftermath of the executive order, we were still greeted with headlines like this one, from *The Texas Tribune:* "Immigrant Toddlers Ordered to Appear in Court Alone."

On a hot, dry day at the end of June, I visited the Otay Mesa Detention Center, not far from the border between California and Mexico. I've seen many prisons. Otay Mesa was identical in appearance. To get in the facility, which is surrounded by chain-link fences and barbed wire, you have to pass through multiple checkpoints. One gate opens, you stand in the middle area, and then it shuts behind you before another opens ahead. For anyone detained there, it sends a strong signal that you are locked away from the world.

Once inside the building, I met with mothers who'd been separated from their children. They were wearing blue jumpsuits with the word DETAINEE in block letters on their backs. I asked the facility staff to give us some privacy. They stood about twenty yards away while I asked the mothers about their experiences and came to understand the deep trauma they had endured.

Olga told me that she hadn't seen her four children—ages seventeen, sixteen, twelve, and eight—in nearly two months and that she wasn't even sure where they were. She had fled domestic violence in Honduras, taking a flight to Mexico. She stopped at the Tapachula shelter, in Mexico, where she learned that there was a caravan helping asylum seekers get to the United States. It wasn't going to cost her any money, and it was going to drop her off in Tijuana just south of the border. They provided her and her family with food on the journey and offered to help her with the process of seeking asylum. She said she traveled by airline, train, and bus and at some points walked, though she was often able to hitchhike. People along the way had wanted to help.

When she arrived in Tijuana, she and her family were taken to churches and shelters, and eventually presented themselves to the U.S. Border Patrol. They were led to a holding cell and told to wait to be processed. That was when her children were taken from her, with no warning or explanation. She pleaded with the Border Patrol agents to tell her where her children had been taken. She presented their birth certificates. She needed answers. Desperately. But no answers were given. All she knew was that her three girls were being held together while her son was all by himself. Eventually a social worker was able to connect her by phone to her kids, who weren't sure exactly where they were. She had come to believe that they were all in New York City, and though they said they were okay, it was hard to imagine that could be true.

Another woman from Honduras had a similar story. She, too, had fled the country because she was being abused, and she had brought her eight-year-old son, Mauro, with her. Her son was also taken from her cell with no explanation. The deportation officers told her that he was in Los Angeles, but even they weren't sure. She had brought him with her because she thought he would be safe in the United States. But now that hope seemed lost.

The Department of Homeland Security had said that families seeking asylum at ports of entry would not be separated from one another. But when another woman at Otay Mesa, Morena, left El Salvador and presented herself with her two boys—ages twelve and five—at the San Ysidro Land Port of Entry processing center, her children were ripped away from her. She pleaded with the agents not to take her kids, but to no avail. She had to wait fifteen days to call her sons, because detainees were charged eighty-five cents per minute for calls and she didn't have any money. She had to earn some by working at the facility. Morena had worked for seven days straight and was paid only four dollars. Olga had worked for twelve days and was also paid just four dollars. They said that when they tried to report abuse, they were yelled at. They told me they'd received a lot of verbal abuse from the officers, and had been forced to work late at night after long days of waiting for their hearings.

Six weeks had passed and Morena was still unable to get in touch with her children. She called the facility where she was told they'd been taken, but the phone just kept ringing, with no answer. She told me that the only time they were allowed to make phone calls was when their kids were in class and unavailable. Morena said she was finding it hard to eat because she was so distraught over not seeing or speaking to her children in such a long time.

When I spoke with the guards at the detention center, I had a lot of questions, and the answers didn't add up. They told me, for example, that videoconferencing with kids was a service they offered that was available anytime and for free. They assured me that phone calls were free, too. But when I asked the mothers if they knew this, they immediately said no. They didn't even know that videoconferencing was available. And when I returned to Washington and took part in a Judiciary Committee hearing with Matthew Albence, executive associate director of enforcement and removal operations at ICE, our exchange on this topic was revealing.

I told Albence how, during my visit to Otay Mesa, I'd learned from the parents being detained that when they were performing labor, such as cleaning toilets or doing laundry, they were paid one dollar a day. "Are you familiar with that policy? Or practice?" I asked.

"Many of the individuals that are in ICE custody are eligible to apply and work in a voluntary work program," Albence replied. "It's not mandatory; it's voluntary if they choose to do so. Many do choose to do so, just to pass the time, while they're awaiting their hearing or their removal—"

"Do you think that people voluntarily choose to clean toilets to pass their time? Is that what you're saying?"

"I can say that we have a large number of individuals within our custody that volunteer to work in the work program."

"To clean toilets? Sir, is that what you're saying?"

"I don't know every task that these individuals are assigned, but again, it's voluntary."

Voluntary? I don't think so.

The most shocking answer I got during my time at Otay Mesa was when I asked the detention facility staff the question many people had asked me: "Who is responsible for leading the process to re-unite these families?" They looked around at one another blankly for a few seconds, until one (who was apparently more senior than the others) answered, "That would be me." He then admitted that he had no idea what the plan was or the status of any reunification efforts.

We would later learn that federal records linking parents and children had disappeared. In some cases, for unfathomable reasons, records had actually been destroyed. When a federal court ruled that families had to be reunited within thirty days, government officials had to resort to DNA tests to try to figure out which children belonged with which family.

Before I left the detention facility, I reassured the mothers that they weren't alone—that there were so many people standing with them and fighting for them, and that I would do everything in my power to help them. As I walked down the long driveway toward the exit, I saw that solidarity personified. Hundreds of people had gathered outside the fence, holding vigil in support of the families. People of all ages and backgrounds—children, students, parents, and grandparents—had traveled to Otay Mesa because they shared the anguish and the heartbreak of the mothers inside.

I joined the throng of supporters, many of whom were carrying signs. ESTAMOS CON USTEDES . . . FAMILIES BELONG TOGETHER . . . WE WON'T BACK DOWN. Beneath the blazing summer sun, I told the press what I had seen.

"These mothers have given their testimony, if you will, have shared their stories, and they are personal stories of a human rights abuse being committed by the United States government. And we are so much better than this, and we have got to fight against this. This is contrary to all of the principles that we hold dear and that give us a sense of who we are when we are proud to be Americans. But we have no reason to be proud of this."

These mothers had made the dangerous journey to America with their children because they knew that the danger of staying in their home country was even worse. They have the legal right to seek asylum, but when they arrive, we call them criminals. We treat them like criminals. That is not the sign of a civil society, nor is it a sign of compassion. The United States government has brought great shame to the American people.

The values at stake here are so much bigger than an immigration debate.

Nothing makes a child feel more secure than being tucked in by a parent at the end of a day, getting a kiss and a hug, a good-night story, falling asleep to the sound of their voice. Nothing is more important to a parent than talking with their child at night before the child goes to sleep, answering their questions, comforting and reassuring them in the face of any fears, making sure they know that everything will be okay. Parents and children everywhere relate to these rituals. They are part of the human experience.

As family reunification began, we heard horrific stories that showed us just how shameful this administration's actions have been. The *Los Angeles Times* reported on a three-year-old boy who was separated from his father at the border. "At night, Andriy sometimes wakes up screaming in the bunk bed he shares with his mother and baby brother." We saw video of six-year-old Jefferson reunited with his father after nearly two months of separation. The child's body was covered in a rash; his face was bruised; his eyes were vacant. His father cried, enveloping the boy in a hug. Jefferson was stiff and expressionless. We also learned, through *PBS NewsHour,* of a fourteen-month-old who was returned to his parents, after eighty-five days, covered in lice, apparently having not been bathed. It is hard to imagine anything crueler than such blatant state-sponsored child abuse.

A mother who was separated from her children said that she had been kept in a cell with nearly fifty other mothers. She recounted that officers told them they weren't allowed to eat because they were asking about their children. A pregnant woman fainted out of hunger. She said of the separated children that they had no shoes or blankets in the detention center and that there were people in the cells who had to sleep on their feet. The children were demeaned, she said, called "animals" and "donkeys." These are surely just the examples we know, representative of horrors in the thousands that we may never hear of. These children, ripped away from their parents, will suffer lifelong trauma because of the actions of this administration. This behavior is not just immoral; it is inhumane. And I've introduced a bill in the Senate to put body cameras on immigration agents so we can deter such bad behavior and create transparency and accountability.

A society is judged by the way it treats its children—and history will judge us harshly for this. Most Americans know that already. Most Americans are appalled and ashamed. We are better than this. And we must make right the wrongs that this administration has committed in our name.

Seven

EVERY BODY

"How are you adjusting?" I asked.

"So far so good," Maya replied. "But we haven't had a winter yet."

It was 2008, and Maya was visiting from New York, where she had recently taken a job as vice president of democracy, rights, and justice at the Ford Foundation. We had lived in different cities before, but for many years our homes were never more than a short car ride away from each other. Now she was almost three thousand miles away. I was adjusting, too.

We were in a restaurant, waiting for our mother, who had asked us to meet her for lunch. All three of us were excited to be back in the same city, even for a brief time. We'd come a long way from the Berkeley flatlands, but we were still Shyamala and the girls.

"The foundation is doing amazing things," she said. "And I'm going to be—"

Maya stopped talking midsentence. She was looking over my shoulder. I turned around. Our mother had just walked in. Mommy—the least vain person I knew—looked like she was ready for a photo shoot. She was dressed in bright silk, clearly wearing makeup (which she never did), her hair professionally blown out. My sister and I exchanged a glance.

"What's going on?" I mouthed to Maya as our mother approached our table. She raised an eyebrow and shrugged. She was just as confused as I was.

We hugged and greeted one another, and our mother sat down. A waiter brought us a basket of bread. We reviewed our menus and ordered our food, making lighthearted conversation.

And then my mother took a deep breath and reached out to us both across the table.

"I've been diagnosed with colon cancer," she said.

Cancer. My mother. Please, no.

I know that many of you can relate to the emotions I felt in that moment. Even just reflecting back on it now, it fills me with anxiety and dread. It was one of the worst days of my life.

And the hard truth of life is that every one of us will go through an experience like this sooner or later, whether it is coming to terms with a loved one's mortal illness or experiencing our own. As my mother herself understood so well from a lifetime of looking at cancer cells under the microscope, no matter who we are or where we are from, our bodies are essentially the same. They work the same way—and they break down the same way, too. No one gets a pass. At some point, nearly all of us will face a prognosis that requires profound interaction with the health care system.

So much comes with this realization: pain, worry, depression, fear.

And it is all made worse by the fact that America's health care system is broken. The United States spends more on health care than any other advanced economy, but we don't see better outcomes in exchange. Incredibly, in many parts of the country, life expectancy is actually shrinking, and when it comes to maternal mortality, the United States is one of only thirteen countries where rates have gotten worse over the past twenty-five years. Meanwhile, working families are overwhelmed by medical bills, which are one of America's leading causes of personal bankruptcy.

I want to be clear that I have tremendous respect for the women and men in the medical profession. For so many of them, the call to medicine stems from a deep desire to help others—from helping a baby come into the world to extending the time that person has on earth. But in our nation's approach to health care, we've created a bizarre dichotomy: we are simultaneously home to the most sophisticated medical institutions in the world and to structural dysfunction that deprives millions of Americans of equal access to health care, a basic human right.

Unlike many other wealthy nations, the United States does not provide universal health care for our citizens. Instead, Americans need some form of private health insurance to cover the costs of their care, unless they are senior citizens, severely disabled, or lower income, making them eligible for Medicare or Medicaid. Generally speaking, private insurance is employer based, and the breadth and depth of coverage varies, as does the portion of the insurance premium that the employee is expected to pay. For years, those premiums have been going up—and doing so much faster than wages. A system where access to health care depends on how much you make has created enormous disparities. A 2016 study found a ten-year gap in life expectancy in America between the most affluent women and the poorest. That means that being poor reduces your life expectancy more than a lifetime of smoking cigarettes.

The Affordable Care Act (ACA), aka Obamacare, went a long way toward making health insurance more accessible and affordable, offering tax credits to those who can't cover their premiums and expanding Medicaid to cover millions of people. But after it passed, Republican leaders made it an intense partisan issue and worked to sabotage, strip, and subvert it; indeed, the Senate leader openly declared that it should be repealed "root and branch." Their arguments ranged from comparing the Affordable Care Act to colonial taxation by King George III to suggesting that the president might somehow, someday decree that the government would pay for only one baby to be born in a hospital per family. But for all their posturing and falsehoods, the GOP hadn't bothered to devise a serious alternative. They were playing politics with people's lives—and they still are.

There have been more than a hundred lawsuits challenging the ACA since its passage. Republican governors blocked seventeen states from expanding Medicaid, leaving millions in places like Florida, Texas, Missouri, and Maine without affordable coverage. In numerous states, Republican lawmakers have passed laws restricting the ability of health care officials to help people enroll in insurance plans, despite a law that provides funding for that explicit purpose.

In 2017, the first executive order from the new administration ordered federal agencies to "exercise all authority and discretion available to them to waive, defer, grant exemptions from, or delay the implementation of any provision or requirement of the [Affordable Care] Act that would impose a fiscal burden." The administration halted ACA cost-sharing payments that would have provided more affordable health insurance for middle-class families and individuals and even canceled an advertising campaign to alert people about the 2017 open enrollment period, going so far as to pull ads that were already fully paid for. The result of these efforts has been deep uncertainty and instability in the insurance markets, which has resulted in soaring premiums, forcing people all over the country to give up their health insurance altogether.

And this was on top of the efforts of congressional Republicans to fully repeal the ACA—more than fifty times. In July 2017, their push to end Obamacare was thwarted by just three votes—but they will surely try again. Repealing the ACA would result in tens of millions of people losing their health insurance. It would allow insurance companies to reinstate lifetime limits, driving countless Americans into bankruptcy, and permit insurance companies to once again deny coverage based on preexisting conditions, from asthma to high blood pressure, diabetes to cancer. We all remember what that was like. We know we can't go back.

In early 2011, just after I was elected attorney general of California, I went in to see my dentist for a checkup. The dental hygienist, Chrystal, and I knew each other from past visits, and it had been awhile since I'd seen her. Chrystal asked me how I'd been. I told her I'd been elected. I asked her how she'd been. She told me she was pregnant. It was great news.

As a dental hygienist, she was working for a few different dentists but wasn't considered a full-time employee of any of them. This was before the ACA was in place, so Chrystal was on private insurance with only basic coverage—just enough to cover her annual exams. When Chrystal found out she was pregnant, she went to her insurance company to apply for prenatal coverage.

But she was denied. They told her she had a preexisting condition.

I was alarmed. "You okay? What's wrong?" I asked. "What's the preexisting condition?" And she told me it was that she was pregnant. That was why the insurer had turned her down. When she applied to another health care company for insurance, again she was denied. Why? Preexisting condition. What was it? She was pregnant. I couldn't believe what I was hearing.

This young woman was forced to go into her sixth month of pregnancy before she received a sonogram. Thankfully, there was a free clinic in San Francisco where she could get her prenatal care. Thank God Chrystal had a strong and beautiful baby named Jaxxen and they're both doing well today.

But think about that for a minute. This is the world we could return to if they abolish the ACA: women denied health care coverage for perpetuating the species. Let's remember the words of Mark Twain: "What, sir, would the people of the earth be without women? They would be scarce, sir, almighty scarce."

The Affordable Care Act provided a lot of relief. But there are still structural realities that make health care too costly for working families. As anyone who's been to the doctor knows, in addition to premiums, there are also deductibles and co-payments for prescription drugs and health care services to worry about, which could end up costing thousands of dollars out of pocket.

Compared with people in other wealthy countries, Americans face extraordinarily high prescription drug prices. In 2016, for example, the same dose of Crestor, a medication that treats high cholesterol, cost 62 percent more in the United States than just across the border in Canada. This disparity exists with drug after drug. Fifty-eight percent of Americans take prescription drugs; one in four take four or more; and among those currently taking prescription drugs, one in four find their medications difficult to afford.

Why are Americans paying so much more for the medicines we need? Because, unlike many other advanced countries, the U.S. government doesn't negotiate prices on prescription drugs. When a government is purchasing medicines in bulk, it can negotiate a better price and pass those cost savings to consumers—much like the cost savings you enjoy at a wholesale grocery like Costco. But the current U.S. health care system doesn't allow for such deal making.

Medicare, which covers about fifty-five million people, could have incredible bargaining power to drive significantly lower prescription prices through negotiation. But lawmakers from both parties, at the behest of the pharmaceutical lobby, have prohibited Medicare from doing so. Individual health insurance plans are allowed to negotiate, but with their relatively small numbers of enrollees, they have little leverage to make a dent in prices.

The alternative to negotiating lower prices ourselves is to import cheaper drugs from countries that do. Imagine, for example, that you need Crestor. What if you could buy it from Canada at a significant discount? One of my very first votes in Congress would have enabled just that by allowing Americans to purchase drugs from our northern neighbor. The amendment I voted for earned significant bipartisan support, but the powerful pharmaceutical lobby helped kill it in its tracks.

Pharmaceutical companies have wielded influence over Congress for years, and their power is intensifying. A report by Citizens for Responsibility and Ethics in Washington (CREW) found 153 companies and organizations lobbying in the area of drug pricing in 2017, a number that had quadrupled over the previous five years. In 2016, fearing that Congress might actually do something to get drug prices under control, PhRMA, the trade association that represents the largest drugmakers, increased its membership dues by 50 percent so it could raise $100 million more with which to fight. It should come as no surprise that over the past decade, pharmaceutical companies have spent about $2.5 billion on lobbying. Imagine the new drug trials they could have funded instead.

These efforts have also helped prop up a system by which pharmaceutical companies can quash competition from generic brands, preventing more affordable versions of a medication from reaching the market for years. And in the meantime, they continue to raise prices without any compunction.

Take pharmaceutical manufacturer Mylan. Mylan raised the price of the EpiPen—a lifesaving treatment for anaphylactic shock—by nearly 500 percent over seven years. Between October 2013 and April 2014, the company increased the price of Pravastatin, a statin that helps reduce cholesterol and prevent heart disease, by 573 percent. During that same period, Mylan jacked the price of Albuterol, a common treatment for asthma, from $11 to $434. You don't need to be a prosecutor to see something wrong with a 4,000 percent price hike.

Prescription medicines are not luxury goods. Quite the opposite. We don't want to need them! No one aspires to be allergic to peanuts, or to suffer from heart disease or asthma. I'll always remember the terror I felt when Meena had a childhood asthma attack so bad that Maya had to call 911. It's heartless and wrong for companies to make a fortune by exploiting the fact that their customers literally cannot live without their products.

At the same time that pharmaceutical companies are dramatically raising their prices, they are also cutting down on the amount they spend on research and development of new drug treatments. In January 2018, for example, Pfizer announced that it would no longer participate in neuroscience research, meaning an end to its work on Alzheimer's disease and Parkinson's disease, which together affect tens of millions of people around the world.

Too many of our fellow Americans are getting crushed under the weight of high drug prices—having to choose between taking the medications they need and buying other essentials like food. And that's not to mention the financial peril they face if they go to the emergency room.

Over the course of six months, *Vox* investigated more than 1,400 emergency room bills and found a series of troubling anecdotes about patients blindsided by outrageous fees. In one example, parents brought their baby to the ER after he fell and hit his head. There wasn't any blood, but the parents were worried, so they had an ambulance take him to the hospital. The doctors determined that the baby was fine. He was given a bottle of formula and discharged less than four hours after he'd arrived. When the bill came, the parents found out they owed the hospital nearly $19,000. In another case, a woman broke her ankle and had emergency surgery. Despite the fact that she had medical coverage, her insurance company decided that the hospital had charged too much money. Instead of paying in full, they passed $31,250 in fees on to her. In still another case, a patient in a motorcycle accident actually confirmed on the phone, before going into surgery, that the hospital he'd been taken to was in his insurance company's network. But the surgeon who operated on him wasn't. As a result, he was expected to pay $7,294.

And what if you are one of the more than forty-three million Americans who require mental health care at some point during the year? Even if you have insurance, it is extremely difficult to find mental health care providers who will take it. Almost half of psychiatrists don't take insurance. On the whole, mental health care providers have no incentive to sign a contract to join an insurance company's network because they are reimbursed at such low rates. As a result, if you need mental health treatment, you are likely to have to go out of network. And because continuous care is incredibly expensive, people tend to forgo it altogether. Depression is increasing in the United States, especially among young people. But more and more, it's only people who can pay out of pocket who can access the care they need.

The problem with mental health care isn't just cost. It's also a general lack of qualified providers. According to the Department of Health and Human Services, the United States will need to add 10,000 mental health care providers by 2025 just to meet the expected demand. And when you focus on the problem on a regional level, the challenge is even greater. Alabama has only 1 mental health professional for every 1,260 people; Texas, just 1 per every 1,070 people; West Virginia, 1 per every 950 people. A report from New American Economy found that roughly 60 percent of America's counties lack a single psychiatrist. In rural counties, home to 27 million people, there are only 590 psychiatrists—that's 1 for every 45,762 people.

Even in Maine, the state with the best access to mental health care, 41.4 percent of adults with mental illness do not receive treatment. Think about that for a minute. Imagine if, in your hometown, four out of every ten broken legs went unaddressed, four out of every ten infections went untreated, four out of every ten heart attacks were ignored. We would say, "That's unacceptable!"—and rightly so. It's just as unacceptable that mental illness goes unaddressed, untreated, and ignored.

My mother's cancer treatment acquired a grim kind of routine. During the day, I would take her to the hospital for chemotherapy. We'd see many of the same people every time—men and women of all different ages, hooked up to a machine that was infusing their bodies with the toxic drugs they hoped would save their lives. It took on a strange familiarity, an abnormal sense of normalcy. If I had to, I'd drop her off and pick her up when chemo was done, but I preferred to wait and keep her company, and she preferred it, too.

Sometimes the chemo would steal her appetite. Other times she was hungry, and I would get her buttery croissants that she loved from a bakery nearby. More than once, she had to be admitted to the hospital with complications, and I remember a lot of hard days and nights under those fluorescent lights. When my mother was asleep, I would walk down the long corridors, glancing into the rooms as I passed. Sometimes people would look up. Sometimes they wouldn't. And all too often, they were lying there alone. I left that experience convinced that no one should have to face a hospital stay without support—and that many do.

My mother's circumstance could feel overwhelming. Chemotherapy is depleting; oftentimes my mother was too wiped out to do anything but sleep. Meanwhile, there were so many medications, possible side effects, counterindications, and things to keep track of. What if she had a bad reaction to a new medicine, as happened more than once? I had to coordinate her care, make sure her doctors were talking to one another, and ensure that she was getting the proper treatment. I often wondered how my mother would have fared if we hadn't been there to speak up on her behalf.

I came away believing that we should mandate patient advocates with medical expertise so that anyone dealing with an acute illness has a trustworthy, capable champion by their side. After all, we have decided that when their liberty is at stake, people are entitled to an attorney. We do this because we understand that most people don't speak the language of the courtroom, and even if they do, in high-pressure situations it's difficult to make objective judgments. The same is true in a hospital. Emotions are running high. People are placed into a new environment where a specialized language is being spoken, with complex, unfamiliar terms and phrases. And they may have to make decisions while they are frightened or in pain or heavily medicated—or all three. They're expected to be strong enough to monitor themselves at a moment when they feel deeply vulnerable. We should have expert advocates to shoulder that burden so that patients and their families can focus on healing.

We should also speak truth about the racial disparities in our health care system. In 1985, then–Secretary of Health and Human Services Margaret Heckler released a pathbreaking Report of the Secretary's Task Force on Black and Minority Health. As she wrote at the time, despite significant progress in the American health picture overall, "there was a continuing disparity in the burden of death and illness experienced by blacks and other minority Americans as compared with our nation's population as a whole." In her words, this disparity was "an affront both to our ideals and to the ongoing genius of American medicine."

I was in college when she commissioned this study. What have we seen in the three decades since then? The gaps have narrowed, but they are pervasive—and communities of color pay the price. According to the 2015 Kelly Report on Health Disparities in America, black Americans have higher mortality rates than any other group in eight of the top ten causes of death.

In segregated cities like Baltimore, there are twenty-year gaps in the life expectancy of those living in poor black American neighborhoods and those living in wealthier and whiter areas. "A baby born in Cheswolde, in Baltimore's far northwest corner, can expect to live until age eighty-seven," writes Olga Khazan in *The Atlantic*. "Nine miles away in Clifton-Berea, near where *The Wire* was filmed, the life expectancy is sixty-seven, roughly the same as that of Rwanda, and twelve years shorter than the American average."

These disparities begin in the delivery room. Black babies are twice as likely as white babies to die in infancy, a stunning disparity that is wider than in 1850, when slavery was still legal. In fact, infant mortality rates for black babies today are higher than they were for white infants at the time of the Heckler Report. In other words, today, black infants are less likely to survive their first year than white babies were in the early 1980s.

Black women are also at least three times as likely to die due to complications relating to pregnancy than white women—a shocking gulf that transcends socioeconomic status. A major five-year study in New York City found that college-educated black women are more likely to face severe complications in pregnancy or childbirth than white women who never made it through high school.

There are a number of factors that put black men, women, and children at a disadvantage. Hundreds of years of institutionalized discrimination in housing, employment, and educational opportunity have left black Americans more likely to lack access to health care, to live in poor neighborhoods with limited healthy food options, and to have fewer community health care resources.

And because black Americans are more likely than their white counterparts to be born and raised in low-income, high-crime neighborhoods, they are more likely to experience a phenomenon known as toxic stress, the result of trauma caused by things ranging from witnessing violence to experiencing it. This causes not just psychological anguish, but also physical changes. To borrow the words of toxic stress expert Dr. Nadine Burke Harris, founder of the Center for Youth Wellness, in Bayview–Hunters Point, "child adversity literally gets under our skin and has the potential to change our health."

One study found that children who go through at least six adverse childhood experiences could see their life expectancy reduced by more than twenty years. Physiological stress leads to hypertension, which results in higher rates of infant and maternal mortality, among other conditions. Research has even found that certain levels of stress shorten our telomeres, which are structures that hold our chromosomes together. As we age, our telomeres naturally get shorter until cells start dying, which leads to disease. A study at the University of Michigan measured the telomere length in hundreds of women and found that black women were biologically more than seven years older than white women their age.

But environmental circumstances alone cannot explain health care disparities.

It's also the case that black Americans experience poorer care when they go to the doctor. White patients are 10 percent more likely to get screened for high cholesterol than black Americans, even though rates of heart disease and stroke are higher among black Americans.

Black patients are also less likely to be treated using procedures to repair blocked arteries. White women are more likely to get breast cancer screenings than black women and Latinas. And women of color are more likely to have their symptoms dismissed by their doctor, regardless of their economic status.

When tennis star Serena Williams, one of the greatest athletes of all time, delivered her baby, she had serious complications. The day after an emergency C-section, Williams started having trouble breathing. She had a history of pulmonary embolisms, or blood clots, and, having experienced them before, she suspected she was having another. She told *Vogue* magazine that she walked out of her hospital room so that her mom wouldn't worry and told her nurse that she needed a CT scan and an IV blood thinner right away. But the nurse was skeptical. She thought Williams must have been confused because of her pain medication. Williams persisted. Rather than give her the CT scan and IV drip, the doctor arrived with an ultrasound machine.

"I was like, a Doppler?" Williams recalled. "I told you, I need a CT scan and a heparin drip," she stressed to the medical team. When they finally sent her for a CT, they discovered that she was right after all. "I was like, listen to Dr. Williams!" she told *Vogue*. There were further complications that required surgery and left her bedridden for six weeks. If someone like Serena Williams can go through such an ordeal, imagine what happens to other patients who articulate symptoms and are ignored.

What accounts for these inequities in the care of our fellow citizens? A growing body of research suggests that part of the problem is unconscious, implicit bias—similar to what we see in police departments. All of us absorb social stereotypes and assumptions, often without ever realizing it. But left unexamined, they risk leading us to behave in discriminatory ways, which can have profound consequences in fields like law enforcement, criminal justice, education, and health.

Some enlightened members of the medical profession are working to address this problem. At UC San Francisco, all first-year medical students take a class on the discriminatory effect of these biases. Before they begin, they are given an implicit bias association test that measures their unconscious attitudes, not just about race but about gender, weight, and age. Research has found that 75 percent of those who take the test—no matter their race—show an unconscious preference for white people.

How do we close the divide? It starts by speaking the uncomfortable truth that it exists, and then we can break the problem into parts we can tackle one by one. First and foremost, we need every medical school in the country to require implicit bias training for their students. When people are given the knowledge that implicit bias is real, and that we all have it, it gives them room to think about it in their daily actions and make better decisions.

We also need medical schools to focus proactively on bringing more diversity into the field. As of 2013, only about 9 percent of our country's physicians are nonwhite, and only 4 percent are black. This is the first gap we need to close if we intend to close the others. It won't be easy. It'll be a generational challenge. But it's time we get started.

Most critically, however, improving health outcomes across the board demands that we transform the health care system itself. I believe that health care should be a right, but in a system where the quality of your care does indeed depend on your station in life, the reality is that health care is still a privilege in this country. And we need that to change. It's why we need Medicare for All.

Imagine if U.S. health care coverage was based not on how much you can pay but instead on your health needs. The purpose of the system would be to maximize good health care outcomes rather than maximizing profits. That, in itself, would be revolutionary. Getting sick would no longer mean risking bankruptcy. Employers would no longer have to spend so much to provide health insurance to their employees. And the system itself would run far more efficiently, as we see when we compare the high administrative costs of private health insurance companies with the lower costs of Medicare.

But even if we could snap our fingers and make Medicare for All a reality, this alone would not alleviate all of the problems in the system.

For starters, we need to dramatically increase funding to the National Institutes of Health to step in and fill the innovation gap that pharmaceutical companies have left. I remember how proud my mother was to work with the NIH as a peer reviewer and collaborator with other experts in her field. She would speak of her time there with such reverence that when I was a girl, I imagined Bethesda, Maryland, where the agency is located, to be a place filled with castles and spires. I might have been wrong about the architecture, but not about the beauty of scientific collaboration—and certainly not about the fact that the NIH is a national treasure. If we want our children to have cures for humanity's most terrible diseases, we should invest in our national medical researchers, instead of relying on companies that would rather funnel money to their shareholders.

We also need to protect patients and taxpayers from fraud. And that means putting bad actors under a microscope. Consider for-profit dialysis companies, which offer one of the worst examples of bad practices.

Dialysis is a process by which a machine cleans the blood of patients who are in kidney failure. Kidney disease remains the ninth leading cause of death in America, but for a person in kidney failure, dialysis is a lifesaving treatment and an important bridge between loss of kidney function and getting a kidney transplant (which is a cheaper alternative with a much better prognosis). Across the country, nearly 500,000 patients are on dialysis, going three times a week to have their blood circulated out of their body through a multi-hour process that mimics a healthy kidney's function.

Who are these patients? Disproportionately, they come from low-income communities. People living in certain zip codes are far more likely to end up with kidney failure, which is most commonly the result of diabetes and high blood pressure. Black Americans develop kidney failure at 3.5 times the rate of white Americans, and they constitute nearly one-third of all U.S. patients who receive dialysis.

The two largest dialysis companies, DaVita Inc. and Fresenius Medical Care, have both found themselves in legal hot water. In 2016, Fresenius agreed to pay $250 million to settle thousands of lawsuits. According to *The New York Times,* "Fresenius's own medical office sent an internal memo to doctors in the company's dialysis centers saying that failure to properly use one of the company's products appeared to be causing a sharp increase in sudden deaths from cardiac arrest." Yet the company chose not to warn doctors in non-Fresenius clinics who were using the product until after the memo had been leaked to the Food and Drug Administration.

In 2014, DaVita agreed to pay $350 million to resolve claims of illegal kickbacks, in a scheme where it allegedly sold an interest in its clinics to physicians and physician groups in exchange for their driving patients to those clinics. In 2015, the company agreed to pay $495 million to settle a whistle-blower case in which it was accused of fraudulently overcharging Medicare. DaVita was sued in 2017 for keeping its clinics so understaffed and requiring such high-speed care and turnover that patients' lives were endangered. It's time to crack down on this kind of behavior.

Finally, we will need to overhaul public health policy so that it does a better job of providing mental health care to all Americans. That effort will have to begin by ensuring that more mental health professionals contract with Medicare in the first place. There's only one way to solve this problem: We need to raise Medicare reimbursement rates. As the largest single payer of health care services, the federal government must lead the way to ensure we pay all mental health professionals what they deserve.

We also need to encourage a new generation of Americans to go into the mental health care field. Let's create a model similar to Teach for America or the Peace Corps—an apprenticeship system that has as its core mission the goal of getting people to serve their country through mental health training.

Let's also do away with laws that strip funding from mental health care services. There's an old law known as the IMD exclusion, for example, that prohibits Medicaid from paying for treatment in mental health facilities with more than sixteen beds. This rule has hollowed out mental health care hospitals and left most people with severe mental health conditions to fend for themselves.

Ultimately, I believe we should provide mental health care on demand. And when I say "on demand," I mean that whoever you are and wherever you are, mental health treatment is available if you need it. In addition to requiring far more practitioners, meeting this goal will require investment in and expansion of telemedicine so patients can access mental health care no matter where they live. This is especially important for people in rural areas, where nearly 100 hospitals have closed over the past several years. So far, studies have shown that telemedicine is generally as effective as in-person treatment. But further research and development can surely improve its value.

I n the days before being sworn in as senator, I read a newspaper profile of Chillicothe, Ohio, a small city in southeastern Ohio's Ross County. It's located in the foothills of the Appalachian Mountains, with sprawling fields of soybeans and corn and a skyline marked by the smokestacks of a paper mill that has operated continually for more than a hundred years. Kenworth has its largest truck-manufacturing plant in Chillicothe and pays middle-class wages. The local hospital is one of the county's largest employers. But the grand history and pride that once defined this classically American town have been replaced by a sense of despair.

Seventy-seven thousand people call Ross County home. In 2015 alone, doctors in the county prescribed 1.6 million opioid pills. That same year, thirty-eight people died from accidental overdose. The following year, another forty lost their lives. "Now you can get heroin quicker in these communities than you can get pizza," Teri Minney, head of Ross County's Heroin Partnership Project, told *The Washington Post.* "They're delivering." According to the *Post,* addicts in Ross

County often shoot up in public places, hoping that if they overdose, paramedics or police officers will revive them. "One day in September, police and paramedics responded to thirteen separate overdose calls, including one fatality: a man who died in an apartment right on Main Street. Meanwhile, a woman overdosed in her car as it idled at a Valero gas station with her two-year-old daughter in the back seat."

As has happened in other areas with heavy opioid use, the violent crime rate has gone up, as have incidents of theft. So have the numbers of opioid-addicted babies born, and of children requiring foster care. According to local officials, two hundred children were placed into state care in 2016, 75 percent of whom had parents with opioid addictions. The surge has required that the county nearly double its child services budget, which now makes up more than 10 percent of the total county budget. What was once one of the happiest places in Ohio is now clouded by a fog of hopelessness.

Similar stories are repeating themselves in every state in America. The human toll has rocked the nation to its core. Entire communities have been destroyed. And the opioid epidemic does not discriminate. It has hit people across every demographic, and infected rural, suburban, and urban areas alike. For so many people, what began as a legitimate desire to reduce pain became an overpowering addiction. Now the pain they feel isn't from the original back injury or post-surgery healing; it is the pain that comes from quitting. "It's like having the flu and laying in the street while people run over you while you're puking," one Chillicothe addict described to *The Washington Post*.

The opioid epidemic has killed more than 350,000 Americans in the past two decades. But the national health crisis we face today is itself the result of a failure of public health intervention, from the moment OxyContin was approved to be sold. It is a different story than the one we witnessed during the crack cocaine epidemic—now, instead of people dealing drugs on the corner, people in suits and ties and white coats are dealing a drug while drugmakers cover up the dangers.

It started in 1995, when the FDA approved OxyContin and allowed its manufacturer, Purdue Pharma, to make the claim that, unlike previous opioids (Percocet and Vicodin), OxyContin was "believed to reduce" appeal to drug abusers because it was longer acting. Purdue Pharma seized on this claim and, in 1996, began the largest marketing campaign in pharmaceutical history based on the idea that OxyContin wasn't addictive. The company's executives testified in Congress to this effect and ran a whole program to convince doctors and patients that pain should be treated more aggressively than in the past, and that it could be done with little fear of addiction, as long as that pain pill was OxyContin. This despite the fact that company officials had received information that pills were being crushed and snorted, and that doctors were being criminally charged with selling prescriptions to patients.

According to a time line developed by *Mother Jones,* by 2002, doctors in the United States were prescribing twenty-three times more OxyContin than they had in 1996. By 2004, the Federation of State Medical Boards actually recommended sanctions against doctors who undertreated pain.

Pill mills started to pop up all over the country, where doctors would sell prescriptions and pills for cash. Between 2007 and 2012, three major drug distributors—McKesson, Cardinal Health, and AmerisourceBergen—made $17 billion by saturating West Virginia with opioids. By 2009, the United States was consuming more than

90 percent of the world's hydrocodone and more than 80 percent of its oxycodone. By 2012, sixteen years after OxyContin reached the market, health care providers had written 259 million prescriptions for opioids. For perspective, there are about 126 million households in America.

By the late 1990s, heroin use in the United States had declined quite dramatically from its 1960s and '70s peak. But as opioid addictions skyrocketed in the early 2000s, heroin traffickers found a highly motivated consumer base for their product, which was significantly cheaper and easier to obtain than prescription medication. According to the National Institutes of Health, roughly 80 percent of Americans who become addicted to heroin start with a prescription for opioids.

The danger worsened in 2013 as fentanyl, an exceptionally deadly synthetic opioid with fifty times the strength of heroin, made its way from China into the American heroin supply. The CDC estimates that there were 72,000 drug overdose deaths in America in 2017 alone. That's nearly twice what it was ten years earlier. And in 2018, the CDC released a report finding that opioid deaths are still rising in nearly every segment of the country.

When I was attorney general, I made the fight against opioids one of my highest priorities. We took down a large-scale transnational drug-trafficking organization in 2011 while sponsoring legislation to make it more difficult to print fraudulent prescription pads. We went after pill mills and shut down so-called recovery centers that were overprescribing, leading to patient deaths. When funding to my department's drug-monitoring program was cut, we fought tooth and nail until I got the budget restored. The system allowed prescribers and pharmacists to quickly access a patient's prescription history and make sure the patient wasn't seeking the same painkillers from different doctors simultaneously. We went after criminals who were selling opioids on Craigslist and filed a lawsuit against a pharmaceutical company for inflating prices for opioid addiction treatment.

How has the federal government responded? Not in the way one would hope. According to a joint investigation by *60 Minutes* and *The Washington Post* in 2017, Congress "effectively stripped the DEA of its most potent weapon against large drug companies suspected of spilling prescription narcotics onto the nation's streets. . . . The law was the crowning achievement of a multifaceted campaign by the drug industry to weaken aggressive DEA enforcement efforts against drug distribution companies that were supplying corrupt doctors and pharmacists who peddled narcotics on the black market."

In 2017, the administration declared the opioid crisis a public health emergency, but the fund they used to deal with it had only—I kid you not—$57,000 in it. That represents less than one dollar for each person who died of a drug overdose that year. It's unconscionable. And if Republicans had succeeded in repealing the Affordable Care Act, they would have taken addiction treatment coverage away from three million Americans.

This is a crisis that deserves a major federal mobilization. We need to declare a national state of emergency, which would provide more funding, right away, to help combat this disease—giving places like Chillicothe, Ohio, more resources to pay for addiction treatment, hospital services, skills training, and more.

We need to address the challenge at every point along the spectrum, beginning with providing supportive treatment programs for those whom experts call "pre-contemplators"—that is, people who are not yet ready to commit to treatment.

Even though my opponent in the 2010 attorney general race declared victory on election night, we knew that it was too close to call. We huddled around computers and checked tallies through the night. It took twenty-one days for all the ballots to be counted and for me to be declared the winner. Every vote counts! From left to right: Justin Erlich, Dereck Johnson, Tony West, me, Meena, Maya, Ace Smith, and Brian Brokaw.

California Supreme Court Justice Tani Cantil-Sakauye swears me in at the Women's Museum in Sacramento. Maya is holding Mrs. Shelton's Bible.

Governor Jerry Brown signs our California Homeowner Bill of Rights. Speaker John Pérez, Senate President Darrell Steinberg, and Assembly Member Nancy Skinner all helped enormously in getting the bill passed.

My team traveled with me to Mexico City to work on our collaboration with Mexican attorneys general to combat transnational criminal organizations. From left to right: Mateo Munoz, Travis LeBlanc, me, Michael Trancoso, Brian Nelson, and Larry Wallace, who was the director of the law enforcement division for the California Department of Justice.

Performing the wedding of Sandy Stier (left) and Kris Perry (right) on the balcony of San Francisco City Hall on June 28, 2013

n September 30, 2013, I stood on the stage of the California Endowment for the statewide launch of our elementary school truancy initiative, where I explained that 82 percent of prisoners are high school dropouts. It was also the day that my team first met Doug.

On October 10, 2013, I announced a lawsuit against for-profit Corinthian Colleges, Inc., which defrauded students and investors across the state. We successfully advocated that the students' loans be forgiven.

One of the most joyful days of my life was marrying my sweetheart, Doug. We were married at the courthouse in Santa Barbara, CA, on August 22, 2014.

At the courthouse on the day of our marriage, with my family. Left to right: Tony, Aunt Chinni, Maya, me, Aunt Sarala, Uncle Subash (Chinni's husband), and Meena.

Doug congratulates me for winning reelection as California's attorney general in November 2014. We're at the Delancey Street Foundation, which is run by my dear friend Mimi Silbert.

Visiting the Pitchess Detention Center in Castaic on March 11, 2015, where we were starting Back on Track–Los Angeles. In partnership with the sheriff's department and the Ford Foundation, we were there to provide services to the inmates to help them with their reentry back into society. Left to right: Me, LA sheriff Jim McDonnell, Dan Suvor, Doug Wood, and Jeff Tsai.

A morning walk along the bay with my dear Ella. (March 2015)

Venus Johnson, my associate attorney general and de facto chief of staff, and me, working on issues related to law enforcement. I can't thank Venus enough for her leadership. (April 201(

Campaigning up and down the state on the Fearless for the People bus, with a Kamoji always waving to passersby. My campaign team, from left to right: Juan Rodriguez, Ellie Caple, Sean Clegg, Jill Habig, and Daniel Lopez.

Chrisette Hudlin, my best friend, got her kids (and my godchildren) Helena and Alexander into the spirit of the campaign. Helena was an active volunteer in the campaign office, where she started her own newsletter, interviewing campaign staff. She was one of the toughest interviews I've ever done.

Doug and me jumping off the Kamoji bus on the last full day of campaigning. Ready for action! (November 7, 2016)

Nathan Barankin and I have come a long way together. He was my number two in the attorney general's office in Sacramento and joined me in Washington, DC, as my chief of staff.

Election Night celebration at Exchange LA. (November 8, 2016)

Vice President Biden swearing me in as a United States Senator in the Old Senate Chamber at the U.S. Capitol. (January 3, 2017)

Members of Congress joined the Women's March on Washington on January 21, 2017. Left to right: Rep. Brenda Lawrence (D-MI), Rep. Yvette Clarke (D-NY), Rep. Barbara Lee (D-CA), Rep. Sheila Jackson Lee (D-TX), Rep. Grace Meng (D-NY), me, Emily's List President Stephanie Schriock, Rep. Jackie Speier (D-CA), and Rep. Doris Matsui (D-CA)

I am a proud graduate of Howard University, an institution that has inspired, nurtured, and challenged its students to take on roles of leadership. I was honored to deliver the commencement speech at my alma mater. (May 13, 2017)

Cole graduated from Colorado College on May 22, 2017. Doug, Kerstin, and I were there to celebrate with him.

The devastation and loss for the victims of the Santa Rosa fire was beyond description.

Visiting with first responders during the Santa Rosa fire in Northern California. This firefighter lost his home in the same blaze he was battling. His bravery and his sacrifice were deeply moving. I'll never forget him. (October 2017)

Traveling with a delegation to Puerto Rico to survey the vast destruction from Hurricane Maria. It was critical to witness the devastation felt by our fellow citizens. (November 2017)

With John Laird, Secretary of the California Natural Resources Agency, touring Lake Oroville, where damage to the reservoir's spillways caused flooding and forced the temporary evacuation of 100,000 people.

On March 20, 2018, the Senate Intelligence Committee held a news conference where we presented our findings and recommendations on threats to election infrastructure. Left to right: Sen. Richard Burr (R-NC), Sen. Susan Collins (R-ME), me, Sen. Mark Warner (D-VA), Sen. James Lankford (R-OK), Sen. Martin Heinrich (D-NM), Sen. Joe Manchin (D-WV), and Sen. Angus King (I-ME).

On March 24, 2018, I joined the millions of people around the county in the March for Our Lives to advocate for reasonable gun safety laws. I attended the Los Angeles march, where I met with young community leaders from The Brotherhood Crusade, who are highlighting the impact of gun violence in the community.

Calling for an end to the barbaric practice of family separation, I visited the Otay Mesa Detention Center in Southern California, where mothers who had been separated from their children were being held, on June 22, 2018. I met with them in the prison and then gave a news conference outside. To my left is a great leader: Angelica Salas of CHIRLA.

With Doug and Meena celebrating the San Francisco Pride Parade. (June 2018)

Marching at the Martin Luther King Day Parade in Los Angeles. Left to right: Heather Hutt, Areva Martin, me, Rabbi Jonathan Klein, Doug, Cole, Ella, and Angelica Salas. (January 15, 2018)

In this crowd are survivors of sexual assault who fearlessly spoke truth to powerful forces and refused to be silenced. I am inspired by their courage.

Hanging with a few Dreamers. Let's find time between the marching and the shouting to dance, sing, and laugh—to be joyful warriors.

We need to make sure that people who are addicted have access to medication-assisted treatment (MAT)—drugs like buprenorphine, which prevents withdrawal symptoms and cravings without producing the kind of high that heroin or OxyContin does. Many insurance companies will cover the cost of opioids while charging more than $200 a month for buprenorphine. That has to change. We have to change it.

At the same time, we need to create a federal standard for substance use disorder treatment. Right now, in many states across the country, it's possible to open an addiction treatment center without being qualified to do so. There are no requirements for proper training or evidence-based treatment. As a result, too many Americans who have worked up the courage and strength to go to rehab arrive only to find that, for all the expense, they are not getting proper care and the treatment doesn't work.

We also need to reinstate the DEA's authority to go after the major pharmaceutical manufacturers and distributors for their role in creating and sustaining the crisis. And we need to invest resources in law enforcement efforts to cut off the supply of fentanyl from China.

Finally, we need to understand that, at its core, this is a public health issue, not a criminal justice issue. We can't keep repeating the mistakes of the failed war on drugs that put so many people addicted to crack in prison. It is normal human behavior to want to stop feeling pain, whether physical or emotional, and people will find ways to do so. Sometimes that will mean getting help, and sometimes it will mean getting hooked on heroin. Our job is not to punish our friends and family members and neighbors by throwing them in prison. It is to put them on a sustainable path to better manage their pain.

. . .

As my mother's condition worsened, she needed more care than we could provide her. We wanted to hire a home health care aide to help her—and me. But my mother didn't want help.

"I'm fine. I don't need anybody," she would say, even though she could barely get out of bed. There was a fight to be had about it, but I didn't want to have it. Cancer—the disease she'd devoted her life to defeating—was now wreaking its havoc on her. Her body was giving out. The medication was making it difficult for her to function—to be herself. I didn't want to be the one who took her dignity away.

So we muddled through. I cooked elaborate meals for her, filling the house with the smells of childhood, which reminded us both of happier times. When I wasn't at the office, I was most often with her, telling stories, holding hands, helping her through the misery of chemotherapy. I bought her hats after she lost her hair, and soft clothes to make her as comfortable as I could.

There isn't a smooth, steady decline, I would learn. The process isn't gradual. My mother would reach a plateau and stay there for weeks or months, then, seemingly overnight, fall to the plateau beneath it. During one especially hard spell, I convinced her to spend two weeks at the Jewish Home for the Aged—a place known for some of the kindest and best care—where she could get the round-the-clock care she needed. We packed her up and drove over to the home. The staff was incredibly kind to our family. They gave my mother a tour of the facility, showed her to her room, introduced her to the doctors and nurses, and explained the routine of her care.

At one point, one of the doctors pulled me aside. "How's my DA?"

she asked. The question caught me off guard. I had been so focused on my mother's well-being I hadn't made room for anything else, but the question cracked through the strength I had mustered and hadn't wanted to betray. I started to choke up. I was scared. I was sad. Most of all, I wasn't ready.

She asked me if I had heard of "anticipatory grief." I hadn't, but the term made perfect sense. So much of me was in denial. I couldn't bring myself to believe that I was going to have to say goodbye. But underneath it, I was aware. And I had started grieving my mother's loss already. There was something validating about that, about understanding what was happening to me. Putting a label on things can help you cope with them, I've learned. It doesn't make you stop feeling your emotion, but you can put it somewhere if you can name it. And now I could.

When the tour was over, I unzipped my mother's suitcase so that I could help her move in. But she had other plans. She was sitting cross-legged on the bed, all five feet of her, when she said firmly, "Okay, this was nice. Let's leave."

"Mommy, you're going to stay here for two weeks, remember?"

"No, I'm not. Nn-nnn. I'm not staying for two weeks." She turned to the medical team, who were still in the room. "This has been great. Thank you. We're leaving."

And so we did.

She ended up in the hospital not long after that. That was when I started to see another change. For as long as I could remember, my mother loved to watch the news and read the newspaper. When Maya and I were kids, she'd insist we sit down in front of Walter Cronkite each night before dinner. She loved to digest everything that was happening in the world. But suddenly, she had no interest. Her mighty brain had decided it had had enough. Though she still had room for us.

I remember that I had just gotten into the attorney general's race and she asked me how it was going.

"Mommy, these guys are saying they're gonna kick my ass."

My mother had been lying on her side. She rolled over, looked at me, and just unveiled the biggest smile. She knew who she had raised. She knew her fighting spirit was alive and well inside me.

When it was time for hospice care, we took her home and, finally, she let a hospice nurse come with us. Maya and I still didn't believe that she could die, to the point that when she said she wanted to go to India, we booked plane tickets and started planning. We worked out how we could get her on a plane, and made arrangements for a nurse to come with us. We were all in a great state of delusion—especially me. I couldn't bear to tell my mother no—not because she couldn't take it, but because I couldn't. Whether it was a question of bringing a nurse home or staying in the nursing home or going to India, I didn't want to accept what saying no to her meant. I didn't want to accept that she was running out of time.

One night, Maya, Tony, Meena, and I were all at my mother's house when Aunt Mary and Aunt Lenore, who had flown into town, came for a visit. I decided to cook again. I'll never forget that night—I was making Alice Waters's recipe for beef stew. I had browned the cubes of beef and they were cooking down in red wine, and all of a sudden my brain figured out what was happening around me. I started to hyperventilate—short breaths in and out. I felt like I might faint. All of a sudden, the delusion was gone. I had to face reality. I was going to lose my mother and there was nothing I could do.

We had called our uncle in India to let him know that she was too sick to make it. He got on a plane from Delhi to see her. I now realize that she waited for his arrival, waited to say goodbye. She passed away the very next morning.

One of the last questions she asked the hospice nurse, the last concern on her mind, was "Are my daughters going to be okay?" She was focused on being our mother until the very end.

And though I miss her every day, I carry her with me wherever I go. I think of her all the time. Sometimes I look up and talk to her. I love her so much. And there is no title or honor on earth I'll treasure more than to say I am Shyamala Gopalan Harris's daughter. That is the truth I hold dearest of all.

Eight

THE COST OF LIVING

W hen I was getting ready to write this book, I spent a good deal of time going through photo albums, reminiscing with Maya, and unpacking old boxes, including things my mother had saved. It's been a blessing. I've had the chance to sit with good memories that don't always make it to the front of my mind.

When we were growing up, our mother always made chiles rellenos around Christmas. After she died, I wanted so badly to find the recipe. I searched everywhere I could, including online, but nothing matched my mother's version. I felt so defeated, as though I'd lost more than just the flavor of her cooking. And then, while I was digging through my cookbooks, I found a notebook, and as soon as I opened it, the recipe fell right out of the pages and onto the floor. I was transported just by reading my mother's handwriting. It was like she was there with me, still responding to my needs.

I also found a couple of pot holders that Maya and I had woven on plastic looms. Any reader who grew up in the 1970s probably knows just what I mean. Our mother made sure our hands were never idle, especially in front of the television. That's where I perfected my crochet shell stitch.

Our mother loved to talk with her hands, and she was always using her hands—to cook, to clean, to comfort. She was always busy. Work itself was something to value—hard work especially; and she made sure that we, her daughters, internalized that message and the importance of working with purpose.

She also showed us, in so many ways, how much she valued all work, not just her own. When something good would happen at the lab, my mother would come home with flowers for our babysitter.

"I wouldn't have been able to do what I did if you didn't do what you do," she would say. "Thank you for everything."

She saw the dignity in the work that society requires to function. She believed that everyone deserves respect for the work they do, and that hard effort should be rewarded and honored.

I'd hear the same thing at Rainbow Sign, where speakers would talk about Dr. King's Poor People's Campaign, about his belief that "all labor has dignity," and his effort to make it so.

As part of that effort, Dr. King had gone to Memphis in 1968 to join black sanitation workers in their fight for basic decency. Day in and day out, these workers rode the trucks that hauled away the city's garbage. The city didn't provide uniforms; instead, workers were forced to befoul their own clothes on the job. They worked long hours without water to drink or a place to wash their hands. "Most of the tubs had holes in them," one sanitation worker recounted. "Garbage leaking all over you." He described how, when the workers got home in the

evening, they'd remove their shoes and clothes at the door and mag-
gots would fall out.

For this hard, indispensable work, they received little more than
minimum wage. They didn't get overtime pay. They had no sick
leave. If they were injured at work and needed time to mend—as happened often—they were likely to be fired. And if bad weather made
trash collection impossible, they were sent home without pay. Many
needed government assistance to feed their families.

When the city refused to compensate the families of two sanitation workers who were crushed to death by their trash compactor, it
became too much for the others to bear. With great courage, 1,300
Memphis sanitation workers went on strike, demanding safer conditions, better pay and benefits, and recognition of their union. They
were on strike for their families, for their children, and for themselves. It was, above all else, a battle for dignity. The signs they held
at marches said simply I AM A MAN.

When King arrived at Bishop Charles Mason Temple, in Memphis, on March 18, 1968, a crowd of 25,000 people had gathered to
hear him speak.

"So often we overlook the work and the significance of those who
are not in professional jobs, of those who are not in the so-called big
jobs," he said. "But let me say to you tonight, that whenever you are
engaged in work that serves humanity and is for the building of humanity, it has dignity and it has worth."

"We are tired," King said to the audience in Memphis. "We are
tired of our children having to attend overcrowded, inferior, quality-
less schools. We are tired of having to live in dilapidated substandard
housing conditions. . . . We are tired of walking the streets in search
of jobs that do not exist . . . of working our hands off and laboring

every day and not even making a wage adequate to get the basic necessities of life."

Sixteen days later, King returned to Memphis to march on behalf of the strikers—speaking again at Bishop Charles Mason Temple, where he declared, "I've been to the mountaintop." The next evening, April 4, 1968, he was killed by an assassin. Two months after that, on June 5, Robert F. Kennedy was murdered as well. The nation's clearest voices and strongest leaders in the fight for economic justice had been suddenly, irrevocably silenced.

That was half a century ago. In some ways, we have come so far since then. And in others, we have barely budged. I remind people that when you adjust for inflation, the federal minimum wage is actually lower now than when Dr. King spoke of "starvation wages" in 1968. What does that say about how our country values the sanctity and dignity of work?

Americans are a hardworking bunch. We pride ourselves on our work ethic. And for generations, most of us have been raised to believe that there are few things more honorable than putting in an honest day's work to take care of our family. We grew up trusting that when we worked hard and did well, we would be rewarded for our effort. But the truth is, for most Americans, it hasn't been that way for an awfully long time.

Whenever there is a major push to pressure Congress into doing the right thing, activists and elected leaders implore the American people to call and write their representatives. These days, the phone lines are overwhelmed by Americans engaged in an extraordinary thing: exercising democracy. And in a number of cases, it has really mattered. I believe that repeal of the Affordable Care Act failed in 2017 because congressional Republicans had taken a non-partisan issue—access to affordable health care—and made it a partisan one, and the people just weren't having it. It activated and energized folks to fight back, and because of the pressure they put on key senators, the people prevailed. That means that millions of people still have health coverage because individual Americans picked up the phone and wrote letters.

For me, reading these letters isn't just about understanding where people stand on major policy issues. It's about understanding what their lives are like, both the joys and the fears. When people write to me, it is often as a last resort. They are struggling, and in real trouble, but nothing else they've tried has worked. And so they turn to me and share with me the things that have upended their lives.

Dear Senator Harris,

My husband and I work full time jobs yet we still struggle every week to make ends meet. I get full [health care] coverage for my two-year-old son [for] which I thank God every day, but can't figure out why my husband and I can't get full coverage either?

. . . We can't get help with daycare because we "make too much money" but yet we can't even afford to pay $50 a month for daycare, so we depend on family, [but] they have their own problems, so there have been too many occasions [when] we lose money because we can't get a babysitter for us to go to work.

. . . I am begging with my life that this needs to change!! Please for the love of God HELP!! This is just not ok! I am confused,

angry, frustrated, and I feel so betrayed by our government! I don't
EVER ask for help unless I need it and I seriously need it!!

Every letter stands on its own. But together, they tell the same story. It is the story of Americans trapped in a cost-of-living crisis, where everything from housing and health care to child care and education is way more expensive than it used to be while wages remain as low as they've been for decades. The letters I receive consistently tell the story of the hollowing out of the middle class, and of an economic life defined by intense struggle.

When I wake up in the middle of the night with a thought on my mind, I remind myself that in countless households around the country, someone else is wide awake, too. Millions of someone elses. And I imagine that the majority of them are asking themselves questions about their greatest fears: Am I going to be able to provide a good life for my children? What if I can never make ends meet? How will I get through the month?

The American people have not given up on the American Dream. I know this to be true. But when you can't sleep at night, how can you dream?

How can you dream when, on average, a year of child care for a baby or toddler is more expensive than a year of in-state public college tuition? How can you dream when the cost of higher education has gone up more than three times faster than wages since I was in school in the eighties? How can you dream when you are drowning in student loan debt?

How can you dream if you make minimum wage and work forty hours a week, knowing that, in 99 percent of U.S. counties, you can't afford the market-rate rent on the average one-bedroom apartment?

How can you dream when your pay barely budges no matter how hard you work, while everything else keeps getting so much more expensive? How can you dream when your son is sick but you can't afford your copay or deductible?

A middle-class life isn't what it used to be. And right now it isn't what it's supposed to be. Being middle-class ought to mean having financial security and stability. But how is that possible when the cost of living is so high that you live one setback away from catastrophe? An injury. An illness. Nobody expects life to be easy, but it's not supposed to be a life-altering crisis when your car's transmission fails.

And yet for so many, it is. One setback and the savings account gets emptied. Another and the retirement account goes, too. Soon you're carrying a bigger balance on your credit card than you know is safe, but what choice do you have? You have to get the car fixed if you're going to keep your job. There is rent or a mortgage to pay.

According to one survey, 57 percent of Americans don't have enough cash to cover a $500 unexpected expense. That's one of the reasons I've introduced the LIFT the Middle Class Tax Act in the U.S. Senate, a bill that creates a major new middle-class tax credit that would provide eligible families up to $6,000 a year—the equivalent of $500 a month. Families would be able to receive the credit as a monthly stipend, rather than wait for a refund the following year. It's a different kind of safety net, one that prevents hardworking people from falling out of the middle class, or gives them a fair shot at attaining it for their families. This is the kind of tax relief we can provide when we stop giving endless tax cuts to corporations and the wealthy.

I think of Mr. and Mrs. Shelton. She was a nursery school teacher and he was a construction worker, and on those incomes they were able to purchase a two-bedroom home that was everything they dreamed of, and everything they had worked for. But at the time of this writing, that house is listed on Zillow at $886,000, which would be impossible to purchase on the salaries of a teacher and a construction worker. I recognize that California has become extraordinarily expensive, but this is a problem in major metropolitan areas all across the country. According to a 2018 analysis by Redfin, in cities like Denver and Phoenix, less than 1 percent of the homes on the market were affordable on the average teacher's salary.

In rural areas, housing affordability issues aren't as severe, but communities have been devastated by a lack of jobs. According to a recent report, only 3 percent of job growth in the twenty-first century has come from rural areas. That has forced people to find work far away from home, which leaves them with an awful choice: endure an hours-long commute every day, or move away from the place where their family has lived for a generation, the place where their friends live, where their kids play little league baseball, where they have always gone to church.

I also think of the workers I've met along the way who are severely undervalued in this economy. Several years ago, I met a woman named Wendy through SEIU and got to spend the day with her, watching her work up close. She had changed jobs when her elderly mother got sick, becoming a home health care worker so she could be the one to take care of her day and night. That meant everything from lifting her mother out of her bed to dressing her, feeding her, assisting her in the bathroom, measuring and tracking her vitals, helping her into her wheelchair and taking her out for a walk, and keeping her cognitively engaged throughout. It was detailed and demanding work, physically, mentally, and emotionally.

And yet, in 2017, the average home health aide in the United States was earning too little to keep a four-person household above the poverty line. And because they are often contractors, they aren't always eligible for employee benefits. That strikes me as outrageous. As the baby boomer generation continues to retire, we're going to need more home health aides—1.2 million by 2026. And this is how we intend to treat them? What does this say about the value we place on caring for older Americans? What does this say about how we honor our elders?

The cost-of-living crisis is especially hard on women. Women are still paid, on average, eighty cents on the dollar compared with men— a gap that is even more punishing for black American women, who are paid only sixty-three cents for every dollar earned by white men. As the National Women's Law Center points out, that means a black woman who works full time, year-round, comes up more than $21,000 behind her white male counterpart. That affects everyone in her home. It's even worse for Latinas, who make just fifty-four cents on the dollar.

Politicians talk a big game about the value of hard work. But it's time we speak some truth. The truth is that the economy stopped rewarding and valuing most hard work a long time ago. And we've got to acknowledge that if we're going to change it.

Let's start by reflecting on how we got here.

For several decades after the Second World War, workers got pay raises when companies did well. And the government gave people a hand up, offering free education through the GI Bill. The productivity gains necessary to grow the economy were remarkable. In the three decades after the war, productivity improved a staggering 97 percent. The difference then was that everyone shared in the bounty.

During that same period, worker wages grew 90 percent. That's how the United States was able to build the world's largest middle class.

But in the 1970s and '80s, corporate America decided to go its own way. Instead of spending their earnings on workers, the corporations decided that their only real obligation was to their shareholders. From big business's perspective, it was those who owned a piece of the company who deserved the lion's share of the riches, not the people who made the company run. So while productivity improved 74 percent between 1973 and 2013, worker compensation rose just 9 percent.

In the 1980s, President Reagan made that idea core to the Republican Party's view of economics. Cut taxes for corporations. Cut taxes for shareholders. Oppose minimum wage increases. Oppose the very idea of a minimum wage. Dismantle organized labor, the most powerful force fighting for workers in Washington. Roll back government oversight. Ignore the collateral damage.

This was the ushering-in of a new era of selfishness and greed. And it was frighteningly effective. Corporate profits have soared, but American workers haven't gotten a meaningful raise in forty years. And yet there is no shame, it seems, in CEOs making more than three hundred times the wage of their average worker.

The goal of economic growth has to be to grow the pie. But if all that's left for workers are the crumbs, what kind of economy are we really building?

This was the context in which we entered the twenty-first century. The American people got sandwiched between forces beyond their control—on one side, outsourcing and offshoring that eviscerated the manufacturing sector, and on the other, the worst recession since the Great Depression. Suddenly, the jobs were gone. Communities turned into ghost towns.

I read so many letters that underscore the significance of the passage of time. A man, sixty-two, who lost everything in the Great Recession, who has nothing left for retirement and is running out of working years. A couple dealing with a family health crisis, who can't afford to pay their medical bills and still cover the monthly rent. They need help right now; they can't wait. Anyone stuck in a cycle of financial desperation will tell you it's an emergency. That there is no time for delay. Dinner has to go on the table tonight. Gas has to go in the tank in the morning. The bills have to be paid tomorrow. The rent is due at the end of the week. There is truly no time to spare.

During this period there have also been a rash of corporate predators who have taken advantage of—and often ruined—vulnerable people. Among the worst examples of these predators are the for-profit colleges that became the darlings of Wall Street during this time. Generations of Americans have been told that their best shot at opportunity is to get a degree. And a lot of folks took that advice to heart and went for it, sometimes at great cost to themselves and their families.

Dear Senator Harris,

At one point, I considered getting two jobs to provide for my son and me. I concluded the best solution for me was to go back to school and continue to work my minimum wage job, so my son wouldn't miss out on quality time with me. I decided I would struggle through poverty long enough to complete school. This is a reality for a lot of Americans.

The problem is that a lot of people signed up at for-profit colleges that promised them a great education and a great future, when, in truth, the degrees they were offering weren't worth much of anything.

When I was attorney general of California, we took on Corinthian Colleges Inc., one of the largest for-profit college scams in the country. In order to get students and investors to sign up, Corinthian representatives lied incessantly. They told investors that more than 60 percent of their students were successfully placed in sustainable jobs. They charged the students enormous amounts for their degrees and told them that some programs had 100 percent job placement rates, even when there was no evidence that a single graduate had received a job. They advertised programs they didn't offer and penalized their telemarketers if they revealed the truth to prospective students.

Even more venal was the way Corinthian went after vulnerable people. They targeted people living at the poverty line; people who had decided to go back to school and earn a degree so they could better take care of themselves and the people they loved; people who had lost jobs during the Great Recession and who believed their best chance in the job market was to acquire a new set of skills. Corinthian's internal documents betrayed the company's attitude toward its own students: they called their target demographic "isolated," "impatient" men and women with "low self-esteem," who have "few people in their lives who care about them" and who are "stuck" and "unable to see and plan well" for their own future. As far as I was concerned, this conduct was no different from the criminal predators I've known—purposely targeting those most in need.

Of course, most public companies don't act in such a predatory way. But a central tenant of corporate governance—to create value for shareholders even if it's to the detriment of workers—has created a great deal of harm of its own.

For example, to raise stock prices, executives engage in a concept called "buybacks," in which a company buys its own stock off the market, often causing the stock price to jump. Putting aside whether or not buybacks are ever an appropriate tool, let's acknowledge how extreme its use has become.

Between 2003 and 2012, S&P 500 companies spent 91 percent of their earnings on buybacks and dividends for shareholders. That leaves 9 percent to invest across the entire company, in everything from research and development to worker wages.

What's the result of all this? It's been great for the richest 1 percent of American households, who now own 40 percent of the nation's wealth, which adds up to roughly $40 trillion. But it's been a financial nightmare for the middle class. According to research done by United Way, 43 percent of households can't afford basic expenses: a roof over their head, food on the table, child care, health care, transportation, and a cell phone.

What are people supposed to think about a government that has left them behind? How are you supposed to feel when you're drowning and no one is coming to your aid, and then you turn on the television and hear that the economy is doing great? Great for whom?

It's not great for people who have had to move hours away from their job just to find an affordable place to live. It's not great for people who are dropping out of the workforce because they can't afford child care. It's not great for the people who are giving up on their dream of going to college because they know they can't afford it.

And yet with millions of Americans hanging by a thread, the White House reached for scissors. In 2017, the administration cut taxes for people who didn't need it and raised taxes on people who can't afford it. They sabotaged the Affordable Care Act, driving up premiums. They ignited a trade war that could lead to higher prices on things we all buy, from groceries to cars. They nominated judges intent on destroying organized labor. They canceled a pay raise for federal civil servants—everyone from transportation security officers to food inspectors, park rangers, medical personnel, and more. They even halted the debt relief policy that we put in place to help Corinthian Colleges' victims. And for good measure, they did away with net neutrality, which will allow internet companies to charge a premium for popular websites for the first time, adding an unacceptable new bill to the stack.

Dear Senator Harris,

I'm a high school student and most of my school work depends on the internet and the tools it gives us. My school is small and doesn't have much money, plus I come from a poor background and my parents struggle to make ends meet. If you take away Net Neutrality, you're basically taking away all the tools the internet provides students like me to succeed in school and adding more problems to poor families all over the nation.

We are running out of time. That's the hard truth. And not just in terms of dealing with what is so urgent right now. We are running out of time to deal with major changes to come. With the rise of artificial intelligence, we are likely to face an automation crisis in this country, with millions of jobs on the line.

Industries are changing. Self-driving trucks could cost 3.5 million truck drivers their jobs. The entire tax preparation business could disappear, too. The McKinsey Global Institute found that as many as 375 million people worldwide will need to switch jobs because of automation and predicts that 23 percent of current working hours could become automated by 2030. Another analysis suggests that automation could displace 2.5 million jobs a year in the near term. We have seen, already, the cost of displacement. But nothing has yet prepared us for what is to come.

We will also have to cope with the realities of climate change, which is as much an economic crisis as it is an environmental one. In 2017, extreme weather events in America—things like hurricanes, tornadoes, droughts, and floods—killed more than 362 people, displaced more than one million, and caused more than $300 billion in damage. Experts predict that over time, things will get much worse. The economic toll will follow—hitting states in the South and the lower Midwest the hardest. After Hurricane Harvey hit the Gulf Coast in 2017, a study found that in Houston, three of every ten affected residents fell behind on their rent or mortgage; 25 percent had trouble paying for meals.

Climate change imperils industries, too. Temperature and current changes in the oceans are already hurting the fishing industry. The agriculture industry faces dangers on multiple fronts: a rise in invasive species, pests, fungus, and disease; changing weather patterns that will lower yields; and the constant fear of drought.

Put bluntly, we have work to do. Hard work. Indispensable work. We have everything we need—all of the raw ingredients—to build an economy for the twenty-first century that is fair and sturdy, an economy that rewards the work of those who sustain it. But we have to hurry. And we have to be willing to speak truth.

We need to acknowledge that the jobs of the future are going to require people to earn an education after high school, whether it's a certification or a university degree. This isn't optional anymore. If we want to be true to the principle that all Americans deserve access to public education, then we can't stop funding it after high school. We need to invest in our workforce, now and in the future, and that means we're going to have to invest in more post–high school education, too. It means, among other things, that we have to make debt-free college a reality.

Let's speak truth about housing affordability. We can't have a functioning society if people can't afford to live in it. The housing crisis is not something we can just shrug off as if it is a fact of nature. We've got to make a major effort, from changing zoning laws to encourage new and affordable housing to giving relief to people who are struggling—right now—to pay their rent. For starters, I introduced a Senate bill that would give overburdened renters some relief. If someone is paying more than 30 percent of their income in rent and utilities, they would receive a new refundable tax credit to help defray their housing costs. But there's much more to do.

Let's speak truth about child care. If we don't find a way to make it affordable, we're not only subjugating people in financial crisis; we are also making it harder for women to stay in the workforce when they want to. This is one of the systemic barriers to women's growth and success in the workplace. We need to tear it down.

And let's speak truth about what we have to build up. To put people to work in well-paid jobs, and to prevent our economy from lagging, we should be investing in rebuilding our nation's infrastructure. We have roads and bridges that need building and upgrading. We have broadband internet infrastructure to build in rural areas that still lack it. We have new wind farms and transmission lines that need installing. We have airports that need modernizing and subways in dire need of repair. If not for ourselves, shouldn't we at least do this work for our children and grandchildren?

Let's also speak truth about organized labor, which has been systematically dismantled by the Republican Party. Less than 7 percent of the private workforce is represented by unions today, and a 2018 Supreme Court ruling is likely to decimate public sector union membership as well. Many people have already written the obituary for the labor movement. But we can't accept that. Unions are the ones lobbying in Washington exclusively on behalf of workers. They are the only ones who have given the power to the people in the workplace. In the midst of a Republican effort to hollow out the middle class, it is the unions that have successfully compelled management to pay better wages and provide better benefits. We need a rebirth of organized labor in America.

And let's speak one final truth: big corporations and the richest people in the richest country in the world can afford to pay their fair share of taxes so that we can fix the economy. It's necessary, it's moral, and it's wise.

Nine

SMART ON SECURITY

When I arrived in the Senate, I was surprised to learn that there was a seat open on the Senate Select Committee on Intelligence. I asked outgoing senator Barbara Boxer why this was. She told me that the committee's work was fascinating, meaningful, and critical to the country, but that most of it took place behind closed doors. Members of the committee couldn't talk publicly about their activities, because reviewing the country's most sensitive intelligence involved the highest levels of security clearance. Consequently, she explained, there usually wasn't much of a spotlight on the committee.

That didn't matter to me. I knew that, by the very nature of the job, if I had something important to say, I could find a bouquet of microphones to speak into. But when it came to the daily work, I wanted to be informed in real time about the threats facing my constituents and our country.

So I joined the Senate Intelligence Committee, fully expecting the work to be done in the shadows, away from the press and outside the day-to-day focus of the national conversation. But days after I was sworn in as a United States senator, those expectations were upended. On January 6, 2017, the intelligence community released a public assessment that determined that Russia had conducted multiple cyber operations against the United States, with the intent of influencing the outcome of the 2016 presidential election. Suddenly our work—an investigation into what had gone so terribly wrong—would become one of the most consequential undertakings in the history of the Senate.

Most of what I do on the committee involves classified information, so there's a real limit to what I can write about here. But there are times when the intelligence community releases its assessments to the public, stripped of the information sources and methods by which the information was obtained, and meticulously written to avoid revealing anything that could compromise national security or endanger people's lives. And there are times when our committee works in close coordination with the intelligence community to release our own assessments publicly so that we can balance the critical need for the American people to know what is happening from our oversight perspective against the equally critical need to keep our intelligence-gathering efforts covert. I can—and will—reference that work.

Twice a week, for two hours at a time, members of the Intelligence Committee get together behind closed doors to speak with the men and women who lead our seventeen intelligence agencies and receive briefings on the latest information. I can't tell you the details of what we talk about, but I can tell you what it's like. For starters, the room we gather in is known as a SCIF, which stands for Sensitive Compartmented Information Facility. It has been designed to prevent eavesdropping of any kind. Before we enter, we have to put our cell phones in a cupboard outside the door. Inside, we take classified notes by hand, and even those must be kept locked away in the SCIF.

When the committee holds public hearings, Democrats sit on one side of the dais and Republicans on the other as we face witnesses and cameras. But inside the SCIF and away from the cameras, it is a very different environment. Often senators take off their jackets. We get down to business. It is not just the absence of cameras and the seating arrangement that changes the dynamic; it is the work itself. The rigid partisanship that has paralyzed much of Washington somehow fades as we enter the room. We are, all of us, keenly focused on the weight of the work we are undertaking and its consequences. There is simply no room for anything other than a focus on America's national security and the protection of Americans' privacy and civil liberties. The public can't be there, nor the media, nor other senators who aren't on the committee. It's just us, to do oversight with global reach. It is invigorating, even inspiring. It is a scene I wish the American people could see, if just for a moment. It is a reminder that even in Washington, some things can be bigger than politics.

My work on the Intelligence Committee and the Homeland Security Committee covers a broad range of issues, from building and maintaining counterterrorism capability at home and abroad to the work of disrupting and destroying ISIS; to protecting and securing our borders; to the challenge of nuclear proliferation; and to the ever delicate balance between gathering intelligence and protecting civil liberties. But rather than run through the laundry list of issues we deal with in all their complexity, I want to focus on a few of the threats that keep me up at night.

First and foremost, I think of cybersecurity—a new front in a new kind of battle. If we had a daily visual of attacks under way—of explosions in our cities, of Russian, Chinese, North Korean, and Iranian warplanes overhead—the American people would insist that we respond, clear in the knowledge that the future of the American experiment was very much at risk. But cyber warfare is silent warfare, and its consequences are often difficult to grasp before the damage is done. I sometimes refer to it as a war without blood: there are no soldiers in the field, no bullets and bombs. But the reality is cyber warfare aims to weaponize infrastructure and, at its worst, could result in casualties. Imagine, for example, a cyberattack on railroad switching signals or hospital generators or a nuclear power plant.

The intelligence community and private companies alike are waging a defensive battle against cyberattacks on a minute-by-minute basis. But the reality is that we still remain unprepared for this new kind of terrain. Our systems and infrastructure need to be seriously upgraded.

We are currently under attack. Our elections are top of mind, especially given the nefarious—and effective—attacks by the Russian government. The January 2017 assessment found that "Russian President Vladimir Putin ordered an influence campaign in 2016 aimed at the U.S. presidential election. Russia's goals were to undermine public faith in the U.S. democratic process, denigrate Secretary Clinton, and harm her electability and potential presidency." Though many have become numb to it through the news cycle, the significance of this finding is hard to overstate. The intelligence community assessed, with a high degree of confidence, that Russia's intelligence services conducted cyber operations to hack into a U.S. presidential campaign and to release data they gathered with the intent of influencing the outcome of the election.

Russian agents and propagandists exploited U.S. social media platforms such as Facebook, Twitter, and YouTube to spread false and inflammatory information about Secretary Clinton and to stoke divisions in the United States. And what I think is very telling is exactly how they went about it.

They focused on hot-button issues, from race to LGBTQ and immigrant rights. This means that they knew that racism and other forms of hate have always been our nation's Achilles' heel. They knew precisely where to strike us, deliberately targeting—and tearing away at—some of the most painful, divisive parts of our nation's history.

I first made this point during an Intelligence Committee meeting. A few days later, I was sitting at my desk on the Senate floor, the last one in the far back. I had chosen the desk for two reasons: it wasn't visible on the C-SPAN cameras, which made it easier for me to concentrate on the work at hand. But, more important, it was the desk closest to the candy drawer.

I looked up and noticed that Senator James Lankford, a Republican from Oklahoma, was walking toward me, literally crossing the aisle so we could have a conversation.

"Kamala, I've been listening to what you've been saying about race as our Achilles' heel, and I think you're on to something important," he said. "Personally, I think it starts with the question 'Have you had a family over to your house that doesn't look like you? Have you ever really had that kind of interaction? I think that's a good place to start."

"I'm glad to hear you say that," I told him. "We have to start somewhere."

Lankford and I sat across from each other in closed sessions of the Intelligence Committee, and though there are very few things we agree about when it comes to policy, I found him to be genuinely kind and thoughtful. It didn't take long for us to build a friendship.

Together with our colleagues on the committee, we spent more than a year working with the intelligence community to understand the information that led to the January 2017 assessment about Russian attacks. Of particular interest to me was the threat of Russian penetration of our election equipment itself. In May 2018, we released our preliminary findings on the issue of election security. We let the public know that in 2016, the Russian government had conducted a coordinated cyber campaign against the election infrastructures of at least eighteen individual states, and possibly as many as twenty-one. Other states also saw malicious activity, which the intelligence community has been unable to attribute to Russia. What we do know is that Russian operatives scanned election databases looking for vulnerabilities. They attempted to break in. And in some cases, they were actually successful in penetrating voter registration databases. Thankfully, as of May 2018, our committee had not seen any evidence that actual vote tallies or voter registration rolls were changed. But given our limited information on state audits and forensic examinations of states' own election infrastructures, we cannot rule out that activities were successfully carried out that we just don't know about yet.

In our report, we raised concerns about a number of potential vulnerabilities that remain in our election infrastructure. Voting systems are outdated, and many of them do not have a paper record of votes. Without a paper record, there is no way to reliably audit a vote tally and confirm that numbers haven't been changed. We found that thirty states use paperless voting machines in some jurisdictions, and that five states use them exclusively, leaving them vulnerable to manipulation that cannot be reconciled and reversed. We also found that many of our election systems are connected to the internet, leaving them open to hacking. Even systems not regularly connected to the internet are nevertheless updated by software that must be downloaded from the internet.

It's misleading to suggest that impenetrable cybersecurity is possible; our focus must be on defending against, detecting, deterring, managing, and mitigating any effort to do us harm. There's a grim joke: What's the difference between being hacked and not being hacked? Knowing you've been hacked. The truth hurts—but we simply can't afford to be naive.

To help members of Congress and their staffs understand the nature of the risk, I invited a computer science and engineering professor from the University of Michigan to visit the Capitol and demonstrate the ease with which a hacker could change an election's outcome. We gathered in a room in the Capitol Visitor Center, where the professor had set up a paperless voting machine used in numerous states, including swing states like Florida, Pennsylvania, and Virginia. Four senators participated—Senators Lankford, Richard Burr, Claire McCaskill, and me—and the room was filled with staffers who had come to better understand the process.

The professor simulated a vote for president, where we were given a choice between George Washington and the infamous Revolutionary War traitor Benedict Arnold. As you might imagine, all four of us voted for George Washington. But when the result came back,

Benedict Arnold had prevailed. The professor had used malicious code to hack the software of the voting machine in a way that assured Arnold's victory, no matter how the four of us had voted.

He told us that the machine was very easily hacked, enough so that, in a demonstration elsewhere, he turned one into a video game console and played *Pac-Man* on it. Can you imagine?

America's electoral infrastructure consists of outdated machines and local officials who often have little or no cyber-threat training. When you consider how many major corporations have experienced data breaches, despite having invested in the best cybersecurity money can buy, our vulnerability becomes all the more stark. Some might think it is alarmist to be talking this way, but I think we should be preparing to defend against the worst-case scenario: that foreign actors will target these outmoded machines and manipulate vote tallies. Given Russia's unprecedented effort to undermine confidence in our election system while attempting to interfere with the outcome of a presidential election, there's no question that the Kremlin is emboldened—along with other state and nonstate actors—to try again.

At the time, James Lankford and I were the only members of the Senate who served on both the Homeland Security and Intelligence Committees. As such, we were uniquely suited to come together in a nonpartisan way to develop legislation to combat these attacks. At the end of December 2017, together with other senators, we introduced a bill—the Secure Elections Act—that would protect the United States from future foreign interference in our elections.

The legislation—which grew out of hearings and testimony in front of both the Homeland Security and Intelligence Committees, would improve cybersecurity information sharing between federal

and state agencies. It would create a process by which election officials could receive top-secret security clearance, allowing them to
have timely access to classified material (as in a case where we learned
that Russia had attacked their machines). It would establish clear expert guidelines for securing election systems—including, for example, the need for paper ballots. Russia might be able to hack a machine
from afar, but it can't hack a piece of paper. And it would provide
$386 million in grants for cybersecurity improvements.

It would also establish what's known as a bug bounty program for
election infrastructure. Commonly used in tech firms, a bug bounty
is a system by which altruistic hackers are paid for identifying software vulnerabilities. It's an economically efficient way to quickly
patch bugs that could be exploited by malicious actors. We owe it to
ourselves to continually test our system's security, just as we'd test the
smoke alarm in our home. No one wants to wait for the house to
catch on fire in order to realize the battery's dead.

Remarkably, despite the bill's bipartisan support, as of this writing, it has yet to receive a vote in the United States Senate. Though it
was introduced nearly a year before the 2018 midterm elections, the
White House opposed the bill, and the Senate majority leader refused
to bring it to the floor. And so I am, indeed, kept up at night, knowing the scale of our vulnerabilities and knowing that actions we
should be taking immediately have stalled out without any justifi-
cation.

It's also important to remember that election systems aren't the
only area in which we are vulnerable to foreign interference.

In March 2018, for example, the Department of Homeland Security and the FBI issued a joint alert that showed that Russian hackers
had gained access to the computer systems of organizations and U.S.

government entities in sectors ranging from energy and water to aviation and manufacturing. DHS and the FBI described the actions as a "multi-stage intrusion campaign by Russian government cyber actors who targeted commercial facilities' networks and staged malware, conducted spear phishing, and gained remote access into energy sector networks." After they got access, the Russians did extensive reconnaissance. They were able to gain access to at least one power plant's control system. And they placed tools in the systems that would allow them, in certain cases, to shut down power plants at will.

This is, needless to say, an extraordinary vulnerability. Millions of Americans recall the blackout of August 2003, when an electricity surge overloaded the grid covering parts of eight northeastern states. Major cities were plunged into darkness. Fire departments rushed to free people from elevators as building temperatures rose. Hundreds of trains were stopped in their tracks, and thousands of passengers had to be rescued from darkened subway tunnels. Waste treatment plants lost power; 490 million gallons of raw sewage were spilled in New York City alone. Cell phone service was disrupted. ATMs went down. Hospitals had to rely on generators to care for vulnerable patients. Analysts later concluded that mortality rates in New York City rose 28 percent during the two-day blackout.

In the intelligence community's Worldwide Threat Assessment in 2018, the director of national intelligence detailed increased risks to critical infrastructure over the coming year. "The use of cyberattacks as a foreign policy tool outside of military conflict has been mostly limited to sporadic lower-level attacks," the report explained. "Russia, Iran, and North Korea, however, are testing more aggressive cyberattacks that pose growing threats to the United States and U.S. partners."

Iran, which in the past has attacked a large U.S. corporation and stolen personal data, is expected to continue its work penetrating the United States' cyber infrastructure. North Korea, which conducted a destructive attack on Sony in November 2014, and which the U.S. government identified as responsible for a massive cyberattack in the United Kingdom that paralyzed that country's health care system, is expected to use its cyber operations to steal money in the wake of sanctions, as it did in 2016, when it took $81 million from the Bangladesh Bank. China, meanwhile, has been advancing its own cyberattack capabilities since 2015 and has directed attacks at U.S. private industry, particularly defense contractors and IT and communications firms whose products and services support worldwide networks. An investigation by the Office of the United States Trade Representative found that Chinese theft of American intellectual property costs us more than $200 billion annually.

And then there are nonstate actors. As the DNI threat assessment indicates, "Transnational criminals will continue to conduct for-profit cyber-enabled crimes, such as theft and extortion against US networks." This is costly business: in February 2018, cybersecurity software provider McAfee and the nonpartisan Center for Strategic and International Studies released a report that put such cybercrime's toll in North America at $140 billion to $175 billion. And we can also expect state actors to fund such criminal activity, which represents both an inexpensive and deniable way for them to pursue their malicious aims.

Cybersecurity has to become one of our highest priorities in this new age. It's not enough to make sure that our troops have the very best weapons when they go into battle. We also have to make sure our military, intelligence community, and private sector have the very best cyber defenses to protect against these new and ever-changing threats. As General Keith Alexander, former NSA director and inaugural head of U.S. Cyber Command, said in 2016, Department of Defense systems are probed by hackers about 250,000 times an hour. That's six million times each day.

In a world where tech can be weaponized, we need to deploy the very best technology in order to respond. And that means constantly upgrading our efforts so that we are always a step ahead.

I remember that when I first became attorney general, in 2011, I was shocked by what we lacked in terms of technology. So I put together a team, led by Special Assistant Attorney General Travis LeBlanc, to upgrade and overhaul our system so that we could better fight crime in the digital era. In my first year in office, we organized an "eCrime Unit," which we staffed with attorneys and investigators who focused on technology-related crimes like identity theft and cyber exploitation. I spent much of the remainder of my tenure working to institutionalize California's technological advantages. Those efforts culminated in the creation of our Cyber Crime Center, which gave all of our tech crime fighters access to state-of-the-art digital forensics capabilities, making California one of the first states to do so.

But in addition to deploying our best technology now, we need to invest in the innovations and breakthroughs that we'll need in order to stay protected down the line. That's one of the reasons I've put forward a bill to invest in quantum computing, a frontier technology that would put the United States at the forefront of the race for technological superiority. Our pursuit of innovation cannot be viewed from an economic lens alone. It matters to national security, too. It's also one of the reasons I believe we must be a country that welcomes highly skilled students and professionals from around the world to study at our universities and work at our companies.

Ultimately, I believe we are going to need to develop a cyber doctrine. As a matter of principle, we will have to decide when and whether a cyberattack is an act of war, and what kind of response it warrants.

On January 12, 2017, Mike Pompeo came before the Senate Intelligence Committee for his confirmation hearing as CIA director. By tradition, questions at public hearings are asked in order of seniority, so, as the newest member of the committee, I questioned Pompeo last. Throughout the hearings, I listened as my colleagues asked Pompeo a wide range of questions, touching on traditional issues ranging from intelligence sharing and collection to preventing terrorist attacks in the United States and abroad. When it was finally my turn, I focused on a subject area that seemed to surprise Pompeo and others on the committee. I wanted to know how his public position rejecting the science of climate change was going to impact his role at the top of America's intelligence apparatus.

Right-wing pundits from Fox to the Heritage Foundation took great pleasure in calling my questions "dumb," "ridiculous," and "off-base." Evidently, they felt my concerns were divorced from issues of national security. But they were wrong. This was about analytic objectivity and not politicizing intelligence. The CIA had already made an unclassified assessment regarding the threat of climate change. Pompeo's previous statements disregarded the CIA assessment. How would he brief the president? Would he let his personal views override the findings of CIA professionals when it came to climate change—and, if so, what would that mean for other dire threats against our nation?

Climate change can be seen from many angles. Some see it purely as an environmental issue. They point to the destruction of habitats, the melting of ice sheets, and a coming mass extinction of species. Others see it as a public health issue that demands a world where clean air and clean water are readily available. There is also the economic dimension of climate change: ask farmers about the complexity of their work, about their precise and measured focus on weather patterns, about the incredibly narrow margins that exist between a successful harvest and a ruinous one, and you will come to understand that extreme weather events and unpredictable shifts in the climate are nothing to dismiss.

But when you speak to generals, when you speak to senior members of the intelligence community and experts on international conflicts, you will find that they look at climate change as a national security threat—a "threat multiplier" that will exacerbate poverty and political instability, creating conditions that enable violence, despair, even terrorism. An unstable, erratic climate will beget an unstable, erratic world.

For example, climate change will lead to droughts. Droughts will lead to famine. Famine will drive desperate people to leave their homes in search of sustenance. Massive flows of displaced people will lead to refugee crises. Refugee crises will lead to tension and instability across borders.

Climate change also increases the risk of deadly global pandemics making their way to the United States. The Centers for Disease Control and Prevention reported that between 2006 and 2016, the number of Americans infected by diseases like West Nile, Zika, and Lyme more than tripled. As temperatures continue to warm, diseases are flourishing in parts of America where they wouldn't have been able to survive in the past. In fact, the CDC has already identified nine types of infections that had never been seen before in the United States.

The hard truth is that climate change is going to cause terrible instability and desperation, and that will put American national security at risk. That's why former CIA director John Brennan has said that when CIA analysts look for deeper causes of rising instability in the world, one of the causes they point to is climate change. That's why, as part of President Obama's national security strategy, climate change was identified as a national security threat of the highest priority. That's why the Pentagon has been ahead of the curve in developing resilience to the effects of climate change, including strategies to protect the dozens of military bases that will be affected by rising seas and extreme weather events. And it's why I didn't hesitate in asking the person who would become the nation's CIA director how and whether climate change would be a factor in his strategy to protect the American people.

This isn't the stuff of science fiction or of a dystopian novel set far in the future. Climate-driven crisis is already on the rise. In late 2017, for example, water reserves fell so low in Cape Town, South Africa, that the city of more than three million people, South Africa's second largest, was at risk of having its taps run dry. Residents started showering over buckets so that they could reuse the water in their washing machines. Farmers had to abandon about a quarter of their crops.

This is an issue we will face at home, too, and it's a matter of national security that we prepare for it. We need a diversified water security strategy to ensure a reliable, sustainable supply. Growing up in California, I understood from an early age that the water supply is precious and precarious. In elementary school, my classmates and I studied ecology; I remember my mother smiling when she had to explain to me the difference between a *conservative* and a *conservationist*. I saw the drought of 1976–77 through a child's eyes—unflushed toilets, shower timers, and dried-out brown lawns. I think a lot about water security, and I never take it for granted.

A diversified approach would work on multiple fronts simultaneously. Conservation is the cheapest, most effective way to increase our water resources. But we also need to update our aging water infrastructure, improve our storm water capture and storage capacity, and make smart investments in water recycling, purification, and desalination.

There's a lot we can learn from friends and partners who have already made such investments—especially Israel, a global leader on water security issues. In February 2018, I traveled to Israel and toured its Sorek desalination plant, which uses reverse osmosis to produce clean drinking water from the sea. I had a glass. It tasted as good as any water I've ever had.

And that's not all. As many have said, the Israelis have made the desert bloom. They've done so in part by successfully reclaiming 86 percent of their wastewater and purifying it for agricultural reuse. By contrast, the United States, which produces 32 billion gallons of municipal wastewater each day, reclaims only 7 to 8 percent. Surely we can do better than that.

Conserving water and safeguarding against scarcity must be a top priority. The same can be said, in this era of climate change, for the need to protect against floods. In India, Bangladesh, and Nepal, flooding in the summer of 2017 killed 1,200 people and affected more than 40 million. Nearly 1 million homes were destroyed. In 2010, flooding in Pakistan rocked 20 percent of the country, killing more than 1,700 people and affecting at least 12 million. Here at home, the destructive force of Hurricane Maria left the island of Puerto Rico in ruins. I visited Puerto Rico in November 2017 and saw some of that devastation firsthand—homes obliterated, roads collapsed and destroyed, and a community in crisis. It was disheartening. The official death toll has been revised from 64 to more than 2,900, but a report from scientists at Harvard's T. H. Chan School of Public Health estimates that the storm and its aftermath were responsible for the deaths of at least 4,600 American citizens in Puerto Rico.

And if it isn't floods, it's fires. Fires aren't caused by climate change, but they are exacerbated by it. Higher temperatures and longer dry spells turn our forests into kindling. California has always had wildfires, but because of climate change, they are becoming more frequent and getting bigger and bigger. When I was attorney general, I had toured a fire overhead by helicopter. From that height, the scale of the devastation came into view—entire streets, entire neighborhoods burned to the ground. It looked like a graveyard, with chimneys as headstones.

In August 2018, I flew home to California to meet with firefighters and evacuees from the Mendocino Complex Fire, which burned more than 450,000 acres, making it the largest fire in the state's history.

When I arrived in Lake County, I went to a convention center where evacuated families were being sheltered temporarily. Some of them knew they had lost their homes and all of their possessions. Others were left to wonder. I met a mom who was pregnant with her third child. She was trying to keep her family's spirits up. I remember how proud her daughter was to show me how neatly she had tidied the sheets on top of the Red Cross cots where they now slept.

A year earlier, I met a firefighter who lost his own home in a fire he was fighting. He said he had always thought he understood the pain of losing everything, given how often he had seen it happen to others—but that it was so much worse than he imagined. Still, he reminded himself and me, it wasn't as bad as the families that got the call that their husband or son had been one of the many firefighters who lost their lives that year.

There is a theme that runs through all of these issues, be it cyber-security or climate change or keeping aggressors like Russia and North Korea in check. Though the United States is a superpower, there are real limits to what we can do alone. In order to keep the American people safe, in order to ensure that our national interests and homeland are secure, we must work in partnership with our allies—economically, diplomatically, and militarily. We must protect NATO, the most important defensive treaty the world has ever known, especially in the face of Russia's increasingly flagrant aggression. We must rejoin the Paris Agreement, because only together can we reverse the trends of climate change and prevent some of its more terrifying outcomes. And we must remind ourselves that the work we do to protect the American people must also be in service of American values. That the actions we take project a message to the world about who we are.

It was that final truism that I held in mind when Gina Haspel came before our committee in a confirmation hearing to replace Mike Pompeo as CIA director. Haspel, a thirty-three-year veteran of the CIA, had been at the agency during a time when prisoners were tortured. She had been asked many questions about this work by other senators—about whether her actions had been legal; about whether she would ever authorize such actions again.

When it was my turn to speak, I underscored that this hearing wasn't about the incredible and unquestionable importance of the service and sacrifice of the men and women of the CIA, nor was it about the agency's mission, both of which I wholeheartedly support. The hearing, I explained, was about her suitability to be the director of the CIA, and it was our job, as senators, to understand that who we chose for that position would send a signal to the men and women of the agency, the American people, and our neighbors around the world about our values and our moral authority. With that in mind, I initiated what became a revealing exchange:

"So one question I have not heard you answer is: Do you believe that the previous interrogation techniques were immoral?"

Haspel paused as she considered the answer. "Senator, I believe that CIA officers to whom you refer—"

"It's a yes-or-no answer. Do you believe the previous interrogation techniques were immoral? I'm not asking do you believe they were legal; I'm asking do you believe they were immoral?"

She paused again. "Senator, I believe that CIA did extraordinary work to prevent another attack on this country, given the legal tools that we were authorized to use."

"Please answer yes or no. Do you believe in hindsight that those techniques were immoral?"

"Senator, what I believe sitting here today is that I support the higher moral standard we have decided to hold ourselves to."

"Can you please answer the question?"

"Senator, I think I've answered the question."

"No, you have not. Do you believe the previous techniques—now armed with hindsight—do you believe they were immoral? Yes or no?"

"Senator, I believe that we should hold ourselves to the moral standard outlined in the Army Field Manual."

Shortly after Haspel refused to answer the question, the late Senator John McCain, who had been subjected to five years of brutal torture as a prisoner of war in North Vietnam, released a statement saying that he would not support her confirmation as CIA director.

"Like many Americans, I understand the urgency that drove the decision to resort to so-called enhanced interrogation methods after our country was attacked," McCain wrote. "I know that those who used enhanced interrogation methods and those who approved them wanted to protect Americans from harm. I appreciate their dilemma and the strain of their duty. But as I have argued many times, the methods we employ to keep our nation safe must be as right and just as the values we aspire to live up to and promote in the world.

"I believe Gina Haspel is a patriot who loves our country and has devoted her professional life to its service and defense," he continued. "However, Ms. Haspel's role in overseeing the use of torture by Americans is disturbing. Her refusal to acknowledge torture's immorality is disqualifying. I believe the Senate should exercise its duty of advice and consent and reject this nomination."

We live in an uncertain world, one filled with complexity and danger. The challenges we face in the future will be new and nuanced, and they will require us to mobilize based on being smart, not on being afraid. There will be hard decisions to make, to be sure, of the kind that no previous generation has had to consider. And yet it will serve us well to remember what it was that helped us protect the American people and secure the peace in the generations leading up to this moment. We must remember that we are a nation of laws, that we stand for the rule of law. We must remember what we have worked and in some cases bled for: an international order that promotes peace and cooperation; a commitment to democracy, here and around the world; a rejection of despots and tyrants and dictators who rule their countries based on their self-interest alone, not the interests of the people they are meant to serve. Imperfect though we have been, ours is a history in pursuit of a better, safer, freer world. In the years to come, with all the challenges to come, we cannot lose sight of who we are and who we can be.

Ten

WHAT I'VE LEARNED

Early in my career, one of the first cases I tried was a hit-and-run case in Judge Jeffrey Horner's Oakland courtroom. To illustrate my argument, I had printed out a map on a large sheet of paper, which I pinned to an easel with butterfly clips. I needed the map so that I could show the jury the driver's path.

I don't remember all the details of the case, but I do remember this map, because I kept stumbling over north, south, east, and west. To acknowledge my own gaffes, at some point in the proceedings I cracked a self-deprecating joke before the jury. Not long after, during a break, Judge Horner called me into his chamber. "Don't you ever do that again," he said. "You figure it out. Figure it out."

His words stuck with me, along with so many lessons I've absorbed along the way—foundational wisdom from my mother; encouragement and guidance from family members, friends, and trusted mentors; and the powerful examples I've witnessed, both good and bad, that have shaped my understanding of what it takes to lead effectively, what it takes to achieve one's objectives, and what we owe to one another in the process.

These lessons have been informed by my own life experience and leavened by their application over the course of my career. Today they find expression in a series of brief phrases, ones my team members hear so often they'll probably laugh when they read this chapter. One year, my team even had blue stress balls made, with NO FALSE CHOICES emblazoned in white letters.

Of course, it isn't possible to reduce the complexity of leadership to simple slogans. But my team and I rely on these mantras as touchstones and guideposts—as starting points for policy conversations and as ways to determine whether we're on the right track. I'm sharing them here because they say a lot about my personal philosophy and style. And maybe they will help to shape your thinking in some way, as the wisdom earned by other people has helped shape mine.

TEST THE HYPOTHESIS

When I was a kid, I used to accompany my mother to the lab, where she'd give me jobs to do. Cleaning test tubes, mainly. I think she probably knew early on that I wasn't going to follow her into the sciences. It was the humanities and the arts that spoke to me, even as I was in awe of my mother and her colleagues and their work.

But when you're the daughter of a scientist, science has a way of shaping how you think. Our mother used to talk to Maya and me about the scientific method as if it were a way of life. When I'd ask her why something was the way it was, she wasn't content to just give me the answer. She wanted me to formulate my own hypothesis, to use that as a starting point for further investigation, and to challenge my assumptions. This was how she did her work in the lab. The experiments she ran each day were aimed at figuring out whether her ideas would stand after being tested. It was about kicking the tires. She would collect and analyze the data, and draw conclusions from that evidence. If the results didn't support the hypothesis, she would reevaluate.

Innovation is the pursuit of what can be, unburdened by what has been. And we pursue innovation not because we're bored but because we want to make things faster, more efficient, more effective, more accurate. In science, in medicine, in technology, we embrace the culture of innovation—hypotheses, experiments, and all. We expect mistakes; we just don't want to make the same mistake twice. We expect imperfections; it's basic for us. We've gotten used to the idea that software will need to be tweaked and updated. We don't have any problem with the concept of "bug fixes" and upgrades. We know that the more we test something, the clearer we'll understand what works and what doesn't, and the better the final product or process will be.

But in the realm of public policy, we seem to have trouble embracing innovation. That's in part because when you're running for public office and you stand before the voters, you aren't expected to have a hypothesis; you're expected to have "the Plan." The problem is, when you roll out any innovation, new policy, or plan for the first time, there are likely to be glitches, and because you're in the public eye, those glitches are likely to end up on the front page in bold lettering. When the HealthCare.gov website crashed two hours after it launched in 2013, the problem, though temporary, became a stand-in for describing the entire pursuit of affordable health care coverage as folly.

The point is, when you are in public office, there really is a lot of risk associated with pursuing bold actions. Even so, I believe it is our obligation to do so. It is inherent in the oaths we take.

The point of being a public official is to find solutions to problems, especially the most intractable, and to have a vision for the future. I've always said that political capital doesn't gain interest. You have to spend it, and be willing to take the hit. You have to be willing to test your hypothesis and find out if your solution works, based on metrics and data. Blind adherence to tradition should not be the measure of success.

Michael Tubbs, the mayor of Stockton, California, understands this idea better than just about anyone I know. He became mayor, at twenty-six, of a city that had been hammered by the foreclosure crisis and forced into bankruptcy. His city still contends with high poverty and crime and, now, rising rents. Tubbs asked a team of researchers to identify novel ways he could fight poverty, and one of the ideas they came back with was a guaranteed income program. The concept is that giving people direct cash payments can help them make ends meet while giving the economy a boost. And that was a hypothesis he was willing to test. The city is putting together a pilot program, beginning in February 2019, in which it will give a random group of a hundred residents $500 a month for eighteen months to spend however they want. Researchers will check in with the participants regularly during the program. At the end of that time, the city will have a trove of data that will help the mayor—and countless political leaders—determine the effectiveness of such a model.

Another much discussed idea for helping the American workforce is to create a jobs guarantee program. Rather than guarantee a base cash payment, a federal jobs guarantee could ensure that anyone who wants to work will have a good-paying job with dignity. It's an idea straight out of President Franklin Roosevelt's Economic Bill of Rights. Is it possible? Would it work? If it's part of "the Plan" you're running on, you're compelled to say yes. But the better answer is "Let's find out." I signed on to legislation in the Senate to create a model program that will help us do just that. One way or the other, I am confident that the data that comes from such a program will inform our approach.

GO TO THE SCENE

There's a small community in Southern California called Mira Loma that sits just north of the Santa Ana River, at the western edge of Riverside County. It was, for a long time, a rural community, a place of grape vineyards and dairy farms, a place where people loved to ride horses and to raise their children away from the smog of industrial Los Angeles. But in the late 1980s, things started to change.

The rise of globalization meant that the United States would start importing a lot more goods from around the world, and many of those shipping containers from Asia were ending up at Southern California harbors. So nearby Riverside County started approving huge warehouse projects and distribution centers into which trucks would drop off the cargo they picked up at the docks. By the time I was attorney general, there were approximately ninety such mega-complexes in Mira Loma.

Life was transformed for the 4,500 families living in Mira Loma. Farms were dug up and paved over. Traffic became unbearable. The quiet rural community was swallowed up by an industrial warehousing district. And the air turned toxic. Every day, trucks made more than 15,000 trips on Mira Loma's main roads, bringing with them soot and other particulate matter. Soon Mira Loma had one of the highest rates of diesel pollution in the state—well beyond state and federal air quality standards.

Researchers at the University of Southern California conducted a study that found that pollution was linked to poor lung development and other serious illnesses in Mira Loma children. The federal Environmental Protection Agency had already expressed its own concerns about health dangers associated with such filthy air. But things were only getting worse.

The circumstances of Mira Loma were brought to my attention when I learned that the county had approved another complex of warehouses, which would facilitate another 1,500 truck trips through Mira Loma every day. Residents sued to stop it, arguing that the county had failed to take the health concerns seriously and hadn't done the work to mitigate the harm this would cause to a population already experiencing dangerous health impacts. They argued that the county had failed to follow state standards meant to protect communities like theirs. After reviewing the documents, I agreed.

"I want to join the lawsuit," I told my team. "Let's show those families the state has their back."

That could have been the end of it. I was confident that, with state resources behind them, the community would have what it needed to prevail. But taking action wasn't enough. Understanding the circumstances strictly through the lens of briefing documents and discussions with lawyers wasn't enough. I wanted to go to the scene.

As we approached Mira Loma, I could see a towering mass of haze and smog enveloping the community and the surrounding areas. The sun shone through, but with a gray, refracted tint as the toxic cloud settled in. When I got out of the car, the pollution stung my eyes. I could taste it in the air. I could wipe the dust and soot off surfaces with my fingers.

I went into a small meeting room where members of the community had gathered to tell me their stories. One person told me that every day, when the wind changes, he started breathing the fumes. Another told me that it's not safe for children to play outside. More than half the households had children under eighteen, and they were stuck indoors. A soft-spoken woman told me that she was glad I was there, because they had been fighting for a long time and no one ever seemed to listen.

One man told me that they have to wash the soot off their driveways, and clean their clotheslines before they hang any clothes. He worried about the trees in his backyard, which had stopped bearing fruit and were dying. And he expressed his concern for people in the community who were suffering from higher rates of cancer, asthma, and heart disease.

At first, that was all he said. But when the microphone came back to him, the group encouraged him to tell the more personal story that had brought him to the meeting.

"It's hard for me to talk about it. . . . But, I mean, I'll do it to help this community."

Through tears, he began. "I had a daughter . . . and she died before she was fifteen years old. And instead of planning for her fifteenth birthday . . . I was planning for her funeral. . . . She died of lung cancer. Sometimes it's hard for me to talk about it. But if this can help, I'm just telling my story."

It did help. The fight against the county would take place in courtrooms and conference rooms, and we would be not just the voice but the vessel through which the community's story would be told. To really understand the pain that a community is coping with, it's not enough to imagine what it must be like. Smart policies cannot be created in an ivory tower, and arguments aren't won by facts alone. What matters just as much is being there whenever possible, in person, ears and eyes wide open, talking to the folks living closest to the challenge. It mattered that we were there to hear this anguished father's story and the stories of other families in Mira Loma.

It mattered when I visited soldiers in Iraq who were waiting for their next mission, and sailors in San Diego, preparing to deploy for months on a nuclear submarine. It is one thing to talk about the needs of the military and intelligence communities in a Senate hearing room. It is another to go to the scene and make real, in-person connections with the men and women who are serving. I spent a good deal of time with the troops, talked about their specialties and their training, about the challenges of their work and how a combination of bravery and duty had led them to this life. But we talked about other things, too: what they missed, what they feared, what they had left behind, the sacrifice their families had to make while they were gone. It was personal, and that mattered.

It mattered when I visited a Syrian refugee camp in Jordan so that I could get an up-close view of what life was like for the people trapped there—70 percent of them women and children. We drove around the encampment, which seemed to stretch endlessly in all directions, each makeshift dwelling representing a family that had fled war and slaughter. I insisted that we get out of the cars. We walked down a street they had nicknamed the Champs-Élysées, after the famous shopping street in Paris, and we admired the stalls of clothes and food.

At one point, three kids ran up and started talking to me. One of them, a ten-year-old in a blue soccer shirt, took a real liking to me. We took a selfie together and then he asked, through interpreters, if I would come meet his family. I said of course, and I followed him through the camp to where they were living.

When I got there, a large extended family was there to greet me. They had two small dwellings between them and had created a little courtyard between the two, with a board as an overhang. His grandparents were there—the matriarch and patriarch of the family—and they were incredibly welcoming when I arrived.

"Will you stay for tea?" the grandfather asked me. "I'd be honored," I replied.

The grandmother went behind the hut, where there was a water spigot and a small gas camp stove. The next thing I knew she was back, bearing a tray with beautiful glasses, a plate of sweets, and a teapot.

We were all sitting there cross-legged, drinking our tea. I was ready to ask all about them—the story of how they got there, the experience of living in the refugee camp—when the grandfather started to speak.

"Okay, I've invited you into my home. I've given you tea. I've fed you. Now tell me, who are you?"

EMBRACE THE MUNDANE

Bill Gates is obsessed with fertilizer. "I go to meetings where it's a serious topic of conversation," he writes. "I read books about its benefits and the problems with overusing it. It's the kind of topic I have to remind myself not to talk about too much at cocktail parties, since most people don't find it as interesting as I do." Why the fascination? He explains that 40 percent of people on earth owe their lives to higher crop outputs that were made possible only because of fertilizer. It was the literal fuel for the Green Revolution, which helped lift hundreds of millions of people out of poverty. What Gates understands is that there is a big difference between announcing a plan to end world hunger and actually ending it. And closing the gap depends on seemingly mundane details like fertilizer and weather patterns and the height of wheat.

Politics is a realm where the grand pronouncement often takes the place of the painstaking and detail-oriented work of getting meaningful things done. This isn't to say that there's anything inherently wrong with grand pronouncements. Good leadership requires vision and aspiration. It requires the articulation of bold ideas that move people to action. But it is often the mastery of the seemingly unimportant details, the careful execution of the tedious tasks, and the dedicated work done outside of the public eye that make the changes we seek possible.

Embracing the mundane also means making sure that our solutions actually work for the people who need them. When I was attorney general of California, for example, and I went after the for-profit Corinthian Colleges, I was concerned about what would happen to students who'd been defrauded. The students had the right to transfer to another school, get their loan discharged, or get their money back, but the paperwork involved was quite complicated. Most students had no idea how to begin, or even that they had these options in the first place.

We had prevailed in the case, but the students wouldn't actually receive the benefit of the financial relief unless they could navigate the bureaucracy. So my office created a website that walked students, step by step, through this complex process. I wanted to make it as simple as possible for someone to exercise their rights and get actual relief. As we were developing the website, I'd often have our team show it to me, and I'd literally click through the process myself. More than once, I hit a snag. I'd tell them, "If I don't understand it, how will the students?" That meant the team had to rework the interface and the text. But as frustrating as the exercise might have been, it resulted in a better product. Taking the time to perfect the details made the tool more relevant for the students who needed it.

My point is: you have to sweat the small stuff—because sometimes it turns out that the small stuff is actually the big stuff. I read a story once about a principal at a St. Louis elementary school who wanted to take on rampant truancy in her school. When she talked to parents, she realized that many of the kids didn't have clean clothes. Either they didn't have access to washing machines or their families couldn't afford detergent or the power had been shut off. Students were embarrassed to show up at school in dirty clothes. "I think people don't talk about not having clean clothes because it makes you want to cry or go home or run away or something," a student explained. "It doesn't feel good."

So the principal had a washer and dryer installed at her school, and she invited students who had missed more than ten days of class to do their laundry on campus. According to *CityLab,* in the first year of the initiative, more than 90 percent of the students they tracked boosted their attendance.

WORDS MATTER

Words have the ability to empower and to deceive, the power to soothe and to hurt. They can spread important ideas and wrongheaded ones.

They can spur people to action, for good or ill. Words are incredibly powerful, and people in power, whose words can carry furthest and fastest, have an obligation—a duty—to speak them with precision and wisdom. Scripture tells us, "The one who has knowledge uses words with restraint, and whoever has understanding is even-tempered."

I am keenly aware of the potential power that lives in my words—as someone who represents nearly forty million people, who seeks to give voice to the voiceless. And so when I speak, I do so with the knowledge that the words I choose matter.

First, what we call things, and how we define them, shapes how people think about them. Too often, words are used to degrade our impressions of issues, or of one another. It's why I insisted on better terminology in my work with sexually exploited youth. It was not right to refer to these individuals as "teen prostitutes." They were young people who were being exploited and preyed upon by adults.

When I was attorney general, I prosecuted a case against a man who had started a website called UGotPosted.com, which invited people to upload sexually explicit content featuring their former sexual partners. The man who ran the website would then demand payment from those who had been exploited in exchange for removing the images. In the press, and in common parlance, the act of posting the images was described as "revenge porn." In my office, people shorthanded the case as the "revenge porn" case.

I wasn't having any of that. Revenge is something you inflict on someone who has wronged you. These people hadn't wronged their perpetrators. It wasn't revenge. Nor was it pornography. The victims had never intended for the images to be publicly displayed. It was internet-based extortion, plain and simple, so we referred to it as cyber exploitation. I directed my team that we were not to use the term "revenge porn." I encouraged the media not to use the term, either. And I did so for one fundamental reason: words matter.

Second, I choose to speak truth. Even when it's uncomfortable. Even when it leaves people feeling uneasy. When you speak truth, people won't always walk away feeling good—and sometimes you won't feel so great about the reaction you receive. But at least all parties will walk away knowing it was an honest conversation.

That is not to say that all truth is uncomfortable, or that the intention is to cause discomfort. Many truths are incredibly hopeful. I am simply saying that the job of an elected official is not to sing a lullaby and soothe the country into a sense of complacency. The job is to speak truth, even in a moment that does not welcome or invite its utterance.

SHOW THE MATH

Many of us remember taking math tests in grade school, where it wasn't enough to simply answer a question. You had to show your work. That way, your teacher could see how your logic unfolded, step by step. If you got the solution right, the teacher would know that you hadn't just made a lucky guess. And if you got it wrong, she could see exactly where and why—and help you correct your mistake.

"Showing the math" is an approach that I've embraced throughout my career. In part, it's a methodology that helps me and my team test the logic of our own proposals and solutions. When we force ourselves to lay out our assumptions, we often find that there are certain parts of our arguments that assume things they shouldn't. So we go back and revisit them, we revise them, we dive deeper so that when we are ready to put forth a proposal, we can be confident in its soundness.

At the same time, I think leaders who are asking for the public's trust have a responsibility to show the math, too. We can't make other people's decisions for them, but we have to be able to show how we reached ours.

That's why, when I taught young lawyers how to put together a closing argument, I would remind them that it wasn't enough to get up in front of the jury and just tell them, "You must find eight." Their job was to get up there and show the jury that two plus two plus two plus two leads, categorically, to eight. I'd tell them to break down every element. Explain the logic of their argument. Show the jury how they reached their conclusion.

When you show people the math, you give them the tools to decide whether they agree with the solution. And even if they don't agree with everything, they may find that they agree with you most of the way—a kind of policy-making "partial credit" that can form the basis for constructive collaboration.

NO ONE SHOULD HAVE TO FIGHT ALONE

In the spring of 1966, Cesar Chavez led a 340-mile march of Latinx and Filipino farmworkers from California's Central Valley to its state capital in an effort to spur action and direct the country's eyes at the unconscionable ways that farmworkers were being treated. That summer, the United Farm Workers was formed, and under Chavez's leadership, it would become one of the most important civil rights and labor rights organizations in the country.

At the same time, two thousand miles away, Martin Luther King

Jr. was leading the Chicago Freedom Movement. Through speeches and rallies and marches and meetings, he demanded everything from the end of housing discrimination to the need for high-quality education for all.

In September 1966, King sent Chavez a telegram. He wrote about the many fronts on which the battle for equality must be fought—"in the urban slums, in the sweat shops of the factories and fields. Our separate struggles are really one—a struggle for freedom, for dignity, and for humanity."

That is the sentiment I believe we all must embrace. There are so many ongoing struggles in this country—against racism and sexism, against discrimination based on religion, national origin, and sexual orientation. Each of these struggles is unique. Each deserves its own attention and effort. And it would be wrong to suggest that the differences don't matter, or that one solution or one fight will alone solve them all. But at the same time, we should embrace the point that King made to Chavez—that what these struggles have in common is the pursuit of freedom, of basic human dignity. Black Lives Matter can't just be a rallying call for black people, but a banner under which all decent people will stand. The #MeToo movement cannot make lasting structural changes for women in the workplace unless the effort is joined by men. Victories by one group can lead to victories for others, in the courts and in society as a whole. None of us—none of us—should have to fight alone.

And if we are lucky enough to be in a position of power, if our voice and our actions can mobilize change, don't we have a special obligation? Being an ally can't just be about nodding when someone says something we agree with—important as that is. It must also be about action. It's our job to stand up for those who are not at the table where life-altering decisions are made. Not just those people who look like us. Not just those who need what we need. Not just those who have gained an audience with us. Our duty is to improve the human condition—in every way we can, for everyone who needs it.

IF IT'S WORTH FIGHTING FOR, IT'S A FIGHT WORTH HAVING

"On Monday, I stood in front of your office," a protester named Ana Maria Archila exclaimed to Republican senator Jeff Flake, of Arizona, as he got into an elevator. "I told the story of my sexual assault. I told it because I recognized in Dr. Ford's story that she is telling the truth. What you are doing is allowing someone who actually violated a woman to sit on the Supreme Court! This is not tolerable!"

As she spoke, Senator Flake nodded his head but didn't make eye contact. Then another survivor, Maria Gallagher, spoke up: "I was sexually assaulted and nobody believed me. I didn't tell anyone, and you're telling all women that they don't matter, that they should just stay quiet because if they tell you what happened to them you are going to ignore them. That's what happened to me, and that's what you are telling all women in America, that they don't matter."

Senator Flake continued to avoid the woman's gaze. "Look at me when I'm talking to you!" she said, her voice breaking. "You are telling me that my assault doesn't matter, that what happened to me doesn't matter, and that you're going to let people who do these things into power. That's what you're telling me when you vote for him. Don't look away from me!" The elevators closed, and Senator Flake made his way to the room where the Judiciary Committee was holding a vote on the confirmation of Brett Kavanaugh.

I had been appointed to the Judiciary Committee ten months earlier and had expected, at some point, to be part of a Supreme Court confirmation process. But when Anthony Kennedy announced his retirement on June 27, 2018, I counted myself among the millions of people who were stunned and dismayed, especially when we learned that Judge Kavanaugh had been chosen to replace him.

Before we ever knew the name Christine Blasey Ford, we knew from Judge Kavanaugh's public statements, his writings, and his judicial record that he was hostile to civil rights and voting rights and reproductive rights. We knew he would be a reliable vote against unions, against the environment, against corporate regulation.

We knew before his first set of confirmation hearings that there was something in his past that Judge Kavanaugh and the White House were trying to hide. We knew it because 90 percent of Judge Kavanaugh's record was withheld from members of the Judiciary Committee.

We knew after those first hearings that Brett Kavanaugh had misled the Senate under oath: about his involvement with stolen documents, about his work with controversial judicial nominees, about his role in Bush-era warrantless wiretapping.

We knew all of this first. And then we learned her name. And then we learned her story.

We learned that when she was in high school, Christine Blasey Ford had gone to a gathering at a house with several people, where Brett Kavanaugh had forced himself on top of her, had grinded against her, and had groped her while trying to take off her clothes. We learned that when she tried to scream, he had put his hand over her mouth, that she believed he was going to rape her, that she feared he might inadvertently kill her.

"I was able to get up and run out of the room," Dr. Ford explained as she testified under oath in front of the Judiciary Committee about the attack. "Directly across from the bedroom was a small bathroom. I ran inside the bathroom and locked the door. I heard Brett and Mark leave the bedroom laughing and loudly walk down the narrow stairs, pinballing off the walls on the way down.

"I waited, and when I did not hear them come back up the stairs, I left the bathroom, ran down the stairs, through the living room, and left the house," she continued. "I remember being on the street and feeling an enormous sense of relief that I had escaped from the house and that Brett and Mark were not coming after me."

I watched her in such awe as she told her story. In front of Dr. Ford sat all twenty-one members of the Senate Judiciary Committee, looking down from a raised dais. Behind her sat an audience of many strangers. To her left was Rachel Mitchell, an Arizona prosecutor who would question Dr. Ford instead of the Republican committee members—all men—who apparently doubted their own ability to question her. There were bodyguards in the room, too, whose protection Dr. Ford now needed. And, of course, there were the cameras, broadcasting every moment, every movement, every word spoken and tear shed in front of a national audience. This was no place for a person to have to talk about the worst day of her life.

And yet there she was in front of us and the world—even after death threats, even after having to leave her home, even after countless vile attacks hurled at her online. Christine Blasey Ford came to Washington out of a sense of what she called her civic duty and testified in one of the most extraordinary displays of courage I have seen in my lifetime.

Then Judge Kavanaugh responded.

"This whole two-week effort has been a calculated and orchestrated political hit," Kavanaugh railed at the committee, "fueled with apparent pent-up anger about President Trump and the 2016 election, fear that has been unfairly stoked about my judicial record, revenge on behalf of the Clintons, and millions of dollars in money from outside left-wing opposition groups!" Fuming, he declared that "the behavior of several of the Democratic members of this committee at the hearing a few weeks ago was an embarrassment." He went on for forty-five minutes. And that was just his opening statement.

"I like beer. I like beer," Kavanaugh said in response to a question from Senator Sheldon Whitehouse, a Democrat from Rhode Island. "I don't know if you do. Do you like beer, Senator, or not? What do you like to drink? Senator, what do you like to drink?"

Minnesota senator Amy Klobuchar, also a Democrat, asked, "So you're saying there's never been a case where you drank so much that you didn't remember what happened the night before, or part of what happened?"

"It's—you're asking about, you know, blackout," he said, with visible frustration. "I don't know. Have you?"

"Could you answer the question, Judge? I just—so you—that's not happened. Is that your answer?"

"Yeah," he said smugly. "And I'm curious if you have."

"I have no drinking problem, Judge," she said, not moments after having described how alcoholism had deeply affected her father.

"Yeah, nor do I," he retorted. It was, if anything, a revealing moment from a man who had sworn up and down that he always treats women with respect.

Near the end of the hearing, it was my turn to question the witness. As everyone was aware, Dr. Ford had taken and passed a polygraph examination. She had called for outside witnesses and expert witnesses to testify. And, most important, she had called for an FBI investigation. I asked Kavanaugh if he would do the same. He repeatedly evaded answering—just as he had done on many questions from my colleagues up to that point. The contrast between Dr. Ford's sincerity and Judge Kavanaugh's caginess was striking.

As was his willingness to mislead the committee. He gave patently false statements about the meanings of certain terms he'd written in his high school yearbook. He downplayed key aspects of his drinking. He was dishonest about the kinds of gatherings he attended in high school.

And that temper. Judge Kavanaugh's flagrant behavior was so outside the norms of judicial standards that in the days after the hearing, the American Bar Association reopened its evaluation of him, and more than 2,400 academics signed an open letter to the Senate saying they were "united, as professors of law and scholars of judicial institutions, in believing that he did not display the impartiality and judicial temperament requisite to sit on the highest court of our land."

And yet from the moment the hearing was over, it seemed the Republican caucus was ready and eager to move on, and that, despite Kavanaugh's performance and despite Dr. Ford's testimony, the committee would push forward with a vote. Shortly after Judge Kavanaugh finished testifying on Thursday night, Republican leaders scheduled a committee vote on his nomination for Friday morning.

There are many reasons why survivors of sexual assault don't report, and one is the fear—or assumption—that they will not be believed. "I was calculating daily the risk/benefit for me of coming forward, and wondering if I would just be jumping in front of a train that was going where it was going anyway," Dr. Ford had testified that morning, "and that I would just be personally annihilated."

As Republican senators pressed ahead, that fear seemed all too justified. Those senators were choosing not to believe Christine Blasey Ford, even though she had risked everything to warn them about what she knew, even though she had reached out before Judge Kavanaugh had even been nominated, even though she had no reason to lie.

They chose not to believe Dr. Ford even as they refused to do a real investigation, even though she had corroborating information that backed up her claims, even though Judge Kavanaugh had more than one accuser. For Judge Kavanaugh's defenders, the cost of believing her—the cost of the truth itself—was simply too high.

"This has been about raw power," I said the next morning after leading a walkout of the committee hearing. "You're seeing that on display in the hearing this morning; you're seeing that in the process from the beginning. . . . This is a failure of this body to do what it has always said it is about, which is to be deliberative."

When I returned to the chamber, there were rumblings. It appeared that Senator Flake had been affected by the survivors who'd stopped him in the elevator on the way to the hearing that morning. After consultation with Senator Chris Coons, a Democrat from Delaware, and others, Senator Flake called for a delay to the final vote so the FBI could be given a week to investigate further. It gave us an unexpected reprieve.

We know now that the victory felt in that moment was fleeting—but that does not diminish its significance. Two survivors of sexual assault standing in front of an elevator seemed to change the mind of a senator whom most saw as immovable, securing an FBI investigation and forcing a delay in an out-of-control process. In that moment, those two brave women were more powerful than all the Democratic senators on the Judiciary Committee. Together they paused history—and gave us one last chance to prevail.

But the White House had one more card to play. The administration limited the scope of the investigation, dictating whom the FBI could speak to, even preventing agents from following up with Dr. Ford and Judge Kavanaugh themselves. And yet for key swing senators, the fact that there had been an investigation of any kind was enough. On October 6, 2018, I stood on the Senate floor and watched as Judge Kavanaugh got confirmed.

I have been writing these words in the days since, even as I finish this manuscript. Like many Americans, I am still processing what our country has just been through. But for now, I will say this: It would be a mistake to downplay the consequences of having Justice Kavanaugh on the Supreme Court. With this lifetime appointment, he will be in a position, along with the conservative majority on the court, to end a woman's right to choose as we know it; to invalidate the Affordable Care Act; to undo the legal basis by which corporations are regulated; to unravel fundamental rights to vote, to marry, and to privacy.

I worry about the ways his partisanship and temperament will infect the court, how it will color his decision making, how it will disadvantage so many who seek relief in the courts. I worry about what it will do to the court itself to have a man credibly accused of sexual assault among its justices. I worry about the message that has been sent yet again to Americans and the world: that in our country, today, someone can rage, lash out, resist accountability, and still ascend to a position of extraordinary power over other people's lives.

But here's what I am not worried about: I am not worried about our commitment to the fight for a better country. I am not worried that this experience has diminished our will. We chose this fight not because we were sure we could win but because we were sure it was right. Because that should be all that matters. And I know it is no bromide of consolation to say what is certainly true: that even though we didn't prevail, this fight mattered.

Dr. Ford did not come forward in vain. As Senator Patrick Leahy said of her decision to speak, "Bravery is contagious." The cameras and microphones that Dr. Ford never sought carried her story and her message far beyond our committee room, inspiring women and men to tell the stories of their sexual assaults, many for the first time. On the day that Dr. Ford testified, the National Sexual Assault Hotline saw a 200 percent increase in calls. Women were calling in to C-SPAN to share their stories. Writing op-eds. Telling their husbands and fathers. They were speaking their truth—and, in so doing, making plainer than ever the pervasiveness of sexual violence.

These survivors took no pleasure in reliving their own pain. Many who came forward had no intention of seeking justice, much less an expectation of receiving it. But they spoke out, like the survivors of Harvey Weinstein, Larry Nassar, and Bill Cosby, like survivors of abuse in the Catholic Church, to help ensure that this conversation will never again be limited to whispers. Sexual violence is real. It is wrong. It affects men as well as women. And no one should suffer in silence. The faces, the voices, the crowds who filled the hearing room and the Hart Building and the streets outside the Supreme Court, the people who flooded social media with messages of solidarity and shared anguish, all command us to listen, to respect, to believe, and to act. Their voices, like Dr. Ford's, will have lasting reach.

Indeed, though this battle is over, the scope of its impact is yet to be seen. History has shown that one person's willingness to stand up for what is right can be the spark that ignites far-reaching change. Anita Hill's testimony wasn't enough to keep Clarence Thomas off the Supreme Court in 1991, but it brought the term "sexual harassment" into the mainstream and started a national conversation. Less than two months after Hill's testimony, Congress passed the Civil Rights Act of 1991, which expanded the remedies available to victims of sexual harassment. The following year, Democratic women took the 1992 elections by storm, doubling the number of women in the House and tripling the number of women in the Senate.

I am not naive. I walk the same halls where one Republican senator told survivors of sexual assault to "grow up," and where another described protesting survivors as a "mob," even as the president he serves was inciting a crowd to humiliate Dr. Ford. I know—we all know—that there are miles still to go before women are accorded the full respect and dignity we deserve. But I am heartened by the unprecedented numbers of women running for office, and the many more who have been politically energized. I am heartened by the new bonds being forged across boundaries of race, age, background, experience, and gender as women and men stand shoulder to shoulder for justice, equality, and basic rights.

This progress is the product of a movement. A movement that started before Anita Hill ever testified and will continue long after Dr. Ford becomes a hero in our children's history books. We will grow stronger through every effort, even when we face setbacks. We will draw wisdom from every chapter, even when those lessons are hard. We will face what is to come with conviction that change is possible—knowing that truth is like the sun. It always rises.

YOU MAY BE THE FIRST.
DON'T BE THE LAST.

I was in the middle of my first campaign for district attorney when I got a call from an old law school friend, Lisa, who was working as a career counselor at a nearby law school. She had met a young black woman named Venus Johnson, a second-year law student who had grown up in Oakland, the child of an immigrant, with dreams of becoming a prosecutor. Not surprisingly, when my friend heard Venus's story, she thought of me.

We arranged to spend a day together in the fall of 2003, and from the moment I shook Venus's hand, I could feel this incredible sense of commonality. I could see myself in her. She was kind enough to spend the day following me around while I campaigned and ran errands. At one point, we ended up shopping for a wedding present for one of my dear friends. (I settled on bedding.) At another, we drove past a storefront that had a sign for my opponent in the window.

"Come on, let's go," I told Venus as I grabbed one of my own signs out of the trunk. We went in and I shook hands with the store owner and asked him for his support.

"But . . . um . . . I have another candidate's sign in my window," he said, not sure what to make of me. "That's okay," I told him. "You can put mine in the window, too!" He agreed, and we were on our way.

Over lunch, Venus and I talked about the reasons she wanted to be a prosecutor, and the kind of work she had hoped to do. I learned that her father had a long career in law enforcement, and that she always imagined herself fighting on behalf of victims. I told her that I had taken a similar path and recommended she follow her instincts and join the Alameda County District Attorney's Office. I'd be happy, I told her, to make some calls on her behalf.

She seemed to wonder why I was doing this for her. I told her that there was something my mother used to say that I always held close. "You may be the first. Don't be the last." My mother had gotten to where she was because of the help of mentors. I had gotten to where I was because of mentors, too. And I intended to be a mentor to as many people as I could during the course of my career.

A few years after my first conversation with Venus, she got the job she'd been dreaming of in the Alameda County DA's Office. She worked there for eight years, and, like me, she specialized in helping victims of sexual violence. We spoke regularly over those years. In 2014, she joined me in the attorney general's office, and about one year into her working for me on legislative matters, I had a specific request for her.

I called her into my office. "I want you to be my associate attorney general and my de facto chief of staff." There was a pregnant pause. "Me?" she asked. "Yes, you!" I've had a lot of good fortune in my life, but I'm not sure I've ever felt as lucky as the moment she said yes. She was as wonderful at the job as I thought she would be. In addition to keeping things moving, staffing me, and being the last person in line to ensure that I was prepared for meetings and press conferences, she helped to manage a complex bureaucracy and lead major initiatives on my behalf as a legal and policy adviser. I couldn't have asked for a better member of the team.

During those years, we spent a lot of time together. We've continued to speak since our time in the attorney general's office. Sometimes about her cases. Sometimes about career moves she was considering. Once about a recipe for a really amazing chicken broth.

Venus was part of the inspiration for a speech I often give, especially in front of groups of young women. I like to induct them into what I call the Role Models Club.

I tell them that, whatever profession they choose, they've got to keep raising their hands, to share—and take credit for—their good ideas, and to know that they deserve to rise as high as they dare to climb. I also tell them that when they see others in need, they've got to go out of their way to lift them up.

I tell them that sometimes members of the Role Models Club can feel alone. Sometimes they may think, "Do I have to carry this burden by myself?" The fact is, they will find themselves in rooms where no one else looks like them. And breaking barriers can be scary. When you break through a glass ceiling, you're going to get cut, and it's going to hurt. It is not without pain. But I ask them to look around at one another and hold that image in their brains and their hearts and their souls. I tell them to remember that they are never in those rooms alone—that we are all in there with them, cheering them on. And so when they stand up, when they speak out, when they express their thoughts and feelings, they should know that we're right there in that room with them and we've got their back. I know Venus always has mine.

I've seen a lot in my years of public service. And what I've learned can't all be boiled down. But I've come away with the firm belief that people are fundamentally good. And that, given the chance, they will usually reach out a hand to help their neighbor.

I've learned, through history and experience, that not all progress is gradual or linear. Sometimes it simply goes from one plateau to another. Sometimes we fall back tragically. Sometimes we leap forward and achieve things beyond the realm of what we thought possible. I believe that our job is to provide the force propulsion that will get us to a higher plane.

We have yet to achieve that perfect union. Alongside the great achievements of the American experiment lies a dark history that we have to deal with in the present. In the face of powerful headwinds, it's easy to become tired. To become overwhelmed. But we cannot give up. The beginning of our downfall comes when we stop aspiring.

Let me speak one final truth: For all of our differences, for all the battles, for all the fights, we are still one American family, and we should act like it. We have so much more in common than what separates us. We need to paint a picture of the future in which everyone can see themselves, and everyone is seen. A vibrant portrait of a vibrant United States, where everyone is treated with equal dignity and each of us has the opportunities to make the most of our own lives. That is the vision worth fighting for, born out of love of country.

It is an age-old fight. And what we know about it is this: Victories won can be lost in complacency. Battles lost can be won with new effort. Every generation has to recommit to the work, to the effort, and to the true meaning of the word "patriot." A patriot is not someone who condones the conduct of our country, whatever it does; it is someone who fights every day for the ideals of the country, whatever it takes.

What I have seen, especially since becoming a United States senator, is that this is a fight born out of optimism, too. I see hundreds of Dreamers walking the halls of the Capitol who believe that if they are heard, they can make a difference. And they will. I see it in the parents who traveled from all over the country to Washington with their disabled children, to show Congress the faces of those who would lose coverage if the Affordable Care Act was repealed. I see it in the women who fight every day for the right to make their own decisions about their bodies. I see it in the Parkland survivors, who march and fight and organize for gun safety laws, and who have achieved significant victories that tell them a better future is possible.

When I travel our country, I see that optimism in the eyes of five- and seven- and ten-year-olds who feel a sense of purpose in being part of the fight. I see it, and feel it, in the energy of the people I meet. Yes, people are marching. Yes, people are shouting. But they are doing it from a place of optimism. That's why they've got their babies with them. That's why my parents took me in a stroller to civil rights marches. Because as overwhelming as the circumstances may be, they believe, as I do, that a better future is possible for us all.

My daily challenge to myself is to be part of the solution, to be a joyful warrior in the battle to come. My challenge to you is to join that effort. To stand up for our ideals and our values. Let's not throw up our hands when it's time to roll up our sleeves. Not now. Not tomorrow. Not ever.

Years from now, our children and our grandchildren will look up and lock eyes with us. They will ask us where we were when the stakes were so high. They will ask us what it was like. I don't want us to just tell them how we felt. I want us to tell them what we did.

ACKNOWLEDGMENTS

When I sat down to write about my life, I didn't expect the process to become a life experience of its own. During one of the most tumultuous years in recent memory, my weeks started early and ended late, and I spent most weekends working on this book: recalling the professional experiences that had led up to it; revisiting the childhood that formed my way of thinking; and reflecting on what this inflection point represents. Writing this book has reinforced for me what drew me to public service and what will always be worth fighting for, and I am so grateful to everyone in my life who helped me along the way. There are a lot of you to thank.

First, I want to thank the people of California, whom I've been so honored to represent. Thank you for believing in a brighter future for our state and our nation, and for working so hard to make it so. Thank you for believing in me, for putting your trust in me all these years. I want you to know that I try hard to earn it every day. And I want to especially thank the people who wrote letters to me and let me share excerpts in this book. Your stories matter.

I also want to thank my extraordinary Senate staff, in Washington and California, for the critical work you do each day on behalf of the American people. I am so grateful for your sense of purpose and your dedication. I know this work is personal to each of you. In particular, I want to thank Tyrone Gale, who started with me as my press secretary on day one in the Senate, and whom we recently lost to cancer. Tyrone is irreplaceable. He was an exceptional talent and an exceptional person—kind, warm, generous, and deeply committed to public service. Those of us who knew him will carry his memory forward, and try each day to live up to the example he set.

Like everything in my life, this book would not have been possible without the love, support, and help of family. Doug, thank you for your advice, encouragement, and feedback on this project. Cole and Ella, you are an endless source of love and pure joy for me. As I watch you enter the world, choosing your own unique paths, it makes me so proud, every day, to be your Momala.

Maya, writing this book was like reliving our childhood. The list of things I have to thank you for is too long for these pages. So let me use this simply to thank you for the input and insights you offered throughout this process. Thank you, also, for bringing me a brother in Tony, and for Meena. Meena, I remember you at two years old, walking around the house, literally in my shoes. Now you're a leader in your own right who has forged an important path and whose advice I cherish. Thank you for everything, especially for my baby nieces, Amara and Leela, and their amazing dad, Nik.

Thank you to my father, who, when I was a young girl, encouraged me to be fearless. Thank you to my Chittis, Sarala and Chinni, and to my uncle Balu, for the love you've shared with me across great distances. Thank you to Auntie Lenore for being such an important part of my life, and to Uncle Aubrey, for sharing memories of those early days during the writing process. And thank you to Mimi and Denise for always encouraging me.

To Chrisette and Reggie, thank you for encouraging me to write this book at the earliest stage. I've mentioned many of my dearest personal friends in this book and could have written volumes more about the experiences we've shared. Suffice it to say, I am so grateful to Amy, Chrisette, Lo, Stacey, Vanessa, and everyone (too many to mention here) with whom I've been blessed to travel this journey of life. When people ask me the secret to life, I tell them it's having good friends who become your family. That's what you've all been for me, and what I've tried to be for you. And thank you for all the godchildren you've brought into my life.

This book would not have been possible without the support of my broader family, too—staff and former staff who have been at my side throughout the years.

Thank you to my longtime advisers, Ace Smith, Sean Clegg, and Juan Rodriguez, for always being there for me, and for your insights and perspectives through the years.

I am deeply grateful to my former staff from my days as attorney general and district attorney. You've all gone off to do such wonderful things but have remained part of the family. There are so many to whom I am grateful. Special thanks to Venus Johnson, Debbie Mesloh, Brian Nelson, Lateefah Simon, Dan Suvor, Michael Troncoso, and others for all your help with this project. And thank you to Josie Duffy Rice, who is like a niece to me, for your comments and suggestions on the manuscript. I have so much respect for your perspective and your perceptions. I also want to thank John Pérez, whom I still refer to as Mr. Speaker, as well as Marc Elias for your wise counsel.

Of course, none of this would be possible without the extraordinary team at Penguin, led by Scott Moyers. Scott, you were the best editor a person could have asked for, and I will always be grateful to you for understanding the vision of the book I wanted to write. Thank you to Creative Artists Agency, in particular to Mollie Glick, David Larabell, Craig Gering, Michelle Kydd Lee, and Ryder White, for all of your work to make this happen.

I want to thank my collaborators, Vinca LaFleur and Dylan Loewe, for your commitment, compassion, and yes, your patience. You made this process a joy.

And a big thank-you to their research and fact-checking team: Brian Agler, Zach Hindin, Steven Kelly, Machmud Makhmudov, Maggie Mallon, and Raul Quintana. And thank you to Dorothy Hearst for our important early work together on this project

Finally, I want to thank all the people I love that are no longer with us. I don't know what kind of book distribution Penguin has in heaven, but, Aunt Mary, Uncle Freddy, Uncle Sherman, Mr. and Mrs. Shelton, Aunt Chris, Auntie Bea, Henry Ramsey, Jim Rivaldo, Mrs. Wilson, and my grandparents: this book is a tribute to how much you meant to me, how much of my life was shaped by you, how much you mattered.

Mommy, you are the star of this book because you were the reason for everything. It's been almost ten years since we lost you, and I miss you so much. Life without you is still hard to accept. But I believe you are staring down at us. When I am stuck with a hard decision, I ask, "What would Mommy think?" And in that way, you are here. It is my sincerest hope that this book will help those who never met you understand the kind of person you were. What it meant to be Shyamala Harris. And what it means to be her daughter.

NOTES

PREFACE

xiii **Shortly after, the Associated Press:** Phil Willon, "Kamala Harris Breaks a Color Barrier with Her U.S. Senate Win," *Los Angeles Times,* November 8, 2016, http://www.latimes.com/politics/la-pol-ca-senate-race-kamala-harris -wins-20161108-story.html.

xv **"We cannot play ostrich," he said:** Thurgood Marshall, "The Meaning of Liberty," acceptance speech after receiving the Liberty Award on July 4, 1992, http://www.naacpldf.org/press-release/thurgood-marshalls-stirring -acceptance-speech-after-receiving-prestigious-liberty-award-on-july-4-1992.

CHAPTER 1: FOR THE PEOPLE

8 **They met on Sundays:** Donna Murch, "The Campus and the Street: Race, Migration, and the Origins of the Black Panther Party in Oakland, CA," *Souls* 9, no. 4 (2007): 333–45, https://doi.org/10.1080/10999940701703794.

9 **SFSU had a student-run:** Martha Biondi, *The Black Revolution on Campus* (Berkeley: University of California Press, 2012), 47.

17 **Pollar once told a journalist:** Richard Ramella, "The Rainbow Sign Can Use Some Help," *Berkeley Gazette*, April 18, 1975, 14.

32 **"The penal code was not created":** Scott Duke Harris, "In Search of Elusive Justice," *Los Angeles Times Magazine,* October 24, 2004, http://articles .latimes.com/2004/oct/24/magazine/tm-kamala43.

34 **She was a groundbreaker:** Harris, "In Search of Elusive Justice."

CHAPTER 2: A VOICE FOR JUSTICE

40 **toxic waste polluted the soil:** *Pollution, Health, Environmental Racism and Injustice: A Toxic Inventory of Bayview Hunters Point, San Francisco* (San Francisco: Hunters Point Mothers Environmental Health and Justice Committee, Huntersview Tenants Association, and Greenaction for Health & Environmental Justice, 2012), http://greenaction.org/wp-content /uploads/2012/08/TheStateoftheEnvironment090204Final.pdf.

45 **I introduced criminal justice reform legislation:** A Bill to Clarify the Rights of All Persons Who Are Held or Detained at a Port of Entry or at Any Detention Facility Overseen by U.S. Customs and Border Protection or U.S. Immigration and Customs Enforcement, S. 349, 115th Cong. (2017–2018), https://www.congress.gov/bill/115th-congress/senate-bill/349.

47 **95 percent of our country's:** Nicolas Fandos, "A Study Documents the Paucity of Black Elected Prosecutors: Zero in Most States," *New York Times*, July 7, 2015, https://www.nytimes.com/2015/07/07/us/a-study-documents -the-paucity-of-black-elected-prosecutors-zero-in-most-states.html.

48 **All told, we had more:** The University of London, Institute of Criminal Policy Research, *World Prison Brief,* accessed October 25, 2018, http://www .prisonstudies.org/highest-to-lowest/prison-population-total?field_region _taxonomy_tid=All.

53 **In 2004, for example:** Lee Romney, "Bill Would Fight Child Prostitution," *Los Angeles Times,* September 5, 2004, http://articles.latimes.com/2004 /sep/05/local/me-child5.

54 **Lateefah was a teenager:** Kevin Cartwright, "Activist Awarded for Work with Troubled Youth," *The Crisis* 111, no. 1 (January/February 2004): 9, https://books.google.com/books?id=Ice84BEC2yoC&pg.

54 **"I saw resilience in these young women":** Carolyn Jones, "Lateefah Simon: Youth Advocate Nominated as Visionary of the Year," *SFGate*, January 5,

2015, https://www.sfgate.com/visionsf/article/Lateefah-Simon-Youth-advocate
-nominated-as-5993578.php.

55 **nearly 70 percent commit a crime:** "NRRC Facts and Trends," National
Reentry Resource Center, Council of State Governments Justice Center,
https://csgjusticecenter.org/nrrc/facts-and-trends.

58 **Another among them was:** Bob Egelko, "Judge Thelton Henderson Ending
Long Career Rallying for Oppressed," *San Francisco Chronicle,* January 15,
2017, https://www.sfchronicle.com/bayarea/article/Judge-Thelton
-Henderson-ending-long-career-10859424.php; Associated Press, "Judge
Thelton Henderson, Lawyer Fired for Loaning MLK a Car, Retiring,"
Al.com, January 20, 2017, https://www.al.com/news/birmingham/index.ssf
/2017/01/judge_thelton_henderson_lawyer.html; and Jenifer Warren, "Judge
Is No Stranger to Controversy," *Los Angeles Times,* December 16, 1996,
http://articles.latimes.com/1996-12-16/news/mn-9670_1_federal-judges.

59 **It represented smart, effective stewardship:** U.S. Department of Justice,
Office of Justice Programs, *Back on Track: A Problem-Solving Reentry Court,*
by Jacquelyn L. Rivers and Lenore Anderson, FS 00316 (Washington, DC,
September 2009), https://www.bja.gov/Publications/backontrackfs.pdf.

64 **the median savings account:** Board of Governors of the Federal Reserve
System, Survey of Consumer Finances, 2016 (Washington, DC, 2016),
https://www.federalreserve.gov/econres/scfindex.htm.

64 *The New York Times Magazine* **told:** Nick Pinto, "The Bail Trap," *New York
Times Magazine,* August 13, 2015, https://www.nytimes.com/2015
/08/16/magazine/the-bail-trap.html.

65 **Latino men pay nearly:** Kamala Harris and Rand Paul, "To Shrink Jails,
Let's Reform Bail," op-ed, *New York Times,* July 20, 2017, https://www
.nytimes.com/2017/07/20/opinion/kamala-harris-and-rand-paul-lets-reform
-bail.html.

66 **According to the FBI, more people:** Christopher Ingraham, "More People
Were Arrested Last Year over Pot Than for Murder, Rape, Aggravated
Assault and Robbery—Combined," *Wonkblog, Washington Post,* September
26, 2017, https://www.washingtonpost.com/news/wonk/wp/2017/09/26/more
-people-were-arrested-last-year-over-pot-than-for-murder-rape-aggravated
-assault-and-robbery-combined.

66 **Between 2001 and 2010:** "Marijuana Arrests by the Numbers," ACLU,
https://www.aclu.org/gallery/marijuana-arrests-numbers.

66 **93 percent of the people:** John Annese, "NYPD Ripped for 'Racially Biased Practices' After Stats Show Cops Still Targeting Minorities for Pot Arrests," *New York Daily News,* April 27, 2018, http://www.nydailynews.com /new-york/nyc-crime/nypd-targeting-minorities-marijuana-arrests-2018 -article-1.3957719.

67 **In the decade after we:** *33 States Reform Criminal Justice Policies Through Justice Reinvestment* (Philadelphia: Pew Charitable Trusts, November 2016), http://www.pewtrusts.org/~/media/assets/2017/08/33_states_reform _criminal_justice_policies_through_justice_reinvestment.pdf.

67 **And since 2010, twenty-three states:** Chris Mai and Ram Subramanian, *The Price of Prisons: Examining State Spending Trends, 2010–2015* (New York: Vera Institute of Justice, May 2017), https://www.vera.org/publications /price-of-prisons-2015-state-spending-trends.

68 **Nearly four years after Ferguson:** Jim Salter, "Missouri Report: Blacks 85 Percent More Likely to Be Stopped," AP News, June 1, 2018, https://apnews .com/58d9ad846ef14b93915ee26d3cf4663e.

68 **three times more likely to:** C.K., "Black Boys Are the Least Likely of Any Group to Escape Poverty," *The Economist,* April 2, 2018, https: //www.economist.com/blogs/democracyinamerica/2018/04/broken-ladder.

68 **they are arrested twice as often:** C.K., "Black Boys."

68 **six times as likely as white men:** Janelle Jones, John Schmitt, and Valerie Wilson, *50 Years After the Kerner Commission* (Washington, DC: Economic Policy Institute, February 26, 2018), https://www.epi.org/publication /50-years-after-the-kerner-commission.

68–69 **sentences nearly 20 percent longer:** American Civil Liberties Union, "Written Submission of the American Civil Liberties Union on Racial Disparities in Sentencing Hearing on Reports of Racism in the Justice System of the United States," submitted to the Inter-American Commission on Human Rights, 153rd Session, October 27, 2014, https://www.aclu.org /sites/default/files/assets/141027_iachr_racial_disparities_aclu_submission _0.pdf.

CHAPTER 3: UNDERWATER

76 **"Garden of the Sun":** Wallace Smith, *Garden of the Sun: A History of the San Joaquin Valley, 1772–1939,* ed. William B. Secrest Jr., 2nd ed. (Fresno, CA: Craven Street Books, 2004).

76   **nearly 40 percent Latinx:** Michael B. Teitz, Charles Dietzel, and William Fulton, *Urban Development Futures in the San Joaquin Valley* (San Francisco: Public Policy Institute of California, 2005), 18, http://www.solimar.org /pdf/urbandevsanjoaquin.pdf.

78   **lost more than half their value:** Bonhia Lee, "Emerging from the Bust, Fresno Housing Market Is Healthiest Nationwide," *Fresno Bee,* January 5, 2016, https://www.fresnobee.com/news/business/article53168660.html.

78   **the unemployment rate had soared:** U.S. Bureau of Labor Statistics, *Unemployment Rate in Fresno, CA (MSA),* retrieved from FRED, Federal Reserve Bank of St. Louis, https://fred.stlouisfed.org/series/FRES406UR.

78–79   **Ten years after purchasing their home:** Alana Semuels, "The Never-Ending Foreclosure," *The Atlantic,* December 1, 2017, https://www.theatlantic.com /business/archive/2017/12/the-neverending-foreclosure/547181.

79   **the Humane Society was reporting:** "Hidden Victims of Mortgage Crisis: Pets," NBC News, January 29, 2008, http://www.nbcnews.com/id/22900994 /ns/business-real_estate/t/hidden-victims-mortgage-crisis-pets/#. W2dfby2ZOEI; and Linton Weeks, "The Recession and Pets: Hard Times for Snoopy," *All Things Considered,* NPR, April 6, 2009, https://www.npr .org/templates/story/story.php?storyId=102238430.

79   **Roughly 5 million homeowners:** "2010's Record-Breaking Foreclosure Crisis: By the Numbers," *The Week,* January 14, 2011, http://theweek.com /articles/488017/2010s-recordbreaking-foreclosure-crisis-by-numbers.

79   **And 2.5 million foreclosures:** "2010's Record-Breaking Foreclosure Crisis."

81   **to speed up the foreclosure process:** " 'Robo-Signers' Add to Foreclosure Fraud Mess," NBC News, October 13, 2010, http://www.nbcnews.com/id /39641329/ns/business-real_estate/t/robo-signers-add-foreclosure-fraud-mess.

83   **"a woman running for attorney general":** ProsperitasMember, "Pundits Explain Why Kamala Will Never Win (Oops)," YouTube video, 3:00, posted December 7, 2010, https://www.youtube.com/watch?v=1HemG2iLkTY.

86   **I was now ahead in the race:** Jon Brooks, "Video: Steve Cooley Prematurely Declares Victory Last Night," KQED News, November 3, 2010, https: //www.kqed.org/news/4195/video-steve-cooley-prematurely-declares-victory -last-night.

87   **Of the nearly nine million ballots cast:** Jack Leonard, "Kamala Harris Wins Attorney General's Race as Steve Cooley Concedes [Updated]," *Los Angeles Times,* November 24, 2010, http://latimesblogs.latimes.com/lanow/2010/11 /steve-cooley-kamala-harris-attorney-general.html.

89 **37,000 homeowners lined up:** CBS News, "The Next Housing Shock," *60 Minutes* report, YouTube video, 14:06, posted April 3, 2011, https://www .youtube.com/watch?v=QwrO6jhtC5E.

89 **"In the 1930s, we had bread lines":** Ryan Chittum, "*60 Minutes* with a Good Look at the Foreclosure Scandal," *Columbia Journalism Review,* April 5, 2011, https://archives.cjr.org/the_audit/60_minutes_with_a_good_look _at.php; and CBS News, "The Next Housing Shock."

90 **the lender said they could help:** California Department of Justice, "Attorney General Kamala D. Harris Convenes Roundtable with Foreclosure Victims," YouTube video, 15:59, posted November 22, 2011, https://www .youtube.com/watch?v=QbycqFzva5Q.

94 **which owned 62 percent of new mortgages:** Douglas J. Elliott, "The Federal Role in Housing Finance: Principal Issues and Policy Proposals," in *The Future of Housing Finance: Restructuring the U.S. Residential Mortgage Market,* ed. Martin Neil Baily (Washington, DC: Brookings Institution Press, 2011), https://www.brookings.edu/wp-content/uploads/2016/07 /thefutureofhousingfinance_chapter.pdf.

100 **in December 2011 she and I:** State of California Department of Justice, Office of the Attorney General, "Attorneys General of California and Nevada Announce Mortgage Investigation Alliance," press release, December 6, 2011, https://www.oag.ca.gov/news/press-releases/attorneys -general-california-and-nevada-announce-mortgage-investigation-alliance.

107 **Parents' dreams of financing:** Janis Bowdler, Roberto Quercia, and David Andrew Smith, *The Foreclosure Generation: The Long-Term Impact of the Housing Crisis on Latino Children and Families* (Washington, DC: National Council of La Raza, 2010), https://communitycapital.unc.edu /files/2010/02/Foreclosure-Generation.pdf.

107 **"the rise in US unemployment":** Aaron Reeves et al., "Increase in State Suicide Rates in the USA During Economic Recession," *The Lancet* 380, no. 9856 (November 24, 2012): 1813–14, https://www.thelancet.com/journals /lancet/article/PIIS0140-6736%2812%2961910-2/fulltext.

107 **In Fresno, the overwhelming majority:** Patrick Clark, "Most U.S. Homes Are Worth Less Than Before the Crash," Bloomberg, May 3, 2017, https: //www.bloomberg.com/news/articles/2017-05-03/most-u-s-homes-are-worth -less-than-before-the-crash.

107 **the burden hit black families disproportionately:** Sarah Burd-Sharps and Rebecca Rasch, *Impact of the US Housing Crisis on the Racial Wealth Gap*

Across Generations (New York: Social Research Council, June 2015), https: //www.aclu.org/files/field_document/discrimlend_final.pdf.

108 **$345 billion in subprime loans:** Peter Rudegeair, Rachel Louise Ensign, and Coulter Jones, "Big Banks Find a Back Door to Finance Subprime Loans," *Wall Street Journal,* April 10, 2018, https://www.wsj.com/articles/big-banks -find-a-back-door-to-finance-subprime-loans-1523352601.

CHAPTER 4: WEDDING BELLS

112 **eighteen thousand same-sex couples:** "Fed Court OKs Immediate Gay Marriages in California; SF Conducts 1st," KPIX CBS San Francisco, June 28, 2013, http://sanfrancisco.cbslocal.com/2013/06/28/federal-court-oks-gay -marriage-to-resume-in-california-immediately.

115 **Justice Stephen Breyer questioned:** *Hollingsworth v. Perry,* 558 U.S. 183 (2010), oral arguments, March 26, 2013, https://www.supremecourt.gov /oral_arguments/argument_transcripts/2012/12-144_5if6.pdf.

116 **"not because it is old":** Franklin D. Roosevelt, "Address on Constitution Day, Washington, D.C.," speech delivered September 17, 1937, American Presidency Project, http://www.presidency.ucsb.edu/ws/?pid=15459.

119 **hundreds of weddings that day:** Malia Wollan, "California Couples Line Up to Marry After Stay on Same-Sex Marriage Is Lifted," *New York Times,* June 29, 2013, https://www.nytimes.com/2013/06/30/us/california-couples-line -up-to-marry-after-stay-on-same-sex-marriage-is-lifted.html.

123 **by 2009, we had reduced truancy:** Jill Tucker, "Pressuring Parents Helps S.F. Slash Truancy 23%," SFGate, June 9, 2009, https://www.sfgate .com/news/article/Pressuring-parents-helps-S-F-slash-truancy-23-3228481 .php.

125 **Our first report, the results:** State of California Department of Justice, Office of the Attorney General, "Report on California Elementary School Truancy Crisis: One Million Truant Students, Billions in Economic Harm," press release, September 30, 2013, https://oag.ca.gov/news/press-releases/report -california-elementary-school-truancy-crisis-one-million-truant-students.

CHAPTER 5: I SAY WE FIGHT

147 **more than half of Silicon Valley's:** Farhad Manjoo, "Why Silicon Valley Wouldn't Work Without Immigrants," *New York Times,* February 8, 2017,

https://www.nytimes.com/2017/02/08/technology/personaltech/why-silicon
-valley-wouldnt-work-without-immigrants.html.

147 **She wanted to be able to tell:** Phil Willon, "Newly Elected Kamala Harris Vows to Defy Trump on Immigration," *Los Angeles Times,* November 20, 2016, http://www.latimes.com/politics/la-pol-ca-senate-kamala-harris-trump -20161110-story.html.

147 **nearly six million American children:** Leila Schochet, "Trump's Immigration Policies Are Harming American Children," Center for American Progress, July 31, 2017, https://www.americanprogress.org/issues /early-childhood/reports/2017/07/31/436377/trumps-immigration-policies -harming-american-children.

148 **the fear of deportation:** Randy Capps et al., *Implications of Immigration Enforcement Activities for the Well-Being of Children in Immigrant Families: A Review of the Literature* (Washington, DC: Urban Institute and Migration Policy Institute, September 2015), https://www.urban.org/sites/default /files/alfresco/publication-exhibits/2000405/2000405-Implications -of-Immigration-Enforcement-Activities-for-the-Well-Being-of-Children-in -Immigrant-Families.pdf; and Seline Szkupinski Quiroga, Dulce M. Medina, and Jennifer Glick, "In the Belly of the Beast: Effects of Anti-Immigration Policy on Latino Community Members," *American Behavioral Scientist* 58, no. 13 (2014): 1723–42, https://doi.org/10.1177 /0002764214537270.

153 **in the first hundred days:** Schochet, "Trump's Immigration Policies."

153 **arrested ninety-seven workers:** Caroline Scown, "Countering the Effects of Trump's Immigration Policies in Schools," Center for American Progress, May 3, 2018, https://www.americanprogress.org/issues/education-k-12/news /2018/05/03/450274/countering-effects-trumps-immigration-policies -schools.

153 **20 percent of the Latinx students:** Scown, "Countering the Effects."

153 **In 2016, a quarter of all kids:** Leila Schochet, "Trump's Attack on Immigrants Is Breaking the Backbone of America's Child Care System," Center for American Progress, February 5, 2018, https://www.americanprogress.org /issues/early-childhood/news/2018/02/05/445676/trumps-attack-immigrants -breaking-backbone-americas-child-care-system.

154 **20 percent of early childhood educators:** Schochet, "Trump's Attack on Immigrants."

154 **those numbers have tripled:** Schochet, "Trump's Attack on Immigrants."

CHAPTER 6: WE ARE BETTER THAN THIS

161 **"somehow they knew"**: Sankar Raman, "A Cardiac Scientist with Heart," *The Immigrant Story*, July 10, 2017, http://theimmigrantstory.org/scientist.

162 **as much as $460 billion**: Zoe Henry, "800,000 Workers, $460 Billion in Economic Output, Dozens of Entrepreneurs: What the U.S. Loses if DACA Goes Away," *Inc.*, March 5, 2018, https://www.inc.com/zoe-henry/dreamer -entrepreneurs-respond-to-daca-uncertainty.html.

166 **There's a region in Central America**: Rocio Cara Labrador and Danielle Renwick, "Central America's Violent Northern Triangle," Council on Foreign Relations, June 26, 2018, https://www.cfr.org/backgrounder/central -americas-violent-northern-triangle.

167 **nearly fifty thousand people were murdered**: Labrador and Renwick, "Violent Northern Triangle."

167 **MS-13 and the Mara 18**: Labrador and Renwick, "Violent Northern Triangle."

167 **violent deaths of women in Honduras**: "Special Rapporteur on Violence Against Women Finalizes Country Mission to Honduras and Calls for Urgent Action to Address the Culture of Impunity for Crimes Against Women and Girls," Office of the United Nations High Commissioner for Human Rights, https://www.ohchr.org/EN/NewsEvents/Pages/DisplayNews .aspx?NewsID=14833.

167 **an eleven-year-old girl in Honduras**: Sonia Nazario, "The Children of the Drug Wars," *New York Times*, July 11, 2014, https://www.nytimes .com/2014/07/13/opinion/sunday/a-refugee-crisis-not-an-immigration-crisis .html.

167 **If there was a ground zero**: Labrador and Renwick, "Violent Northern Triangle."

169 **about a 50 percent chance**: *Continued Rise in Asylum Denial Rates: Impact of Representation and Nationality,* Transactional Records Access Clearinghouse (TRAC) at Syracuse University, December 13, 2016, http: //trac.syr.edu/immigration/reports/448.

170 **some 350,000 immigrants**: Labrador and Renwick, "Violent Northern Triangle."

170 **dropped by 10 percent**: Anneliese Hermann, *Asylum in the Trump Era* (Washington, DC: Center for American Progress, June 13, 2018), https: //www.americanprogress.org/issues/immigration/reports/2018/06/13/452025 /asylum-trump-era.

171 **seven hundred children had been separated:** Caitlin Dickerson, "Hundreds of Immigrant Children Have Been Taken from Parents at U.S. Border," *New York Times,* April 20, 2018, https://www.nytimes.com/2018/04/20/us /immigrant-children-separation-ice.html.

171 **the extraordinary stress and trauma:** Colleen Kraft, "AAP Statement Opposing Separation of Children and Parents at the Border," American Academy of Pediatrics, May 8, 2018, https://www.aap.org/en-us/about-the-aap /aap-press-room/Pages/StatementOpposingSeparationofChildrenandParents .aspx.

174 **"Persons who violate the law":** Julie Zauzmer and Keith McMillan, "Sessions Cites Bible Passage Used to Defend Slavery in Defense of Separating Immigrant Families," *Washington Post,* June 15, 2018, https://www.washingtonpost.com/news/acts-of-faith/wp/2018/06 /14/jeff-sessions-points-to-the-bible-in-defense-of-separating-immigrant -families.

174 **Sessions got rid of the right:** Katie Benner and Caitlin Dickerson, "Sessions Says Domestic and Gang Violence Are Not Grounds for Asylum," *New York Times,* June 11, 2018, https://www.nytimes.com/2018/06/11/us/politics /sessions-domestic-violence-asylum.html.

178 **"I don't know every task":** Kamala D. Harris, U.S. Senator for California, "At Hearing on Family Separations, Harris Blasts Immoral Separations and Inhumane Detention of Pregnant Women," press release, July 31, 2018, https://www.harris.senate.gov/news/press-releases/at-hearing-on-family -separations-harris-blasts-immoral-separations-and-inhumane-detention -of-pregnant-women.

179 **resort to DNA tests:** Caitlin Dickerson, "Trump Administration in Chaotic Scramble to Reunify Migrant Families," *New York Times,* July 5, 2018, https://www.nytimes.com/2018/07/05/us/migrant-children-chaos-family -separation.html.

179 **"These mothers have given":** "Sen. Kamala Harris Visits Otay Mesa Detention Center," NBC 7 San Diego, June 22, 2018, https://www .nbcsandiego.com/on-air/as-seen-on/Sen_-Kamala-Harris-Visits-Otay-Mesa -Detention-Center_San-Diego-486286761.html.

180 **"At night, Andriy sometimes":** Brittny Mejia, "A 3-Year-Old Was Separated from His Father at the Border. Now His Parents Are Dealing with His Trauma," *Los Angeles Times,* July 3, 2018, http://www.latimes.com/local /lanow/la-me-ln-separation-trauma-20180627-story.html.

180 **Jefferson was stiff:** Esmeralda Bermudez, "'I'm Here. I'm Here.' Father Reunited with Son amid Tears, Relief and Fear of What's Next," *Los Angeles Times,* July 15, 2018, http://www.latimes.com/local/california/la-me-family -reunion-20180715-htmlstory.html.

181 **a fourteen-month-old who was returned:** Lisa Desjardins, Joshua Barajas, and Daniel Bush, "'My Son Is Not the Same': New Testimony Paints Bleak Picture of Family Separation," *PBS NewsHour,* July 5, 2018 (updated July 6, 2018), https://www.pbs.org/newshour/politics/my-son-is-not-the-same-new -testimony-paints-bleak-picture-of-family-separation.

181 **A pregnant woman fainted:** Desjardins, Barajas, and Bush, "My Son."

181 **The children were demeaned:** Desjardins, Barajas, and Bush, "My Son."

181 **Most Americans are appalled:** Eleanor O'Neil, "Immigration Issues: Public Opinion on Family Separation, DACA, and a Border Wall," *AEIdeas* (blog), American Enterprise Institute, June 21, 2018, https://www.aei.org /publication/immigration-issues-public-opinion-on-family-separation-daca -and-a-border-wall.

CHAPTER 7: EVERY BODY

185 **the United States is one of only:** Linda Villarosa, "Why America's Black Mothers and Babies Are in Life-or-Death Crisis," *New York Times Magazine,* April 11, 2018.

185 **a ten-year gap in life expectancy:** Dave A. Chokshi, "Income, Poverty, and Health Inequality," *Journal of the American Medical Association* 319, no. 13 (2018): 1312–13, https://jamanetwork.com/journals/jama/fullarticle /2677433.

186 **the Senate leader openly declared:** Jillian Rayfield, "McConnell at CPAC: Repeal Obamacare 'Root and Branch,'" *Salon,* March 15, 2013, https://www .salon.com/2013/03/15/mcconnell_at_cpac_repeal_obamacare_root _and_branch.

186 **comparing the Affordable Care Act:** Jack Gurdon, "Rand Paul: The Republican Frontrunner in Seven Quotes," *Telegraph,* October 2, 2014, https://www.telegraph.co.uk/news/worldnews/us-politics/11134793/Rand -Paul-the-Republican-frontrunner-in-seven-quotes.html.

186 **suggesting that the president might:** "25 Unforgettable Obamacare Quotes," *Politico,* July 16, 2013, https://www.politico.com/gallery /2013/07/25-unforgettable-obamacare-quotes-001595?slide=11.

187 **Repealing the ACA would result:** "H.R. 1628, Obamacare Repeal Reconciliation Act of 2017," cost estimate and analysis, Congressional Budget Office, July 19, 2017, https://www.cbo.gov/publication/52939.

187 **It would allow insurance companies:** U.S. Department of Health and Human Services, Office of Health Policy, *Health Insurance Coverage for Americans with Pre-Existing Conditions: The Impact of the Affordable Care Act* (Washington, DC, January 5, 2017), https://aspe.hhs.gov/system/files/pdf/255396/Pre-ExistingConditions.pdf.

188 **Compared with people in other:** "How Prescription Drug Prices Compare Internationally," *Wall Street Journal,* December 1, 2015, https://graphics.wsj.com/table/GlobalDrug_1201.

188 **the same dose of Crestor:** Rachel Bluth, "Should the U.S. Make It Easier to Import Prescription Drugs?" *PBS NewsHour,* March 22, 2017, https://www.pbs.org/newshour/health/u-s-make-easier-import-prescription-drugs.

188–89 **Fifty-eight percent of Americans take:** "Public Opinion on Prescription Drugs and Their Prices," Henry J. Kaiser Family Foundation, https://www.kff.org/slideshow/public-opinion-on-prescription-drugs-and-their-prices.

189 **One of my very first votes:** Zack Struver, "Klobuchar Drug Importation Amendment Sees Votes Crossing the Aisle," Knowledge Ecology International, January 13, 2017, https://www.keionline.org/23248.

189 **found 153 companies:** John Morgan, *A Bitter Pill: How Big Pharma Lobbies to Keep Prescription Drug Prices High* (Washington, DC: Citizens for Responsibility and Ethics in Washington, 2018), https://www.citizensforethics.org/a-bitter-pill-how-big-pharma-lobbies-to-keep-prescription-drug-prices-high.

190 **increased its membership dues:** Morgan, *A Bitter Pill.*

190 **about $2.5 billion on lobbying:** Morgan, *A Bitter Pill.*

190 **increased the price of Pravastatin:** Morgan, *A Bitter Pill.*

190 **jacked the price of Albuterol:** Morgan, *A Bitter Pill.*

191 **owed the hospital nearly $19,000:** Jenny Gold and Sarah Kliff, "A Baby Was Treated with a Nap and a Bottle of Formula. His Parents Received an $18,000 Bill," *Vox,* July 20, 2018, https://www.vox.com/2018/6/28/17506232/emergency-room-bill-fees-health-insurance-baby.

191 **passed $31,250 in fees:** Gold and Kliff, "Nap and a Bottle."

191 **he was expected to pay $7,294:** Sarah Kliff, "He Went to an In-Network Emergency Room. He Still Ended Up with a $7,924 Bill," *Vox,* May 23,

2018, https://www.vox.com/2018/5/23/17353284/emergency-room-doctor
-out-of-network.

192 **Depression is increasing:** "Depression Is on the Rise in the US, Especially
Among Young Teens," *Science Daily,* October 30, 2017, https://www
.sciencedaily.com/releases/2017/10/171030134631.htm.

192 **Alabama has only 1:** "Mental Health in America, Access to Care Data,"
Mental Health America, http://www.mentalhealthamerica.net/issues
/mental-health-america-access-care-data.

192 **roughly 60 percent of America's counties:** New American Economy, "New
Study Shows 60 Percent of U.S. Counties Without a Single Psychiatrist," press
release, October 23, 2017, https://www.newamericaneconomy.org/press-release
/new-study-shows-60-percent-of-u-s-counties-without-a-single-psychiatrist.

192 **only 590 psychiatrists:** New American Economy, "New Study Shows."

192 **41.4 percent of adults with mental illness:** "The State of Mental Health in
America," Mental Health America, October 7, 2018, http://www
.mentalhealthamerica.net/issues/state-mental-health-america.

194 **"there was a continuing disparity":** U.S. Department of Health and Human
Services, *Report of the Secretary's Task Force on Black and Minority Health,*
vol. 1, by Margaret M. Heckler (Washington, DC, 1985), https://ia800501
.us.archive.org/32/items/reportofsecretar00usde/reportofsecretar00usde.pdf.

195 **black Americans have higher mortality rates:** Robin L. Kelly, *2015 Kelly
Report: Health Disparities in America* (Washington, DC: Office of
Congresswoman Robin L. Kelly, IL-02, 2015), 11, https://robinkelly.house
.gov/sites/robinkelly.house.gov/files/2015%20Kelly%20Report_0.pdf.

195 **"A baby born in Cheswolde":** Olga Khazan, "Being Black in America Can
Be Hazardous to Your Health," *The Atlantic,* July/August 2018, https:
//www.theatlantic.com/magazine/archive/2018/07/being-black-in-america
-can-be-hazardous-to-your-health/561740.

195 **Black babies are twice as likely:** Villarosa, "Why America's Black Mothers
and Babies."

195 **black infants are less likely:** From the Heckler Report: "Moreover, in 1981,
Blacks suffered 20 infant deaths per 1,000 live births, still twice the White
level of 10.5, but similar to the White rate of 1960." U.S. Department of
Health and Human Services, *Black and Minority Health,* 2; "Infant
Mortality," Centers for Disease Control and Prevention, https://www.cdc
.gov/reproductivehealth/maternalinfanthealth/infantmortality.htm.

195 **at least three times as likely:** Villarosa, "America's Black Mothers and Babies."

195 **A major five-year study:** New York City Department of Health and Mental Hygiene, *Severe Maternal Morbidity in New York City, 2008–2012* (New York, 2017), https://www1.nyc.gov/assets/doh/downloads/pdf/data/maternal -morbidity-report-08-12.pdf; and Nina Martin and Renee Montagne, "Black Mothers Keep Dying After Giving Birth. Shalon Irving's Story Explains Why," *All Things Considered,* NPR, December 7, 2017, https://www.npr .org/2017/12/07/568948782/Black-mothers-keep-dying-after-giving-birth -shalon-irvings-story-explains-why.

196 **"child adversity literally":** David Bornstein, "Treating the Lifelong Harm of Childhood Trauma," *New York Times,* January 30, 2018, https://www .nytimes.com/2018/01/30/opinion/treating-the-lifelong-harm-of-childhood -trauma.html.

196 **could see their life expectancy reduced:** Khazan, "Being Black in America."

196 **telomere length in hundreds of women:** Khazan, "Being Black in America."

196 **White patients are 10 percent more likely:** Robert Pearl, "Why Health Care Is Different if You're Black, Latino or Poor," *Forbes,* March 5, 2015, https: //www.forbes.com/sites/robertpearl/2015/03/05/healthcare-black-latino -poor/#650c70d37869.

197 **Black patients are also less likely:** Quinn Capers IV, "To Reduce Health-Care Disparities We Must Address Biases in Medical School Admissions," *The Hill,* April 14, 2018, https://thehill.com/opinion/healthcare/383154-to -reduce-health-care-disparities-we-must-address-biases-in-medical-school.

197 **more likely to get breast cancer screenings:** Pearl, "Why Health Care Is Different."

197 **regardless of their economic status:** Villarosa, "America's Black Mothers and Babies."

197 **Rather than give her the CT scan:** Rob Haskell, "Serena Williams on Motherhood, Marriage, and Making Her Comeback," *Vogue,* January 10, 2018, https://www.vogue.com/article/serena-williams-vogue-cover-interview -february-2018.

197 **If someone like Serena Williams:** Haskell, "Serena Williams," *Vogue.*

198 **Research has found that 75 percent:** April Dembosky, "Training Doctors to Spot Their Own Racial Biases," CNN, September 7, 2015, https://www.cnn .com/2015/09/07/health/healthcare-racial-bias/index.html.

198 **As of 2013, only about 9 percent:** "Diversity in the Physician Workforce:

Facts & Figures 2014," Association of American Medical Colleges, 2014,
http://www.aamcdiversityfactsandfigures.org.

200 the ninth leading cause of death: "End Stage Renal Disease in the United
States," National Kidney Foundation, updated January 2016, https://www
.kidney.org/news/newsroom/factsheets/End-Stage-Renal-Disease-in-the-US.

200 develop kidney failure at 3.5 times: "Low Income Linked to Higher Levels
of Kidney Disease Among African Americans," National Kidney Foundation,
November 5, 2012, https://www.kidney.org/news/newsroom/nr/Low
-Income-Linked-to-Higher-Levels-of-Kidney-Disease.

200 "Fresenius's own medical office": Andrew Pollack, "Dialysis Equipment
Maker Settles Lawsuit for $250 Million," *New York Times,* February 18,
2016, https://www.nytimes.com/2016/02/19/business/dialysis-equipment
-maker-settles-lawsuit-for-250-million.html.

201 DaVita agreed to pay $350 million: U.S. Department of Justice, "DaVita to
Pay $350 Million to Resolve Allegations of Illegal Kickbacks," press release,
October 22, 2014, https://www.justice.gov/opa/pr/davita-pay-350-million
-resolve-allegations-illegal-kickbacks.

202 doctors in the county prescribed 1.6 million: Melanie Saltzman, "Ohio Sues
Big Pharma over Increase in Opioid-Related Deaths," *PBS NewsHour,*
October 7, 2017, https://www.pbs.org/newshour/show/ohio-sues-big-pharma
-increase-opioid-related-deaths.

202 thirty-eight people died from accidental overdose: Joel Achenbach,
"No Longer 'Mayberry': A Small Ohio City Fights an Epidemic of
Self-Destruction," *Washington Post*, December 29, 2016, https://www
.washingtonpost.com/national/health-science/no-longer-mayberry-a-small
-ohio-city-fights-an-epidemic-of-self-destruction/2016/12/29/a95076f2-9a01
-11e6-b3c9-f662adaa0048_story.html.

202 another forty lost their lives: "Fentanyl and Related Drugs like Carfentanil
as Well as Cocaine Drove Increase in Overdose Deaths," in Ohio
Department of Health, *2016 Ohio Drug Overdose Data: General Findings*
(Columbus, 2016), https://www.odh.ohio.gov/-/media/ODH/ASSETS
/Files/health/injury-prevention/2016-Ohio-Drug-Overdose-Report
-FINAL.pdf.

202 "Now you can get heroin quicker": Achenbach, "No Longer 'Mayberry.'"

203 "One day in September": Achenbach, "No Longer 'Mayberry.'"

203 the violent crime rate has gone up: Achenbach, "No Longer 'Mayberry.'"

203 **two hundred children were placed:** Paula Seligson and Tim Reid, "Unbudgeted: How the Opioid Crisis Is Blowing a Hole in Small-Town America's Finances," *Reuters*, September 27, 2017, https://www.reuters.com /article/us-usa-opioids-budgets/unbudgeted-how-the-opioid-crisis-is -blowing-a-hole-in-small-town-americas-finances-idUSKCN1BU2LP.

203 **The surge has required:** Seligson and Reid, "Unbudgeted."

203 **"It's like having the flu":** Achenbach, "No Longer 'Mayberry.'"

204 **Between 2007 and 2012:** Julia Lurie, "A Brief, Blood-Boiling History of the Opioid Epidemic," *Mother Jones*, January/February 2017, https://www .motherjones.com/crime-justice/2017/12/a-brief-blood-boiling -history-of-the-opioid-epidemic.

204 **the United States was consuming:** Lurie, "History of the Opioid Epidemic."

205 **259 million prescriptions for opioids:** Lurie, "History of the Opioid Epidemic."

205 **roughly 80 percent of Americans:** Keith Humphries, "How Legal Drug Companies Helped Revive the Heroin Trade," *Wonkblog, Washington Post,* June 15, 2018, https://www.washingtonpost.com/news/wonk/wp/2018/06 /15/how-legal-drug-companies-helped-revive-the-heroin-trade.

205 **opioid deaths are still rising:** Karen Kaplan, "Opioid Overdose Deaths Are Still Rising in Nearly Every Segment of the Country, CDC Says," *Los Angeles Times,* March 29, 2018, http://www.latimes.com/science /sciencenow/la-sci-sn-opioid-overdose-deaths-20180329-htmlstory.html.

206 **"effectively stripped the DEA":** Scott Higham and Lenny Bernstein, "The Drug Industry's Triumph Over the DEA," *Washington Post,* October 15, 2017, https://www.washingtonpost.com/graphics/2017/investigations /dea-drug-industry-congress.

207 **Many insurance companies will cover:** German Lopez, "She Paid Nothing for Opioid Painkillers. Her Addiction Treatment Costs More Than $200 a Month," *Vox,* June 4, 2018, https://www.vox.com/science-and-health /2018/6/4/17388756/opioid-epidemic-health-insurance-buprenorphine.

CHAPTER 8: THE COST OF LIVING

214 **"Most of the tubs":** Steven Ross, Allison Graham, and David Appleby, *At the River I Stand* (San Francisco: California Newsreel, 1993), documentary film, 56 min., https://search.alexanderstreet.com/preview/work /bibliographic_entity%7Cvideo_work%7C1858429.

215 "So often we overlook": Martin Luther King Jr., "All Labor Has Dignity," King Series, ed. Michael K. Honey (Boston: Beacon Press, 2011).

215 "We are tired," King said: King, "All Labor Has Dignity."

218 a year of child care for a baby: Tanza Loudenback, "In 33 US States It Costs More to Send Your Kid to Childcare Than College," *Business Insider,* October 12, 2016, http://www.businessinsider.com/costs-of-childcare-in-33-us-states-is-higher-than-college-tuition-2016-10.

218 more than three times faster: Michelle Jamrisko and Ilan Kolet, "College Costs Surge 500% in U.S. Since 1985: Chart of the Day," Bloomberg, August 26, 2013, https://www.bloomberg.com/news/articles/2013-08-26/college-costs-surge-500-in-u-s-since-1985-chart-of-the-day.

220 less than 1 percent of the homes: Jenny Luna, "Buying a Home Is Nearly Impossible for Teachers in These Cities," *Mother Jones,* February 4, 2017, https://www.motherjones.com/politics/2017/02/buying-house-nearly-impossible-teachers-these-cities-2.

221 1.2 million by 2026: U.S. Department of Labor, Bureau of Labor Statistics, "Fastest Growing Occupations," *Occupational Outlook Handbook*, April 13, 2018, www.bls.gov/ooh/fastest-growing.htm.

221 more than $21,000 behind: Brandie Temple and Jasmine Tucker, *Equal Pay for Black Women* (Washington, DC: National Women's Law Center, July 2017), https://nwlc.org/resources/equal-pay-for-black-women.

222 worker wages grew 90 percent: Lawrence Mishel, Elise Gould, and Josh Bivens, *Wage Stagnation in Nine Charts* (Washington, DC: Economic Policy Institute, 2015), http://www.epi.org/publication/charting-wage-stagnation.

222 worker compensation rose just 9 percent: Mishel, Gould, and Bivens, *Wage Stagnation.*

222 CEOs making more than three hundred: Diana Hembree, "CEO Pay Skyrockets to 361 Times That of the Average Worker," *Forbes,* May 22, 2018, https://www.forbes.com/sites/dianahembree/2018/05/22/ceo-pay-skyrockets-to-361-times-that-of-the-average-worker.

225 40 percent of the nation's wealth: Christopher Ingraham, "The Richest 1 Percent Now Owns More of the Country's Wealth Than at Any Time in the Past 50 Years," *Wonkblog, Washington Post,* December 6, 2017.

225 adds up to roughly $40 trillion: Harriet Torrey, "Americans' Wealth Surpasses $100 Trillion," *Wall Street Journal,* June 7, 2018, https://www.wsj.com/articles/u-s-net-worth-surpasses-100-trillion-1528387386.

225 **43 percent of households can't afford:** Quentin Fottrell, "50 Million American Households Can't Even Afford Basic Living Expenses," *MarketWatch,* June 9, 2018, https://www.marketwatch.com/story/50-million -american-households-cant-afford-basic-living-expenses-2018-05-18.

227 **375 million people worldwide:** Daniela Hernandez, "Seven Jobs Robots Will Create—or Expand," *Wall Street Journal,* https://www.wsj.com/articles /seven-jobs-robots-will-createor-expand-1525054021.

227 **23 percent of current working hours:** James Manyika et al., *Jobs Lost, Jobs Gained: Workforce Transitions in a Time of Automation* (Washington, DC: McKinsey Global Institute, 2017), https://www.mckinsey.com/~/media /McKinsey/Featured%20Insights/Future%20of%20Organizations/ What%20the%20future%20of%20work%20will%20mean%20for %20jobs%20skills%20and%20wages/MGI-Jobs-Lost-Jobs-Gained-Report -December-6-2017.ashx.

227 **2.5 million jobs a year:** Karen Harris, Austin Kimson, and Andrew Schwedel, "Quick and Painful: Brace for Job Automation's Next Wave," Bain and Company, March 7, 2018, http://www.bain.com/publications/articles /quick-and-painful-brace-for-job-automations-next-wave-labor-2030-snap -chart.aspx.

227 **In 2017, extreme weather events:** Jeff Goodell, "Welcome to the Age of Climate Migration," *Rolling Stone,* February 25, 2018, https://www .rollingstone.com/politics/politics-news/welcome-to-the-age-of-climate -migration-202221.

227 **The economic toll will follow:** Eileen Drage O'Reilly and Alison Snyder, "Where Climate Change Will Hit the U.S. Hardest," *Axios,* June 29, 2017, https://www.axios.com/where-climate-change-will-hit-the-us-hardest -1513303282-6566eea4-6369-4588-88cc-c2886db20b70.html.

227 **After Hurricane Harvey hit:** Goodell, "Age of Climate Migration."

CHAPTER 9: SMART ON SECURITY

240 **490 million gallons:** Andrea Elliott, "Sewage Spill During the Blackout Exposed a Lingering City Problem," *New York Times,* August 28, 2003, https://www.nytimes.com/2003/08/28/nyregion/sewage-spill-during-the -blackout-exposed-a-lingering-city-problem.html.

240 **mortality rates in New York City:** G. Brooke Anderson and Michelle L. Bell, "Lights Out: Impact of the August 2003 Power Outage on Mortality in

New York, NY," *Epidemiology* 23, no. 2 (March 2012): 189–93, https://www.ncbi.nlm.nih.gov/pmc/articles/PMC3276729.

241 **Chinese theft of American intellectual property:** Sherisse Pham, "How Much Has the US Lost from China's IP Theft?" *CNN Business,* March 23, 2018, https://money.cnn.com/2018/03/23/technology/china-us-trump-tariffs-ip-theft/index.html.

241 **cybercrime's toll in North America:** James Lewis, *Economic Impact of Cybercrime—No Slowing Down* (Washington, DC: Center for Strategic and International Studies and McAfee, February 2018), https://www.mcafee.com/enterprise/en-us/assets/reports/restricted/economic-impact-cybercrime.pdf.

242 **six million times each day:** Keith Alexander, "U.S. Cybersecurity Policy and the Role of USCYBERCOM," transcript of remarks at Center for Strategic and International Studies Cybersecurity Policy Debate Series, Washington, DC, June 3, 2010, https://www.nsa.gov/news-features/speeches-testimonies/speeches/100603-alenander-transcript.shtml.

242 **Cyber Crime Center:** State of California Department of Justice, Office of the Attorney General, "Attorney General Kamala D. Harris Announces Creation of eCrime Unit Targeting Technology Crimes," press release, December 13, 2011, https://oag.ca.gov/news/press-releases/attorney-general-kamala-d-harris-announces-creation-ecrime-unit-targeting; and State of California Department of Justice, Office of the Attorney General, "Attorney General Kamala D. Harris Announces California Cyber Crime Center Initiative in Fresno," press release, October 10, 2016, https://oag.ca.gov/news/press-releases/attorney-general-kamala-d-harris-announces-california-cyber-crime-center.

243 **Right-wing pundits from Fox:** Hans A. von Spakovsky, "Nominated for a Cabinet Position? Liberal Senators Just Want to Know Your Position on 'Climate Change,'" Heritage Foundation, February 24, 2017, https://www.heritage.org/environment/commentary/nominated-cabinet-position-liberal-senators-just-want-know-your-position.

243 **"dumb," "ridiculous," and "off-base":** See Andrew Seifter, "Yes, CIA Director Nominee Mike Pompeo Needs to Answer Questions About Climate Change," *Media Matters for America* blog, January 13, 2017, https://www.mediamatters.org/blog/2017/01/13/yes-cia-director-nominee-mike-pompeo-needs-answer-questions-about-climate-change/215013.

244 **diseases are flourishing:** Centers for Disease Control and Prevention, "Illnesses from Mosquito, Tick, and Flea Bites Increasing in the US," press

release, May 1, 2018, https://www.cdc.gov/media/releases/2018/p0501-vs
-vector-borne.html.

245 **the CDC has already identified:** Centers for Disease Control and
Prevention, "Mosquito, Tick, and Flea Bites."

245 **Farmers had to abandon:** Krista Mahr, "How Cape Town Was Saved from
Running Out of Water," *Guardian,* May 4, 2018, https://www.theguardian
.com/world/2018/may/04/back-from-the-brink-how-cape-town-
cracked-its-water-crisis.

246 **reclaims only 7 to 8 percent:** U.S. Environmental Protection Agency and
CDM Smith, *2017 Potable Reuse Compendium (Washington, DC, 2017),
30,* https://www.epa.gov/sites/production/files/2018-01/documents
/potablereusecompendium_3.pdf.

246 **Nearly 1 million homes:** Ben Westcott and Steve George, "Asia Under
Water: How 137 Million People's Lives Are Being Put at Risk," CNN,
August 30, 2017, https://www.cnn.com/2017/07/24/asia/climate-change
-floods-asia/index.html.

247 **The official death toll:** Leyla Santiago, Catherine E. Shoichet, and Jason
Kravarik, "Puerto Rico's New Hurricane Maria Death Toll Is 46 Times Higher
Than the Government's Previous Count," CNN, August 28, 2018, https
://www.cnn.com/2018/08/28/health/puerto-rico-gw-report-excess-deaths.

247 **at least 4,600 American citizens:** See Nishant Kishore et al., "Mortality in
Puerto Rico After Hurricane Maria," *New England Journal of Medicine*
379, no. 2 (July 12, 2018): 162–70, https://www.nejm.org/doi/full/10.1056
/NEJMsa1803972#article_citing_articles.

CHAPTER 10: WHAT I'VE LEARNED

262 **helped lift hundreds of millions:** Bill Gates, "Here's My Plan to Improve
Our World—and How You Can Help," *Wired,* November 12, 2013, https
://www.wired.com/2013/11/bill-gates-wired-essay.

263 **"I think people don't talk":** Mimi Kirk, "One Answer to School Attendance:
Washing Machines," *CityLab,* August 22, 2016, https://www.citylab.com
/solutions/2016/08/school-attendance-washing-machines/496649.

268 **"This is not tolerable!":** Niraj Chokshi and Astead W. Herndon, "Jeff Flake
Is Confronted on Video by Sexual Assault Survivors," *New York Times,*
September 28, 2018, https://www.nytimes.com/2018/09/28/us/politics
/jeff-flake-protesters-kavanaugh.html.

268 **"that they don't matter":** Jesus Rodriguez, "Woman Who Confronted Flake 'Relieved' He Called for Delaying Kavanaugh Vote," *Politico,* September 28, 2018, https://www.politico.com/story/2018/09/28/jeff-flake-protester -kavanaugh-852971.

269 **Kavanaugh had misled the Senate:** Paul Blumenthal and Jennifer Bendery, "All the Lies Brett Kavanaugh Told," *Huffington Post*, October 1, 2018, https://www.huffingtonpost.com/entry/brett-kavanaugh-lies_us _5bb26190e4b027da00d61fcd.

269 **We learned that when she was in high school:** "Kavanaugh Hearing: Transcript," *Washington Post* (transcript courtesy of Bloomberg Government), https://www.washingtonpost.com/news/national/wp/2018/09/27/kavanaugh -hearing-transcript. Subsequent references to information presented during the Kavanaugh hearing may also be found here.

272 **American Bar Association reopened:** Associated Press, "American Bar Association Reopens Kavanaugh Evaluation," *PBS News Hour,* October 5, 2018, https://www.pbs.org/newshour/politics/american-bar-association -reopens-kavanaugh-evaluation.

272 **"united, as professors of law":** Susan Svrluga, " 'Unfathomable': More Than 2,400 Law Professors Sign Letter Opposing Kavanaugh's Confirmation," *Grade Point* (blog), *Washington Post,* October 4, 2018, https://www .washingtonpost.com/education/2018/10/04/unprecedented-unfathomable -more-than-law-professors-sign-letter-after-kavanaugh-hearing.

272 **"I was calculating daily the risk/benefit":** "Kavanaugh Hearing: Transcript."

275 **a 200 percent increase in calls:** Holly Yan, "The National Sexual Assault Hotline Got a 201% Increase in Calls During the Kavanaugh Hearing," CNN, September 28, 2018, https://www.cnn.com/2018/09/24/health/ national-sexual-assault-hotline-spike/index.html.

INDEX